The *III* Insurance

FACT BOOK 2008

III Insurance
Information
Institute

TO THE READER

Since its inception more than 40 years ago, the Insurance Information Institute's Insurance Fact Book has grown each year to reflect trends and developments shaping the insurance industry. Our 2008 edition includes a host of new statistics, from increased data on life insurance investments to expanded information on auto and home insurance claims, as well as a new financial terms glossary and a guide to I.I.I.'s vast print and Web resources.

Among the new charts and tables added this year:
- Life/health insurers, bond portfolio analysis
- Life/health insurance industry premium by line and by state
- Top ten floods
- Top ten most expensive and least expensive states for automobile insurance
- Private passenger collision and comprehensive claims
- Homeowners lightning claims
- Mortgage guaranty insurance premiums and combined ratios
- U.S. death rates by cause

The I.I.I. Fact Book is meant to be used along with the Institute's Web site, www.iii.org, which features a wealth of information for consumers, researchers and businesses alike. I.I.I. also remains a vital source of timely, reliable information for reporters. To help journalists, the I.I.I. has produced new print and Web versions of its Insurance Handbook for Reporters, with concise explanations of auto, home, life, disability and business insurance.

In conclusion, we would like to thank the many associations, consultants and others who collect industry statistics and who have generously given permission to use their data.

Robert Hartwig , Ph.D., CPCU
President
Insurance Information Institute

The I.I.I. Insurance Fact Book is published by the Insurance Information Institute, a primary source for information, analysis and referral on insurance subjects. The Fact Book contains material from numerous sources. Because these sources define and collect data in various ways, and moreover, are constantly refining the data, differences among similar data may occur.

Contents

- World insurance premiums (life and nonlife) totaled $3.7 trillion in 2006, according to Swiss Re.

- Data from Highline/National Association of Insurance Commissioners show U.S. property/ casualty (P/C) insurance premiums (excluding state funds), totaled $448.9 billion in 2006, up 4.6 percent from $429.2 billion in 2005. Premiums in the life/health (L/H) sector totaled $583.6 billion, up 10.5 percent from $528.1 billion in 2005.

- The transaction value of insurance-related mergers and acquisitions totaled $23.6 billion in 2006, down from $49.8 billion in 2005.

- There were 2,648 P/C insurance companies and 1,257 L/H insurance companies in the United States in 2006. Many of these companies were part of larger entities.

- Cash and investment assets of P/C insurers totaled $1.2 trillion in 2006, accounting for 83 percent of total P/C assets. Cash and invested assets of L/H insurers amounted to $2.9 trillion, or 61 percent of total L/H insurance assets.

- The P/C insurance industry's rate of return on a statutory basis increased from 10.7 percent in 2005 to 13.4 percent in 2006. The L/H insurance industry's rate of return on a GAAP basis dropped from 13 percent in 2005 to 12 percent in 2006.

- P/C insurers' aftertax net income rose from $46.4 billion dollars in 2005 to $66.7 billion in 2006, according to Highline/National Association of Insurance Commissioners. L/H aftertax net income fell from $35.9 billion to $34.0 billion.

- Insured catastrophe losses totaled $9.2 billion in 2006, down significantly from $62.3 billion in 2005, the highest on record.

PREMIUMS OF P/C AND L/H INSURANCE INDUSTRIES, 1997-2006

($ billions, excludes state funds)

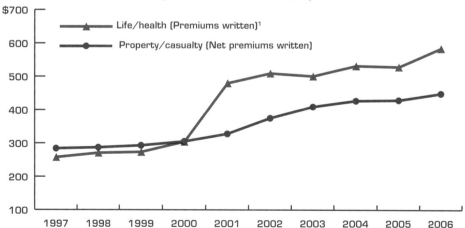

[1]Includes deposit-type funds beginning in 2001.

Source: National Association of Insurance Commissioners (NAIC) Annual Statement Database, via Highline Data, LLC. Copyrighted information. No portion of this work may be copied or redistributed without the express written permission of Highline Data, LLC.

WORLD LIFE AND NONLIFE INSURANCE IN 2006

Outside the United States, the insurance industry is divided into life and nonlife or general insurance rather than life/health and property/casualty.

In 2006 world insurance premium volume, for both sectors combined, totaled $3.72 trillion, up 8.1 percent from $3.45 trillion in 2005, according to Swiss Re. On an inflation-adjusted basis, total insurance premiums grew fastest in Africa, up 17.6 percent, followed by Latin America and the Caribbean, up 11.6 percent, Europe, up 7.5 percent, Asia, up 3.8 percent, North America, up 2.2 percent and Oceania (Australia, New Zealand and other islands), also up 2.2 percent. Inflation-adjusted premiums grew 16.3 percent in emerging markets and 4.0 percent in industrialized countries.

In 2006 life and nonlife insurance premiums (excluding cross-border business) accounted for 16.5 percent of gross domestic product (GDP) in the United Kingdom, the highest share in the Swiss Re study, followed by 16.0 percent in South Africa. Premiums represented 8.8 percent of GDP in the United States.

TOP TEN COUNTRIES BY NONLIFE AND LIFE DIRECT PREMIUMS WRITTEN, 2006[1]
(Direct premiums written, U.S. $ millions)

Rank	Country	Nonlife premiums[2]	Life premiums	Total premiums Amount	Percent change from prior year	Percent of total world premiums
1	United States[3]	$636,452	$533,649	$1,170,101	5.4%	31.43%
2	Japan[4]	97,495	362,766	460,261	-3.8	12.36
3	United Kingdom	106,676	311,691	418,366	24.5	11.24
4	France	73,262	177,902	251,164	13.7	6.75
5	Germany	109,633	94,911	204,544	3.3	5.49
6	Italy	49,103	89,576	138,679	-4.9	3.72
7	South Korea[4]	28,881	72,298	101,179	18.9	2.72
8	Canada[5]	48,988	39,212	88,200	13.0	2.37
9	PR China	25,713	45,092	70,805	17.7	1.90
10	Spain	37,528	28,285	65,813	8.9	1.77

[1]Before reinsurance transactions.
[2]Includes accident and health insurance.
[3]Nonlife premiums include state funds; life premiums include an estimate of group pension business.
[4]April 1, 2006-March 31, 2007.
[5]Life business expressed in net premiums.

Source: Swiss Re, *sigma*, No. 4/2007.

Swiss Re's 2006 world insurance study is based on direct premium data from 147 countries, including 88 countries with premium volume of at least $347 million in 2006. Study findings indicate that premiums increased by 5 percent in 2006, adjusted for inflation. Life insurance premiums increased by 7.7 percent, expanding faster than overall economic activity in most countries. Higher demand for retirement income in countries with aging populations, together with the efforts of governments in some nations to shift from public to private pension programs, boosted demand for life insurance products.

In the United States, the world's largest life insurance market, growth was largely driven by strong sales in wealth accumulation products such as annuities. Robust stock markets in the United Kingdom, Germany and France led to strong sales of life insurance products linked to market indices. While total world nonlife premiums increased by 1.5 percent, adjusted for inflation, most of the growth was in emerging markets, which posted 11 percent growth in contrast with stodgy 0.6 percent growth in premiums in industrialized nations. Swiss Re sees a mixed outlook for 2007, with growth healthy for life insurance and sluggish in the nonlife sector.

WORLD LIFE AND NONLIFE INSURANCE PREMIUMS, 2006

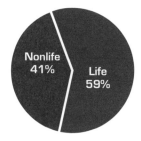

Nonlife 41%
Life 59%

Source: Swiss Re, *sigma*, No. 4/2007.

WORLD LIFE AND NONLIFE INSURANCE PREMIUMS, 2004-2006[1]
(Direct premiums written, U.S. $ millions)

Year	Nonlife[2]	Life	Total
2004	$1,397,522	$1,866,636	$3,264,158
2005	1,442,258	2,003,557	3,445,816
2006	1,514,094	2,209,317	3,723,412

[1]Before reinsurance transactions.
[2]Includes accident and health insurance.

Source: Swiss Re, *sigma* database.

REINSURANCE

Each year the Reinsurance Association of America (RAA) provides an overview of the countries from which U.S. insurance companies obtain reinsurance, i.e., the countries to which
they have ceded, or transferred, some of their risk. The analysis includes premiums that a U.S.
insurance company cedes to "alien," i.e., foreign, reinsurance companies that are not part of
the insurer's own corporate group ("unaffiliated alien reinsurers" in the chart below), as well as
business ceded to overseas reinsurers that are part of the insurer's corporate family ("affiliated
alien reinsurers" in the chart below).

According to the RAA, the role of foreign reinsurers in the U.S. market is growing.
Unaffiliated alien reinsurers' share of the U.S. market increased from 51.8 percent in 2005 to
53.1 percent in 2006. If the domicile of the ultimate parent of the reinsurance company is taken
into account, foreign (or foreign owned) reinsurance companies accounted for 84.5 percent of
the market in 2006, down from 85.4 percent in 2005.

U.S. REINSURANCE PREMIUMS CEDED TO UNAFFILIATED AND AFFILIATED ALIEN REINSURERS BY COUNTRY, 2004-2006[1]

($ millions)

Rank	Country	Unaffiliated alien reinsurers			Affiliated alien reinsurers			2006 total
		2004	2005	2006	2004	2005	2006	
1	Bermuda	$7,795	$8,908	$8,982	$17,031	$18,590	$18,474	$27,456
2	Switzerland	1,533	950	797	7,795	7,664	7,991	8,788
3	U.K.	4,144	4,827	4,630	300	252	346	4,976
4	Germany	2,869	2,529	2,582	3,294	9,401	2,005	4,587
5	Cayman Islands	1,618	1,780	1,806	629	646	435	2,241
6	Barbados	841	837	652	925	917	965	1,617
7	Ireland	852	788	532	177	165	451	983
8	France	401	600	352	198	293	338	690
9	Sweden	NA	NA	NA	38	50	518	518
10	Turks and Caicos	447	382	398	NA	NA	NA	398
11	British Virgin Islands	NA	NA	NA	49	72	327	327
12	Japan	285	273	261	NA	NA	NA	261
	Total, countries shown	20,785	21,874	20,992	30,436	38,090	31,850	52,842
	Total	$21,961	$23,246	$22,214	$31,140	$38,816	$32,470	$54,684

[1]Ranked by 2006 total reinsurance premiums.
NA=Data not available.

Source: Reinsurance Association of America.

THE WORLD'S LEADING INSURANCE COMPANIES

TOP TEN GLOBAL INSURANCE COMPANIES BY REVENUES, 2006[1]
($ millions)

Rank	Company	Revenues[2]	Country	Industry
1	ING Group	$158,274	Netherlands	Life/health
2	AXA	139,738	France	Life/health
3	Allianz	125,346	Germany	Property/casualty
4	American International Group	113,194	U.S.	Property/casualty
5	Assicurazioni Generali	101,811	Italy	Life/health
6	Berkshire Hathaway	98,539	U.S.	Property/casualty
7	Aviva	83,487	U.K.	Life/health
8	Prudential	66,134	U.K.	Life/health
9	Zurich Financial Services	65,000	Switzerland	Property/casualty
10	State Farm Insurance Cos.	60,528	U.S.	Property/casualty

[1]Based on an analysis of companies in the Global Fortune 500. Includes stock and mutual companies.
[2]Revenues include premium and annuity income, investment income and capital gains or losses, but exclude deposits; includes consolidated subsidiaries, excludes excise taxes.

Source: Fortune.

TOP TEN GLOBAL PROPERTY/CASUALTY INSURANCE COMPANIES BY REVENUES, 2006[1]
($ millions)

Rank	Company	Revenues[2]	Country
1	Allianz	$125,346	Germany
2	American International Group	113,194	U.S.
3	Berkshire Hathaway	98,539	U.S.
4	Zurich Financial Services	65,000	Switzerland
5	State Farm Insurance Cos.	60,528	U.S.
6	Munich Re Group	58,183	Germany
7	Millea Holdings	36,067	Japan
8	Allstate	35,796	U.S.
9	Swiss Reinsurance	32,118	Switzerland
10	Hartford Financial Services	26,500	U.S.

[1]Based on an analysis of companies in the Global Fortune 500. Includes stock and mutual companies.
[2]Revenues include premium and annuity income, investment income and capital gains or losses, but exclude deposits; includes consolidated subsidiaries, excludes excise taxes.

Source: Fortune.

TOP TEN GLOBAL LIFE/HEALTH INSURANCE COMPANIES BY REVENUES, 2006[1]
($ millions)

Rank	Company	Revenues[2]	Country
1	ING Group	$158,274	Netherlands
2	AXA	139,738	France
3	Assicurazioni Generali	101,811	Italy
4	Aviva	83,487	U.K.
5	Prudential	66,134	U.K.
6	Nippon Life Insurance	56,624	Japan
7	CNP Assurances	55,584	France
8	MetLife	53,275	U.S.
9	Aegon	45,939	Netherlands
10	Dai-ichi Mutual Life Insurance	40,146	Japan

[1]Based on an analysis of companies in the Global Fortune 500. Includes stock and mutual companies.
[2]Revenues include premium and annuity income, investment income and capital gains or losses, but exclude deposits; includes consolidated subsidiaries, excludes excise taxes.

Source: Fortune.

TOP TEN GLOBAL REINSURERS BY NET REINSURANCE PREMIUMS WRITTEN, 2006
($ millions)

Rank	Company	Net reinsurance premiums written	Country
1	Munich Re	$25,432.7	Germany
2	Swiss Re[1]	23,841.1	Switzerland
3	Berkshire Hathaway Re	11,576.0	U.S.
4	Hannover Re	9,353.5	Germany
5	Lloyd's	8,445.3	U.K.
6	SCOR[2]	4,885.2	France
7	Reinsurance Group of America Inc.	4,343.0	U.S.
8	Everest Re	3,875.7	Bermuda
9	PartnerRe	3,689.5	Bermuda
10	Transatlantic Holdings Inc.	3,633.4	U.S.

[1]Does not reflect full year premiums for GE Insurance Solutions Corp., acquired June 2006.
[2]Based on a pro forma consolidation of SCOR and Revios, acquired in 2006.

Source: Standard & Poors.

TOP TEN GLOBAL INSURANCE BROKERS BY REVENUES, 2006
($ millions)

Rank	Company	Brokerage revenues[1]	Country
1	Marsh & McLennan Cos. Inc.	$10,474.0	U.S.
2	Aon Corp.	6,709.0	U.S.
3	Willis Group Holdings Ltd.	2,341.0	U.K.
4	Arthur J. Gallagher & Co.	1,437.8	U.S.
5	Wells Fargo Insurance Services Inc.	1,008.7	U.S.
6	Brown & Brown Inc.	864.7	U.S.
7	Jardine Lloyd Thompson Group plc	847.0	U.K.
8	BB&T Insurance Services Inc.	842.3	U.S.
9	Hilb Rogal & Hobbs Co.	696.0	U.S.
10	Lockton Cos. L.L.C.	657.2	U.S.

[1]Gross revenues generated by insurance brokerage, consulting and related services.

Source: Business Insurance, July 16, 2007.

TOP TEN GLOBAL REINSURANCE BROKERS BY REINSURANCE REVENUES, 2006
($000)

Rank	Company	Reinsurance revenues	Country
1	Aon Re Global	$942,000	U.S.
2	Guy Carpenter & Co. L.L.C.	880,000	U.S.
3	Benfield Group Ltd.	654,960[1]	U.K.
4	Willis Re	597,700	U.K.
6	Towers Perrin	165,700	U.S.
5	Cooper Gay (Holdings) Ltd.	133,660	U.K.
7	Jardine Lloyd Thompson Group P.L.C.	118,531[1]	U.K.
8	BMS Group	74,734[1]	U.K.
9	Gallagher Re	71,300	U.K.
10	John B. Collins Associates Inc.	64,400	U.S.

[1]Fiscal year 2006.

Source: Business Insurance, October 29, 2007.

FOREIGN SALES BY U.S. INSURANCE COMPANIES

A majority-owned foreign affiliate of a U.S. company is defined as one that is located in another country and is more than 50 percent owned by a U.S. multinational.

SALES OF INSURANCE OVERSEAS BY AFFILIATES OF U.S. INSURANCE COMPANIES, 1997-2004[1]

Year	Life		Nonlife[2]		Total	
	Sales ($ millions)	Percent change from prior year	Sales ($ millions)	Percent change from prior year	Sales ($ millions)	Percent change from prior year
1997	$19,206	NA	$43,661	NA	$62,867	NA
1998	20,727	7.9%	43,137	-1.2%	63,864	1.6%
1999	24,970	20.5	45,271	4.9	70,241	10.0
2000	33,140	32.7	50,743	12.1	83,883	19.4
2001	33,059	-0.2	46,406	-8.5	79,465	-5.3
2002	40,930	23.8	51,908	11.9	92,838	16.8
2003	44,393	8.5	56,015	7.9	100,408	8.2
2004	NA	NA	60,647	8.3	NA	NA

[1]U.S. majority-owned companies. As of 2004, excludes sales by U.S. bank holding companies.
[2]Includes accident and health insurance.
NA=Data not available.

Source: U.S. Department of Commerce, Bureau of Economic Analysis, International Investment Division.

SALES OF INSURANCE IN THE UNITED STATES BY FOREIGN-OWNED COMPANIES

A foreign-owned insurance company is defined as one that is at least 50 percent owned or controlled by a foreign person or business group.

SALES OF INSURANCE IN THE UNITED STATES BY FOREIGN-OWNED COMPANIES, 2002-2004[1]

Year	Life		Nonlife[2]		Total	
	Sales ($ millions)	Percent change from prior year	Sales ($ millions)	Percent change from prior year	Sales ($ millions)	Percent change from prior year
2002	$44,917	NA	$63,619	NA	$108,536	NA
2003	43,869	-2.3%	68,324	7.4%	112,193	3.4%
2004	45,721	4.2	64,232	-6.0	109,953	-2.0

[1]Foreign majority-owned companies. Due to reclassifications resulting from the 2002 benchmark survey, data prior to 2002 are not available.
[2]Includes accident and health insurance.
NA=Data not available.

Source: U.S. Department of Commerce, Bureau of Economic Analysis, International Investment Division.

Over the years, a number of alternatives to traditional commercial insurance have emerged to respond to fluctuations in the marketplace. Captives—a special type of insurance company set up by a parent company, trade association or group of companies to insure the risks of its owner or owners—emerged during the 1980s, when businesses had trouble obtaining some types of commercial insurance coverage. Other so-called alternative risk transfer (ART) arrangements include self insurance, risk retention groups and risk purchasing groups.

LEADING CAPTIVE DOMICILES, 2006

- The number of worldwide captives increased from 3,361 in 1997 to 4,936 in 2006, according to Business Insurance.

Rank	Location	Number of captives	
		2005	2006
1	Bermuda	987[1]	989
2	Cayman Islands	733	740
3	Vermont	542	563
4	British Virgin Islands	380	383[1]
5	Guernsey	382	381
6	Barbados	242	235
7	Luxembourg	208	208
8	Turks and Caicos	166[2]	169[2]
9	Isle of Man	165	161
10	Hawaii	158	160
11	Dublin	154[1]	154[1]
12	South Carolina	122	146
13	Nevada	58	97
14	Arizona	53	74
15	D.C.	59	70
16	Singapore	60	60
17	Switzerland	48	48
18	New York	33	39
19	Utah	15	30
20	Bahamas	22	26
	Total top 20	**4,587**	**4,733**
	Total worldwide	**4,772**	**4,936**

[1]Business Insurance estimate.
[2]Excludes credit life insurers.

Source: Business Insurance, March 12, 2007.

NET PREMIUMS WRITTEN, PROPERTY/CASUALTY AND LIFE/HEALTH

There are three main insurance sectors. Property/casualty consists mainly of auto, home and commercial insurance. Life/health consists mainly of life insurance and annuity products. The third sector, health insurance, is offered by private health insurance companies, as well as by some life/health and property/casualty insurers. The government's large-scale participation in providing health care through Medicaid and Medicare makes it difficult to compare the health care sector with the life/health and property/casualty sectors, which are mostly private.

P/C AND L/H INSURANCE PREMIUMS, 1997-2006
($000)

Year	Property/casualty[1]	Life/health[2]	Total
1997	$283,979,804	$256,774,578	$540,754,382
1998	286,995,396	269,892,499	556,887,895
1999	293,108,867	272,584,233	565,693,100
2000	305,069,884	303,442,516	608,512,399
2001	327,821,992	479,113,800	806,935,792
2002	375,009,622	508,645,715	883,655,337
2003	409,256,440	500,234,206	909,490,647
2004	427,396,262	531,160,266	958,556,528
2005	429,202,836	528,143,125	957,345,961
2006	448,940,226	583,572,554	1,032,512,780
Percent change 1997-2006	**58.1%**	**127.3%**	**90.9%**

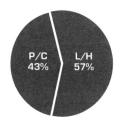

U.S. P/C AND L/H INSURANCE PREMIUMS, 2006

P/C 43% L/H 57%

[1]Net premiums written, excluding state funds. [2]Premiums and annuity considerations (fees for annuity contracts) for life/health insurance companies. Includes deposit-type funds beginning in 2001.

Source: National Association of Insurance Commissioners (NAIC) Annual Statement Database, via Highline Data, LLC. Copyrighted information. No portion of this work may be copied or redistributed without the express written permission of Highline Data, LLC.

PREMIUMS BY TYPE OF INSURER, 2006[1]

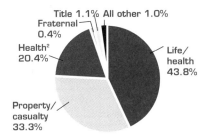

Title 1.1% All other 1.0%
Fraternal 0.4%
Health[2] 20.4%
Life/health 43.8%
Property/casualty 33.3%

- In 2006 net premiums for the property/casualty sector were up 4.6 percent from 2005, according to Highline.

- Life/health insurance premiums and annuity considerations increased 10.5 percent over the same period.

[1]Gross direct premiums. Total premiums for 2006 were $1,409 billion.
[2]Blue Cross/Blue Shield, HMOs and hospital, medical and dental indemnity.
Source: National Association of Insurance Commissioners. Reprinted with permission.

GROWTH IN U.S. PREMIUMS, PROPERTY/CASUALTY AND LIFE/HEALTH INSURANCE, 1997-2006
(Percent change from prior year)

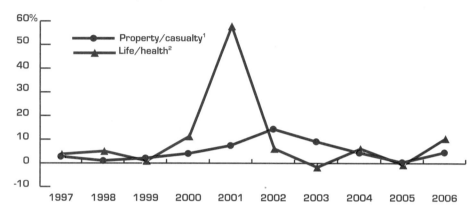

[1]Net premiums written, excluding state funds.

[2]Premiums and annuity considerations for life/health insurance companies. Includes deposit-type funds beginning in 2001.

Source: National Association of Insurance Commissioners (NAIC) Annual Statement Database, via Highline Data, LLC. Copyrighted information. No portion of this work may be copied or redistributed without the express written permission of Highline Data, LLC.

LEADING COMPANIES

LEADING WRITERS OF PROPERTY/CASUALTY INSURANCE BY DIRECT PREMIUMS WRITTEN, 2006
($000)

Rank	Group	Direct premiums written[1]	Market share[2]
1	State Farm Group	$49,614,181	10.0%
2	American International Group	37,859,639	7.6
3	Zurich Insurance Group	28,021,317	5.6
4	Allstate Insurance Group	27,879,416	5.6
5	Travelers Group	22,042,925	4.4
6	Liberty Mutual Insurance Group	18,121,842	3.7
7	Nationwide Group	16,045,069	3.2
8	Berkshire Hathaway Ins. Group	15,211,387	3.1
9	Progressive Group	14,389,701	2.9
10	Hartford Fire & Casualty Group	11,734,580	2.4

[1]Before reinsurance transactions, excluding state funds.
[2]Based on U.S. total including territories.

Source: National Association of Insurance Commissioners (NAIC) Annual Statement Database, via Highline Data, LLC. Copyrighted information. No portion of this work may be copied or redistributed without the express written permission of Highline Data, LLC.

LEADING WRITERS OF LIFE INSURANCE BY DIRECT PREMIUMS WRITTEN, 2006
($000)

Rank	Group	Direct premiums written[1]	Market share[2]
1	American International Group	$44,780,773	8.2%
2	Metropolitan Group	44,499,307	8.1
3	Prudential of America	43,907,439	8.0
4	ING America Insurance Holding Group	29,084,643	5.3
5	John Hancock Group	27,482,404	5.0
6	Hartford Fire & Casualty Group	26,545,649	4.8
7	Aegon US Holding Group	25,550,687	4.7
8	New York Life Group	21,461,127	3.9
9	Principal Financial Group	20,582,781	3.8
10	Lincoln National	18,679,812	3.4

[1]Premium and annuity totals, before reinsurance transactions, excluding state funds.
[2]Based on U.S. total including territories.

Source: National Association of Insurance Commissioners (NAIC) Annual Statement Database, via Highline Data, LLC. Copyrighted information. No portion of this work may be copied or redistributed without the express written permission of Highline Data, LLC.

HEALTH INSURANCE EXPENDITURES

Nearly half of the nation's health care costs are covered under Medcaid, Medicare and other public programs.

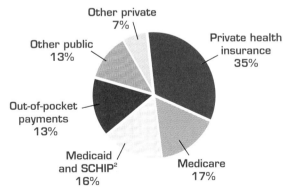

THE NATION'S HEALTH CARE DOLLAR: 2005
WHERE IT COMES FROM[1]

Other private
7%

Other public
13%

Private health
insurance
35%

Out-of-pocket
payments
13%

Medicaid
and SCHIP[2]
16%

Medicare
17%

[1]Does not add to 100 percent due to rounding.
[2]State Children's Health Insurance Program.

Source: Centers for Medicare and Medicaid Services, Office of the Actuary, National Health Statistics Group.

NATIONAL HEALTH CARE EXPENDITURES

According to the U.S. Department of Commerce Centers for Medicare and Medicaid Services, national health care expenditures reached $2.0 trillion, or $6,697 per capita, in 2005, up 6.9 percent from 2004. In 1993, the beginning of the shift to managed care, national health care expenditures were 13.4 percent of the gross domestic product. By 2005 they had grown to 16.0 percent. They are projected to increase to 19.6 percent by 2016.

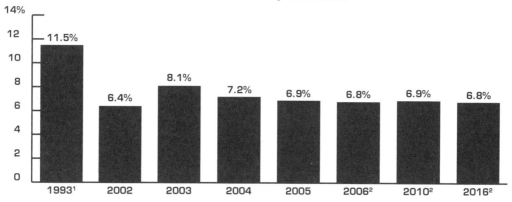

NATIONAL HEALTH CARE EXPENDITURES, AVERAGE ANNUAL PERCENT GROWTH FROM PRIOR YEAR, 1993-2016

[1]Average annual growth from 1970 through 1993; marks the beginning of the shift to managed care.
[2]Projected.

Source: Centers for Medicare and Medicaid Services, Office of the Actuary.

EMPLOYMENT AND OTHER ECONOMIC CONTRIBUTIONS

Property/casualty and life/health insurance contribute to our economy far beyond their core function of helping to manage risk. Insurers contribute about $300 billion to the nation's gross domestic product annually. The taxes they pay include special levies on insurance premiums, which amounted to $15.4 billion in 2006, or 2.2 percent of all taxes collected by the states (see p. 42). Insurance companies invest the premiums they collect in state and local municipal bonds, helping to fund the building of roads, schools and other public projects. They provide businesses with capital for research, expansions and other ventures through their holdings in stocks and bonds, a figure which totaled $3.3 trillion in 2006. The industry is also a major contributor to charitable causes, with donations to U.S. beneficiaries totaling $181.3 million in 2005, placing it among the top 15 contributors, according to a survey of industries by the Conference Board. The sector is also a very large employer, providing some 2.3 million jobs, or 2.0 percent of U.S. employment in 2006.

GROSS DOMESTIC PRODUCT

INSURANCE SECTOR'S SHARE OF GROSS DOMESTIC PRODUCT (GDP), 2001-2005
($ billions)

| Year | Total GDP | Insurance carriers and related activities | |
		GDP	Percent of total GDP
2001	$10,128.0	$234.4	2.3%
2002	10,469.6	237.4	2.3
2003	10,960.8	255.0	2.3
2004	11,712.5	295.6	2.5
2005	12,455.8	296.1	2.4

Source: U.S. Department of Commerce, Bureau of Economic Analysis.

- GDP is the total value of all final goods and services produced in the economy. The GDP growth rate is the primary indicator of the state of the economy.

- The insurance industry contributed $296 billion to the $12.5 trillion GDP in 2005.

EMPLOYMENT IN INSURANCE, 1997-2006
(Annual averages, 000)

| Year | Insurance carriers | | | | Insurance agencies, brokerages and related services | | | Total industry | Insurance and employee benefit funds[3] |
| | Direct insurers[1] | | | | | | | | |
	Life, health and medical	Property/ casualty	Reinsurers	Total	Insurance agencies and brokers	Other insurance-related activities[2]	Total		
1997	797.4	566.9	35.1	1,399.5	559.9	184.2	744.1	2,143.6	38.3
1998	816.8	592.0	34.3	1,443.1	574.9	191.5	766.3	2,209.4	41.4
1999	815.3	603.9	33.5	1,452.7	585.3	198.1	783.4	2,236.1	44.9
2000	808.8	591.6	32.3	1,432.7	587.5	200.3	787.8	2,220.6	46.4
2001	807.7	591.3	31.4	1,430.4	597.9	205.3	803.2	2,233.7	48.4
2002	791.1	590.0	31.7	1,412.8	616.0	204.4	820.4	2,233.2	47.2
2003	789.0	608.6	31.0	1,428.6	628.5	208.9	837.4	2,266.0	47.1
2004	764.4	604.4	29.8	1,398.6	643.3	216.8	860.1	2,258.6	47.0
2005	761.9	595.0	28.8	1,385.7	650.1	223.5	873.6	2,259.3	46.4
2006	797.9	601.0	28.8	1,427.7	659.9	228.3	888.2	2,315.9	48.1

[1]Establishments primarily engaged in initially underwriting insurance policies.
[2]Includes claims adjusters, third-party administrators of insurance funds and other service personnel such as advisory and insurance ratemaking services.
[3]Includes employees of legal entities organized to provide insurance and employee benefits exclusively for the sponsor, or its employees or members. These employees are not included in the total for the insurance industry.

Source: U.S. Department of Labor, Bureau of Labor Statistics.

THE TOP TEN INSURANCE-RELATED MERGERS AND ACQUISITIONS REPORTED IN 2006[1]
($ millions)

- The number of insurance mergers from 2002 to 2006 ranged from a high of 317 in 2006 to a low of 281 in 2002. During the same period, the value of deals fluctuated from a high of $60.0 billion in 2003 to a low of $9.2 billion in 2002.

- Insurance deal value fell from $49.8 billion in 2005 to $23.6 billion in 2006. However, the number of deals rose from 296 in 2005 to 317 in 2006.

Rank	Buyer	Target	Deal value[2]
1	Aviva Plc	AmerUs Group Co.	$2,740.1
2	Protective Life Corp.	Chase Insurance Group	893.0
3	QBE Insurance Group Limited	Praetorian Financial Group Inc.	800.0
4	Principal Financial Group Inc.	WM Advisors Inc.	740.0
5	Onex Corp.	Aon Warranty Group Inc.	710.0
6	Investor group	Scottish Re Group Limited	600.0
7	Prudential Financial Inc.	Variable annuity business	580.5
8	Elara Holdings Inc.	Direct General Corp.	433.7
9	Genworth Financial Inc.	AssetMark Investment Services	340.0
10	Berkshire Hathaway Inc.	Applied Underwriters	339.7

[1]At least one of the companies involved is a U.S.-domiciled company. List does not include terminated deals.
[2]At announcement.

Source: SNL Financial LC.

TOTAL INSURANCE-RELATED REPORTED MERGERS AND ACQUISITIONS, 2002-2006[1]

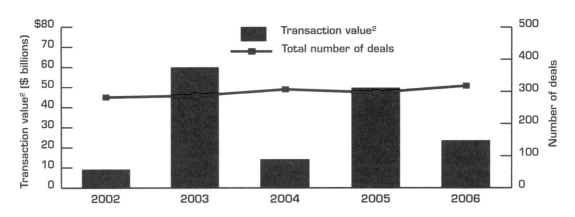

[1]At least one of the companies involved is a U.S.-domiciled company. Does not include terminated deals.
[2]At announcement.

Source: SNL Financial LC.

Insurers are increasingly using multiple distribution channels to sell their products. Traditionally, P/C insurers sold mostly through insurance agents—either captive agents, who sold only the products of one insurance company, or independent agents, who handled the products of many insurers. Companies using captive agents as well as companies selling directly to consumers through the mail, Internet or through telephone solicitations are called direct writers. Blurring the distribution lines, insurers using independent agents are now also selling directly to the consumers.

In 2006 agency writers accounted for 52.3 percent of P/C insurance net premiums written, direct writers accounted for 47.4 percent and other types of writers accounted for 0.3 percent, according to A.M. Best. In the personal lines market, direct writers accounted for 66.9 percent of net premiums written in 2006, agency writers accounted for 33.0 percent and other types of writers accounted for 0.1 percent. In 2006 agency writers, including brokers, accounted for 70.3 percent of commercial property/casualty net premiums written, direct writers accounted for 29.3 percent, and other types of writers accounted for 0.4 percent.

Life insurance was once sold principally by captive agents representing one company. By 2006, independent agents accounted for 56 percent of new life insurance sales, affiliated (i.e., captive) agents held 35 percent of new individual life insurance sales, and others, including stockbrokers, the internet and other direct channels, accounted for the remaining 9 percent, according to LIMRA.

- There were 37,500 independent insurance agencies in 2006, according to the Independent Insurance Agents and Brokers of America, compared with 39,000 in 2004, as agencies increased in size but fell in number.

- In 2006 personal P/C insurance accounted for 44 percent of agency insurance revenues. Commercial lines accounted for 40 percent, life and health insurance for 3 percent, employee benefits for 4 percent and miscellaneous sources for the remainder.

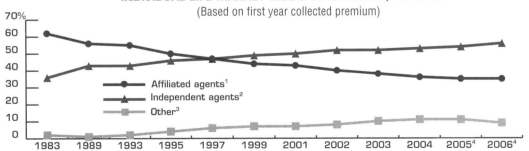

INDIVIDUAL LIFE MARKET SHARE BY CHANNEL, 1983-2006
(Based on first year collected premium)

- Affiliated agents[1]
- Independent agents[2]
- Other[3]

[1]Includes career, multiline exclusive agents and home service. [2]Includes brokers and personal producing general agents. [3]Includes stockbrokers, financial institutions and direct. [4]Estimate.

Source: LIMRA's Market Share by Distribution Channel Survey, LIMRA estimates.

DOMESTIC INSURANCE COMPANIES BY STATE

An insurance company is said to be "domiciled" in the state that issued its primary license; it is "domestic" in that state. Once licensed in one state, it may seek licenses in other states as a "foreign" insurer. An insurer incorporated in a foreign country is called an "alien" insurer in the U.S. states in which it is licensed.

DOMESTIC INSURANCE COMPANIES BY STATE, PROPERTY/CASUALTY AND LIFE/HEALTH INSURANCE, 2006

- According to the National Association of Insurance Commissioners (NAIC), there were 2,648 P/C companies in the United States in 2006, compared with 2,725 in 2005.

- The L/H insurance industry consisted of 1,257 companies in 2006, compared with 1,299 in 2005.

- Many insurance companies are part of larger organizations. According to A.M. Best, in 2006 the P/C insurance industry consisted of 967 organizations, including 584 stock (or public) companies and 315 mutual organizations (firms owned by their policyholders). The remainder consisted of 57 reciprocals, 8 Lloyd's organizations and 19 state funds. (See glossary.)

State	Property/ casualty	Life/ health	State	Property/ casualty	Life/ health
Alabama	23	13	Montana	5	3
Alaska	7	0	Nebraska	33	27
Arizona	45	211	Nevada	13	4
Arkansas	11	35	New Hampshire	30	3
California	120	23	New Jersey	81	6
Colorado	16	10	New Mexico	9	3
Connecticut	67	29	New York	193	82
Delaware	84	36	North Carolina	68	5
D.C.	7	3	North Dakota	17	3
Florida	85	37	Ohio	136	38
Georgia	38	16	Oklahoma	49	28
Hawaii	18	3	Oregon	13	4
Idaho	9	2	Pennsylvania	196	37
Illinois	172	67	Rhode Island	25	4
Indiana	72	42	South Carolina	25	12
Iowa	59	24	South Dakota	19	2
Kansas	25	13	Tennessee	21	15
Kentucky	7	9	Texas	231	151
Louisiana	37	49	Utah	11	16
Maine	21	2	Vermont	16	2
Maryland	43	7	Virginia	15	11
Massachusetts	53	19	Washington	21	10
Michigan	70	28	West Virginia	6	2
Minnesota	51	12	Wisconsin	183	31
Mississippi	15	21	Wyoming	2	0
Missouri	52	31	**United States**[1]	**2,648**	**1,257**

[1]Includes U.S. territories and possessions.

Source: Insurance Department Resources Report, 2006, published by the National Association of Insurance Commissioners (NAIC). Reprinted with permission. Further reprint or redistribution strictly prohibited without written permission of NAIC.

FINANCIAL RESULTS

Whether measured by premium income or by assets, traditional life insurance is no longer the primary business of many companies in the life/health insurance industry. Today, the emphasis has shifted to the underwriting of annuities. Annuities are contracts that accumulate funds and/or pay out a fixed or variable income stream. An income stream can be for a set period of time or over the lifetimes of the contract holder and his or her beneficiaries.

Nevertheless, traditional life insurance products such as universal life and term life for individuals as well as group life remain an important part of the business, as do disability income and health insurance.

Life insurers invest primarily in corporate bonds but also significantly in corporate equities. Besides annuities and life insurance products, life insurers may offer other types of financial services such as asset management.

LIFE/HEALTH INSURANCE INDUSTRY: SELECTED OPERATING DATA, 2004-2006
($ millions)

	2004	2005	2006
Net premiums and annuity considerations[1]	$531,160.3	$528,143.1	$583,572.6
Net investment income	145,544.8	154,600.0	158,116.7
Net gain from operations[2]	41,146.0	41,481.2	38,734.3
Federal and foreign income taxes[3]	10,002.6	8,660.0	11,298.2
Net realized capital gains/losses	1,039.8	3,115.1	6,529.9
Net income after taxes	32,183.3	35,936.3	33,966.0
Dividends to stockholders	17,019.8	15,939.5	16,450.2
Capital and surplus (end of year)	196,843.0	231,115.0	222,335.1

[1]Annuities, life and accident and health policies and contracts.
[2]After dividends to policyholders and before federal income taxes.
[3]Incurred (excluding tax on capital gain).

Source: National Association of Insurance Commissioners (NAIC) Annual Statement Database, via Highline Data, LLC. Copyrighted information. No portion of this work may be copied or redistributed without the express written permission of Highline Data, LLC.

INVESTMENTS, LIFE/HEALTH INSURERS, 2002-2006

Investment type	Amount ($ billions)			Percent of total investments		
	2002	2005	2006	2002	2005	2006
Bonds	$1,706.2	$2,146.2	$2,134.7	73.65%	76.71%	74.28%
Stocks	88.1	94.3	138.6	3.81	3.37	4.82
Preferred stocks	24.7	25.7	64.6	1.07	0.92	2.25
Common stocks	63.4	68.7	74.0	2.74	2.45	2.58
Mortgage loans on real estate	243.5	276.5	294.0	10.23	9.88	10.51
First liens	242.1	275.2	292.9	10.45	9.84	10.19
Other than first liens	1.4	1.3	1.1	0.06	0.05	0.04
Real estate	18.8	19.1	21.8	0.94	0.68	0.65
Properties occupied by company	6.0	5.4	5.7	0.26	0.19	0.20
Properties held for income production	13.5	12.8	12.4	0.58	0.46	0.43
Properties held for sale	2.4	0.9	0.7	0.10	0.03	0.02
Cash, cash eqivalent and short-term investments	84.6	62.0	79.8	3.65	2.22	2.78
Contract loans	104.4	106.4	109.8	4.51	3.80	3.82
Other invested assets	54.3	77.6	80.1	2.34	2.77	2.79
Receivables for securities	3.1	3.0	3.0	0.13	0.11	0.11
Aggregate write-ins for invested assets	10.4	12.5	15.0	0.45	0.45	0.52
Total	**$2,316.5**	**$2,797.7**	**$2,873.8**	**100.00%**	**100.00%**	**100.00%**

Source: National Association of Insurance Commissioners (NAIC) Annual Statement Database, via Highline Data, LLC. Copyrighted information. No portion of this work may be copied or redistributed without the express written permission of Highline Data, LLC.

INVESTMENTS, LIFE/HEALTH INSURERS, BOND PORTFOLIO, 2002 AND 2006

2002

Parents, subsidiaries and affiliates 0.7%
All government and revenue bonds 22.9%
Industrial and miscellaneous 69.3%
Public utilities 7.0%

2006

Parents, subsidiaries and affiliates 1.0%
All government and revenue bonds 21.9%
Industrial and miscellaneous 70.3%
Public utilities 6.7%

Source: National Association of Insurance Commissioners (NAIC) Annual Statement Database, via Highline Data, LLC. Copyrighted information. No portion of this work may be copied or redistributed without the express written permission of Highline Data, LLC.

PREMIUMS BY LINE

Measured by premiums written, annuities are the largest life/health product line, followed by life insurance and health insurance (referred to in the industry as accident and health). Life insurance policies can be sold on an individual, or "ordinary," basis or to groups such as employees and associations. Accident and health insurance includes medical expense coverage, disability income and long-term care. Other lines include credit life, which pays the balance of a loan if the borrower dies or becomes disabled, and industrial life, small policies whose premiums are generally collected by an agent on a weekly basis.

LIFE/HEALTH INSURANCE INDUSTRY PREMIUM BY LINE, 2002-2006
($ millions)

Lines of insurance	2002 Direct premiums written[1]	Percent of total	2005 Direct premiums written[1]	Percent of total	2006 Direct premiums written[1]	Percent of total
Annuities						
Ordinary individual annuities	$176,627.7	33.1%	$177,602.1	31.4%	$193,432.6	31.2%
Group annuities	101,886.8	19.1	110,951.6	19.6	117,152.7	18.9
Total	**$278,514.5**	**52.1%**	**$288,553.6**	**51.0%**	**$310,585.2**	**50.1%**
Life						
Ordinary life	111,733.3	20.9	123,259.4	21.8	129,241.6	20.9
Group life	28,227.7	5.3	30,220.7	5.3	35,255.0	5.7
Credit life (group and individual)	1,778.3	0.3	1,597.7	0.3	1,555.7	0.3
Industrial life	306.0	0.1	250.2	[2]	239.6	[2]
Total	**$142,045.2**	**26.6%**	**$155,328.1**	**27.5%**	**$166,291.9**	**26.8%**
Accident and health[3]						
Group	76,352.9	14.3	78,781.1	13.9	84,235.7	13.6
Other	35,315.2	6.6	40,084.6	7.1	57,169.3	9.2
Credit	1,869.5	0.3	1,495.2	0.3	1,430.7	0.2
Total	**$113,537.6**	**21.3%**	**$120,360.9**	**21.3%**	**$142,835.7**	**23.0%**
All other lines	91.5	[2]	1,325.0	0.2	0.1	[2]
Total, all lines	**$534,188.8**	**100.0%**	**$565,567.7**	**100.0%**	**$619,712.9**	**100.0%**

[1]Before reinsurance transactions.
[2]Less than 0.1 percent.
[3]Does not include A/H premiums reported on the P/C and health annual statements.

Source: National Association of Insurance Commissioners (NAIC) Annual Statement Database, via Highline Data, LLC. Copyrighted information. No portion of this work may be copied or redistributed without the express written permission of Highline Data, LLC.

ANNUITIES

There are several types of annuities. Deferred annuities generally accumulate assets over a long period of time, with withdrawals usually as a single sum or as an income payment beginning at retirement. Immediate annuities allow purchasers to convert a lump sum payment into a stream of income that begins right away.

Deferred and immediate annuities can be either fixed or variable. Generally, interest credited and payments made from a fixed annuity are based on rates declared by the company which can change only yearly. Fixed annuities are considered "general account" assets. In contrast, variable annuity account values and payments are based on the performance of a separate investment portfolio, thus their value may fluctuate daily. Variable annuities are considered "separate account" assets.

Annuities can also be classified by marketing channel—sold to groups or individuals (see the Premiums by Line table, page 19).

INDIVIDUAL ANNUITY CONSIDERATIONS, 2002-2006[1]
($ billions)

- Variable annuity sales grew 16.7 percent in 2006, compared with 3.5 percent in 2005.

- Fixed annuity sales fell for the fourth consecutive year, down 4.2 percent in 2006 after falling 10.2 percent in 2005.

Year	Variable	Fixed	Total Amount	Total Percent change
2002	$116.6	$103.3	$219.9	18.7%
2003	129.4	89.4	218.8	-0.5
2004	132.9	87.9	220.8	0.9
2005	137.6	78.9	216.5	-1.9
2006	160.6	75.6	236.2	9.1

[1]Based on LIMRA's estimates of the total annuity sales market. Includes some considerations (i.e., premiums) that though bought in group settings involve individual buying decisions.

Source: LIMRA International.

ANNUITY DISTRIBUTION SYSTEMS

Insurance agents, including career agents, who sell the products of a single life insurance company, and independent agents, who represent several insurers, account for almost 40 percent of annuity sales. State and federal regulators require sellers of variable annuities, which are similar to stock market-based investments, to register with NASD and the Securities and Exchange Commission.

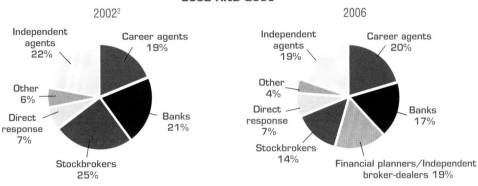

SALES OF INDIVIDUAL ANNUITIES BY DISTRIBUTION CHANNELS, 2002 AND 2006[1]

2002[2]

- Independent agents 22%
- Career agents 19%
- Other 6%
- Direct response 7%
- Banks 21%
- Stockbrokers 25%

2006

- Independent agents 19%
- Career agents 20%
- Other 4%
- Direct response 7%
- Banks 17%
- Stockbrokers 14%
- Financial planners/Independent broker-dealers 19%

[1]Preliminary.
[2]Financial planner sales included with stockbrokers prior to 2003.

Source: LIMRA International.

HEALTH INSURANCE PREMIUMS

Health insurance, referred to in the industry as accident and health (A/H) insurance, includes coverage for medical expenses, disability and long-term care. The chart below shows the premiums of companies whose business is predominantly health insurance. However, property/casualty (P/C) and life/health (L/H) insurers also participate in this market. Total health insurance from the three sectors totaled $451 billion in direct premiums written in 2006, including $303 billion from health insurers, $143 billion from L/H insurers and $5 billion from P/C insurers. As the chart indicates, private health insurers are increasingly participating in goverment programs such as Medicare and Medicaid.

HEALTH INSURANCE DIRECT PREMIUMS WRITTEN, 2002-2006[1]
($000)

Year	Direct premiums written	Government programs[2]	Total
2002	$142,993,077	NA	NA
2003	157,068,238	NA	NA
2004	165,398,197	$68,115,370	$233,513,567
2005	188,332,346	82,383,107	270,715,453
2006	203,050,501	99,704,399	302,754,900

[1]Based on aggregated data from the health insurance annual statement filings; before reinsurance transactions; includes U.S. territories. Includes data for all health insurance companies, Health Maintenance Organizations (HMOs) and Hospital, Medical and Dental/Services or Indemnity (HMDI) companies. [2]Reflects private health insurers' participation in Medicare, Medicaid and the Federal Employee benefit program. NA=Data not available.

Source: National Association of Insurance Commissioners (NAIC). Reprinted with permission Further reprint or redistribution strictly prohibited without written permission of NAIC.

DISABILITY INSURANCE

Disability insurance pays an insured person an income when he or she is unable to work because of an accident or illness.

DISABILITY INSURANCE, NEW ISSUES SALES, 2006[1]

- Annualized premiums for new disability income policies increased by 3 percent in 2006, while the number of policies decreased 2 percent. This follows a 4 percent increase in premiums and a 3 percent increase in policies in 2005.

	Number of policies	Percent change 2005-2006	Annualized premium	Percent change 2005-2006
Noncancellable	171,896	-5%	$310,292,963	2%
Guaranteed renewable	341,458	[2]	199,495,361	5
Total	**513,354**	**-2%**	**$509,788,324**	**3%**

[1]Short-term and long-term individual disability income insurance. Based on a LIMRA survey of 23 personal disability insurance companies.
[2]Less than 1 percent.

Source: LIMRA International.

INDIVIDUAL DISABILITY INCOME INSURANCE IN-FORCE, 2006[1]

	Number of policies	Percent change 2005-2006	Annualized premium	Percent change 2005-2006
Noncancellable	2,618,359	[2]	$3,698,253,752	3%
Guaranteed renewable	1,568,417	2%	942,267,780	7
Total	**4,186,776**	**1%**	**$4,640,521,532**	**4%**

[1]Excludes commercial disability insurance. Based on a LIMRA survey of 27 companies.
[2]Less than 1 percent.

Source: LIMRA International.

LONG-TERM CARE INSURANCE

Long-term care (LTC) insurance pays for services to help individuals who are unable to perform certain activities of daily living without assistance or require supervision due to a cognitive impairment such as Alzheimer's disease. LTC is available as individual insurance or through an employer-sponsored or association plan. According to the National Association of Insurance Commissioners (NAIC), long-term care insurance earned premiums increased by 6.8 percent from $8.8 billion in 2004 to $9.4 billion in 2005.

PERCENTAGE OF WORKERS WITH ACCESS TO LONG-TERM CARE INSURANCE, PRIVATE INDUSTRY, 1999-2006

Year	Percent
1999	6%
2000	7
2003	11
2004	11
2005	11
2006	12

Source: Employee Benefits Survey, U.S. Bureau of Labor Statistics.

- According to the NAIC, 194 insurers wrote LTC insurance in 2005, including 11 P/C insurers, 23 health insurers, 6 fraternal insurers and 154 life, accident and health insurers.

TOP TEN LONG-TERM CARE INSURANCE COMPANIES BY DIRECT PREMIUMS EARNED, 2005

Rank	Company	State of domicile	Parent group	Direct premiums earned	Market share
1	John Hancock Life Insurance Co.	MA	John Hancock Group	$1,544,987,143	16.44%
2	Genworth Life Insurance Co.	DE	Genworth Financial Group	1,315,346,296	14.00
3	Metropolitan Life Insurance Co.	NY	Metropolitan Group	601,925,266	6.41
4	Continental Casualty Co.	IL	CNA Insurance Group	585,978,983	6.24
5	Bankers Life & Casualty Co.	IL	Conseco Group	520,143,941	5.54
6	Unum Life Insurance Co. Of America	ME	UnumProvident Corporation Group	388,402,208	4.13
7	Conseco Senior Health Insurance Co.	PA	Conseco Group	280,281,419	2.98
8	Penn Treaty Network America Ins. Co.	PA	Penn Treaty American Group	275,825,664	2.94
9	Metlife Insurance Co. of CT	CT	Metropolitan Group	253,897,635	2.70
10	IDS Life Insurance Co.	MN	Ameriprise Financial Group	219,371,830	2.33

Source: National Association of Insurance Commissioners (NAIC). Reprinted with permission. Further reprint or redistribution strictly prohibited without written permission of NAIC.

PREMIUMS BY LINE BY STATE

LIFE/HEALTH INSURANCE PREMIUMS AND ANNUITY CONSIDERATIONS BY STATE, 2006[1]

($ millions)

State	Life insurance	Annuities	Accident and health insurance[2]	Deposit-type contract funds	Other considerations	Total
Alabama	$2,017	$2,294	$1,349	$243	$978	$6,881
Alaska	278	364	215	45	148	1,050
Arizona	1,876	4,001	3,212	381	1,677	11,147
Arkansas	868	1,318	1,209	234	447	4,076
California	13,594	20,820	12,945	3,791	13,287	64,437
Colorado	1,838	3,818	2,681	1,587	1,438	11,362
Connecticut	2,397	4,573	2,093	6,569	2,298	17,931
Delaware	3,438	1,796	459	15,502	454	21,649
D.C.	408	532	548	217	671	2,375
Florida	7,338	14,752	8,690	1,632	5,743	38,156
Georgia	3,876	4,185	3,876	1,343	1,582	14,861
Hawaii	624	1,154	314	58	526	2,676
Idaho	439	889	446	276	211	2,261
Illinois	6,063	9,100	6,499	1,734	3,733	27,129
Indiana	2,330	4,598	3,283	1,384	1,467	13,061
Iowa	1,325	2,788	1,404	2,415	768	8,701
Kansas	1,173	1,993	2,522	3,271	597	9,555
Kentucky	1,272	1,907	1,380	177	780	5,517
Louisiana	1,778	2,867	1,597	681	1,209	8,132
Maine	380	805	583	106	336	2,209
Maryland	2,463	4,159	2,011	4,557	2,463	15,653
Massachusetts	3,245	5,559	2,164	1,555	3,026	15,549
Michigan	3,595	8,608	3,601	1,042	2,768	19,613
Minnesota	2,481	4,559	1,661	1,813	1,874	12,389
Mississippi	933	1,127	2,401	154	395	5,009
Missouri	2,374	3,911	4,301	889	1,816	13,290
Montana	250	506	408	25	159	1,349
Nebraska	796	1,550	1,187	779	504	4,817

(table continues)

LIFE/HEALTH INSURANCE PREMIUMS AND ANNUITY CONSIDERATIONS BY STATE, 2006[1] (Cont'd)

($ millions)

State	Life insurance	Annuities	Accident and health insurance[2]	Deposit-type contract funds	Other considerations	Total
Nevada	$804	$1,234	$916	$247	$427	$3,628
New Hampshire	515	1,085	477	42	499	2,619
New Jersey	6,129	10,212	3,521	7,915	3,516	31,292
New Mexico	518	825	554	114	365	2,377
New York	11,974	15,534	5,543	9,522	9,903	52,476
North Carolina	3,993	5,649	4,023	1,596	2,112	17,373
North Dakota	239	513	259	24	153	1,187
Ohio	4,636	8,855	5,223	1,431	3,277	23,422
Oklahoma	1,369	1,634	1,588	273	594	5,459
Oregon	1,112	2,048	1,357	254	1,102	5,872
Pennsylvania	5,915	10,343	3,905	1,387	4,371	25,922
Rhode Island	469	850	373	107	311	2,109
South Carolina	1,660	2,452	1,830	181	787	6,909
South Dakota	384	493	337	45	184	1,444
Tennessee	2,323	3,788	2,616	573	1,850	11,151
Texas	8,376	14,305	12,617	2,015	4,543	41,856
Utah	819	1,625	835	291	542	4,112
Vermont	230	470	307	102	171	1,280
Virginia	3,331	4,809	3,126	2,982	2,074	16,321
Washington	2,242	3,341	2,080	906	1,701	10,271
West Virginia	535	959	620	65	318	2,496
Wisconsin	2,148	4,748	4,042	840	1,578	13,355
Wyoming	198	309	260	68	122	956
United States[3]	**$129,367**	**$210,616**	**$129,445**	**$83,439**	**$91,854**	**$644,721**

[1]Direct premiums written before reinsurance transactions, excluding state funds.
[2]Does not include A/H premiums reported on P/C and health annual statements.
[3]Totals here do not include territories, dividends and other nonstate specific data.

Source: National Association of Insurance Commissioners (NAIC). Reprinted with permission. Further reprint or redistribution strictly prohibited without written permission of NAIC.

TOP TEN LIFE INSURANCE GROUPS BY NUMBER OF INDIVIDUAL TERM LIFE INSURANCE POLICIES ISSUED, 2006

Rank	Company	Number of policies issued	Amount of insurance issued ($000)	Average amount issued per policy
1	State Farm Consolidated	382,044	$79,367,426	$207,744
2	American International Consolidated	378,566	133,836,830	353,536
3	Citigroup Consolidated	259,499	75,825,937	292,201
4	Direct General Group Consolidated	258,480	2,950,590	11,415
5	Liberty National Consolidated	255,598	6,636,489	25,965
6	Genworth Financial Group Consolidated	185,029	82,172,079	444,104
7	American Family Corp. Consolidated	168,657	16,236,462	96,269
8	Protective Life Insurance Consolidated	139,893	65,506,562	468,262
9	Old Mutual Consolidated	130,190	28,599,498	219,675
10	Northwestern Mutual Consolidated	115,849	73,669,181	635,907

Source: National Association of Insurance Commissioners (NAIC) Annual Statement Database, via Highline Data, LLC. Copyrighted information. No portion of this work may be copied or redistributed without the express written permission of Highline Data, LLC.

TOP TEN LIFE INSURANCE GROUPS BY NUMBER OF INDIVIDUAL WHOLE LIFE AND ENDOWMENT INSURANCE POLICIES ISSUED, 2006[1]

Rank	Company	Number of policies	Amount of insurance issued ($000)	Average amount issued per policy
1	Liberty National Consolidated	1,072,960	$19,037,775	$17,743
2	Gerber Life Insurance Company	577,551	4,971,751	8,608
3	American International Consolidated	531,790	26,986,466	50,746
4	State Farm Consolidated	275,206	17,167,091	62,379
5	UnumProvident Life Consolidated	257,001	6,336,959	24,657
6	AEGON USA Incorporated Consolidated	253,848	21,199,043	83,511
7	Mutual of Omaha Consolidated	181,287	3,746,233	20,665
8	Metropolitan Group Consolidated	169,377	28,396,202	167,651
9	New York Life Consolidated	166,587	29,796,194	178,863
10	Unitrin Group Consolidated	146,868	1,194,457	8,133

[1]Benefit is payable either at death or at stated date if policyholder is still alive on that date.

Source: National Association of Insurance Commissioners (NAIC) Annual Statement Database, via Highline Data, LLC. Copyrighted information. No portion of this work may be copied or redistributed without the express written permission of Highline Data, LLC.

LEADING WRITERS OF INDIVIDUAL ANNUITIES BY NET PREMIUMS WRITTEN, 2006
($000)

Rank	Company	Net premiums written
1	Metropolitan Group Consolidated	$16,536,855
2	Hartford Fire and Casualty Consolidated	13,330,114
3	American International Consolidated	12,508,028
4	Lincoln National Consolidated	11,369,824
5	Ameriprise Financial Group Consolidated	10,345,584
6	Allianz Insurance Consolidated	10,219,277
7	Pacific Life Insurance Consolidated	8,713,319
8	Jackson National Consolidated	8,547,867
9	Tiaa Consolidated	7,200,840
10	Prudential of America Consolidated	6,229,465

Source: National Association of Insurance Commissioners (NAIC) Annual Statement Database, via Highline Data, LLC. Copyrighted information. No portion of this work may be copied or redistributed without the express written permission of Highline Data, LLC.

LEADING WRITERS OF GROUP ANNUITIES BY NET PREMIUMS WRITTEN, 2006
($000)

Rank	Company	Net premiums written
1	Prudential of America Consolidated	$15,705,678
2	ING America Insurance Holding Group Consolidated	15,296,875
3	John Hancock Consolidated	13,123,987
4	Axa Insurance Group Consolidated	10,581,706
5	Metropolitan Group Consolidated	7,512,452
6	American International Consolidated	6,414,156
7	Mass Mutual Life Insurance Company Consolidated	6,065,324
8	Hartford Fire and Casualty Consolidated	5,447,600
9	AEGON USA Incorporated Consolidated	5,261,462
10	Great West Life Assurance Consolidated	4,708,655

Source: National Association of Insurance Commissioners (NAIC) Annual Statement Database, via Highline Data, LLC. Copyrighted information. No portion of this work may be copied or redistributed without the express written permission of Highline Data, LLC.

TOP TEN LONG-TERM DISABILITY CARRIERS BY SALES PREMIUM, 2006
($ millions)

Rank	Company	Premiums	Market share
1	Hartford Life	$198.9	15.1%
2	Unum	180.7	13.7
3	Standard	114.1	8.6
4	CIGNA	101.2	7.7
5	Sun Life Financial	81.2	6.1
6	Reliance Standard	81.0	6.1
7	Prudential	76.8	5.8
8	MetLife	71.9	5.4
9	Lincoln Financial Group	71.8	5.4
10	Aetna	54.5	4.1

Source: JHA, Inc., 2006 U.S. Group Disability Market Survey.

TOP TEN SHORT-TERM DISABILITY CARRIERS BY SALES PREMIUM, 2006
($ millions)

Rank	Company	Premiums	Market share
1	Hartford Life	$92.3	15.2%
2	Unum	66.7	11.0
3	Lincoln Financial Group	53.5	8.8
4	Standard	42.1	6.9
5	Guardian Life	37.2	6.1
6	CIGNA	35.0	5.8
7	Reliance Standard	33.6	5.5
8	Principal Financial Group	30.0	4.9
9	MetLife	27.0	4.5
10	Prudential	25.8	4.3

Source: JHA, Inc., 2006 U.S. Group Disability Market Survey.

2006 FINANCIAL RESULTS

The U.S. property/casualty industry posted a $31.2 billion net gain on underwriting for 2006, driven in part by a sharp decline in catastrophe losses from hurricanes and other natural disasters. The net gain on underwriting in 2006 stands in stark contrast to the $5.6 billion net underwriting loss in 2005. The industry's positive underwriting results contributed to net income after taxes of $63.7 billion in 2006, compared with $44.2 billion the previous year. Reflecting the increase in net aftertax income, the industry's rate of return, expressed as net income after taxes as a percent of policyholders' surplus (net worth), rose to 13.4 percent in 2006 from 10.7 percent in 2005. Premiums written rose 4.3 percent in 2006, contrasting with a 0.3 percent rise the previous year.

PROPERTY/CASUALTY INSURANCE INDUSTRY INCOME ANALYSIS, 2002-2006[1]
($ billions)

	2002	2003	2004	2005	2006
Net written premiums	$369.7	$404.4	$424.1	$425.7	$443.8
Percent change	14.3%	9.4%	4.9%	0.3%	4.3%
Earned premiums	$348.5	$386.3	$413.8	$417.7	$435.8
Losses incurred	238.8	238.7	247.8	256.3	231.1
Loss adjustment expenses incurred	44.8	50.0	53.1	55.1	52.6
Other underwriting expenses	93.8	100.7	106.8	109.8	117.5
Policyholder dividends	1.9	1.9	1.7	1.9	3.4
Underwriting gain/loss	-30.8	-4.9	4.3	-5.6	31.2
Investment income	37.2	38.6	40.0	49.7	52.3
Miscellaneous income/loss	-0.8	0.0	-0.3	1.0	1.0
Operating income/loss	5.6	33.8	44.0	45.1	84.6
Realized capital gains/losses	-1.2	6.6	9.1	9.7	3.4
Incurred federal income taxes/credit	1.3	10.3	14.6	10.7	24.2
Net income after taxes	3.0	30.0	38.5	44.2	63.7

[1]2005 results include a special, nonrecurring dividend one insurer received from an investment subsidiary, which when excluded reduces net income to $40 billion. Data in this chart may not agree with similar data shown elsewhere due to different sources.
Source: ISO.

PREMIUMS AND COMBINED RATIO

Insurers use various measures to gauge financial performance. The combined ratio after dividends is a measure of underwriting profitability. It reflects the percentage of each premium dollar an insurer spends on claims and expenses. The combined ratio does not take investment income into account. A combined ratio above 100 indicates an underwriting loss.

NET PREMIUMS WRITTEN AND COMBINED RATIO, PROPERTY/CASUALTY INSURANCE, 1998-2006
($000)

- The property/casualty insurance industry is cyclical. From 1998 to 2006 premium growth ranged from a high of 13.8 percent in 2002 to a low of 0.4 percent in 2005.

- Premiums grew 4.7 percent in 2006, the highest rate since 2003, when premiums rose 9.2 percent.

Year	Net premiums written[1]	Annual percent change	Combined ratio after dividends[2]	Annual point change
1998	$286,265,346	1.0%	105.8	NA
1999	296,560,938	3.6	107.7	1.9 pts.
2000	304,313,600	2.6	109.9	2.2
2001	327,823,226	7.7	115.6	5.8
2002	373,136,894	13.8	107.0	-8.6
2003	407,516,437	9.2	100.2	-6.8
2004	425,741,326	4.5	98.5	-1.7
2005	427,625,417	0.4	100.8	2.3
2006	447,761,985	4.7	92.5	8.3

[1]After reinsurance transactions, excluding state funds. [2]After dividends to policyholders. NA=Data not available. Source: National Association of Insurance Commissioners (NAIC) Annual Statement Database, via Highline Data, LLC. Copyrighted information. No portion of this work may be copied or redistributed without the express written permission of Highline Data, LLC.

WHERE THE UNDERWRITING DOLLAR GOES

The overall cost of underwriting operations in 2006 amounted to $0.86 for every premium dollar collected, compared with $1.01 in 2005. Underwriting operations include claims and their associated expenses, costs involved in sales and administration, dividends to policyholders, and state taxes and licensing fees. They exclude investment income and a margin for profit.

WHERE THE UNDERWRITING DOLLAR GOES, PROPERTY/CASUALTY INSURANCE, ALL LINES, 2006

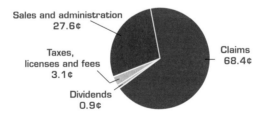

Sales and administration
27.6¢

Taxes, licenses and fees
3.1¢

Dividends
0.9¢

Claims
68.4¢

Source: National Association of Insurance Commissioners (NAIC) Annual Statement Database, via Highline Data, LLC. Copyrighted information. No portion of this work may be copied or redistributed without the express written permission of Highline Data, LLC.

PROFITABILITY: INSURANCE AND OTHER SELECTED INDUSTRIES

According to an analysis conducted by ISO, profitability of P/C insurance companies measured on a GAAP accounting basis lags behind other industries. The return on net worth for Fortune 500 combined companies for the years 1983 to 2006 exceeded that of both large property/casualty insurers and the P/C industry as a whole, in every year except 1986 and 1987.

ANNUAL RATE OF RETURN:
NET INCOME AFTER TAXES AS A PERCENT OF EQUITY, 1997-2006

| Year | Property/casualty insurance | | | Selected other industries[1] | | | Fortune 500 combined industrials and service[6] |
	Statutory accounting[2]	GAAP accounting[3]	Life/health insurance[4]	Diversified financial[5]	Commercial banks	Electric and gas utilities	
1997	11.8%	11.6%	12.0%	14.9%	16.9%	10.4%	13.9%
1998	9.2	8.5	11.0	19.8	16.0	10.2	13.4
1999	6.9	6.0	13.0	21.0	18.0	11.9	15.2
2000	6.8	5.9	10.0	21.3	16.7	11.8	14.6
2001	-1.8	-1.2	7.0	19.3	14.0	10.5	10.4
2002	3.3	2.2	1.0	19.5	17.3	7.9	10.2
2003	8.5	8.9	9.0	19.5	14.9	10.5	12.6
2004	9.3	9.4	11.0	15.0	15.5	10.5	13.9
2005	10.7	9.6	13.0	15.0	16.0	10.0	14.9
2006	13.4	12.2	12.0	15.0	15.0	11.0	15.4

[1]Return on equity on a GAAP accounting basis, Fortune.

[2]Net income after taxes, divided by year-end policyholders' surplus. Calculated by the Insurance Information Institute from Highline Data. Statutory accounting is used by insurers when preparing the Annual Statements they submit to regulators.

[3]Return on average net worth, ISO.

[4]Return on equity on a GAAP accounting basis, Fortune. Combined stock and mutual companies, calculated by the Insurance Information Institute.

[5]Companies whose major source of revenue comes from providing diversified financial services. These companies are not specifically chartered as insurance companies, banks or savings institutions, or brokerage or securities companies, but they may earn revenue from these sources.

[6]Fortune 500 Combined Industrial and Service Businesses median return on equity.

Source: National Association of Insurance Commissioners (NAIC) Annual Statement Database, via Highline Data, LLC. Copyrighted information. No portion of this work may be copied or redistributed without the express written permission of Highline Data, LLC.; ISO; Fortune.

PROPERTY/CASUALTY INSURANCE CYCLE

Most industries are cyclical to some extent. The property/casualty (P/C) insurance industry cycle is characterized by periods of soft market conditions, in which premium rates are stable or falling and insurance is readily available, and by periods of hard market conditions, where rates rise, coverage may be more difficult to find and insurers' profits increase.

A dominant factor in the P/C insurance cycle is intense competition within the industry. Premium rates drop as insurance companies compete vigorously to increase market share. As the market softens to the point that profits diminish or vanish completely, the capital needed to underwrite new business is depleted. In the up phase of the cycle, competition is less intense, underwriting standards become more stringent, the supply of insurance is limited due to the depletion of capital and, as a result, premiums rise. The prospect of higher profits draws more capital into the marketplace leading to more competition and the inevitable down phase of the cycle.

The chart below shows the real, or inflation-adjusted, growth of P/C net written premiums over more than three decades and three hard markets. Premiums can be accounted for in several ways. This chart uses net written premiums, which reflect premium amounts after deductions for reinsurance transactions.

During the last three hard markets, inflation-adjusted net premiums written grew 7.7 percent (1975-1978), 10.0 percent (1984 to 1987) and 6.3 percent (2001 to 2004).

GROWTH IN NET PREMIUMS WRITTEN, PROPERTY/CASUALTY INSURANCE, 1975-2006[1]

(Percent change from prior year)

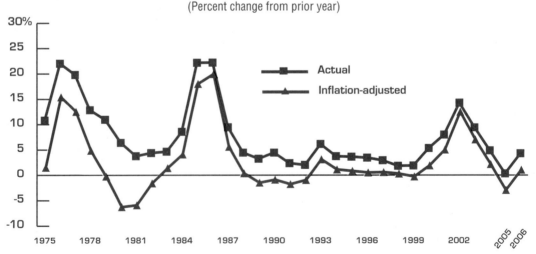

[1]Excludes state funds.

Source: ISO.

OPERATING RESULTS

In most years the insurance industry does not generate profits from its underwriting operations. Investment income from a number of sources, including capital and surplus accounts, money set aside as loss reserves and unearned premium reserves, generally offsets these losses.

OPERATING RESULTS, PROPERTY/CASUALTY INSURANCE, 1999-2006[1]
($ millions)

Year	Net underwriting gain/loss	Net investment income earned	Net realized capital gains	Policyholder dividends	Taxes	Net income after taxes[2]
1999	$18,701	$39,470	$12,971	$3,560	$6,123	$23,208
2000	-26,487	41,511	16,070	4,080	5,655	21,739
2001	-49,760	38,616	6,987	2,397	-81	-5,451
2002	-27,770	39,509	3,209	2,025	2,128	9,782
2003	-3,101	39,758	6,480	1,902	10,760	30,498
2004	5,594	40,327	8,819	1,812	14,275	38,358
2005	-3,625	49,710	11,839	1,986	10,635	46,377
2006	34,754	53,344	3,710	3,612	22,510	66,735

[1]Excludes state funds. [2]Does not equal the sum of the columns shown due to the omission of miscellaneous income.

Source: National Association of Insurance Commissioners (NAIC) Annual Statement Database, via Highline Data, LLC. Copyrighted information. No portion of this work may be copied or redistributed without the express written permission of Highline Data, LLC.

OPERATING RESULTS, PROPERTY/CASUALTY INSURANCE, 1999-2006[1]
($ billions)

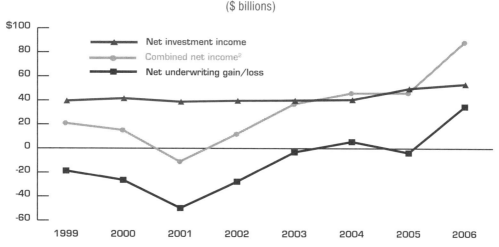

[1]Excludes state funds. [2]Net underwriting gain/loss plus net investment income.

Source: National Association of Insurance Commissioners (NAIC) Annual Statement Database, via Highline Data, LLC. Copyrighted information. No portion of this work may be copied or redistributed without the express written permission of Highline Data, LLC.

POLICYHOLDERS' SURPLUS

A property/casualty insurer must maintain a certain level of surplus to underwrite risks. This financial cushion is known as "capacity." When the industry is hit by high losses, such as a major hurricane, capacity is diminished. It can be restored by increases in net income, favorable investment returns, reinsuring more risk, and/or raising additional capital.

CONSOLIDATED ASSETS AND POLICYHOLDERS' SURPLUS, P/C INSURANCE, 1998-2006[1]

($ millions)

Year	Assets	Annual percent change	Statutory liabilities	Annual percent change	Policyholders' surplus	Annual percent change	Total net premiums written[1]	Annual percent change
1998	$913,134.4	6.0%	$573,493.2	3.5%	$339,530.9	10.5%	$286,265.3	1.0%
1999	911,960.4	-0.1	575,600.2	0.4	336,346.4	-0.9	296,560.9	3.6
2000	914,026.6	0.2	593,870.2	3.2	320,467.4	-4.7	304,313.6	2.6
2001	949,126.5	3.8	654,365.4	10.2	294,856.8	-8.0	327,823.2	7.7
2002	1,013,978.2	6.8	764,494.4	16.8	296,923.0	0.7	373,136.9	13.8
2003	1,194,393.2	17.8	833,706.9	9.1	359,518.8	21.1	407,516.4	9.2
2004	1,301,389.7	9.0	895,870.2	7.5	404,618.9	12.5	425,741.3	4.5
2005	1,399,796.1	7.6	958,376.5	7.0	432,760.5	7.0	427,625.4	0.4
2006	1,483,013.4	5.9	983,604.2	2.6	499,407.0	15.4	447,762.0	4.7

[1]After reinsurance transactions, excluding state funds.

Source: National Association of Insurance Commissioners (NAIC) Annual Statement Database, via Highline Data, LLC. Copyrighted information. No portion of this work may be copied or redistributed without the express written permission of Highline Data, LLC.

NET PREMIUMS WRITTEN AND POLICYHOLDERS' SURPLUS, PROPERTY/CASUALTY INSURANCE, 1998-2006[1]

(Percent change from prior year)

- Policyholders' surplus dropped substantially in 2001, following the World Trade Center terrorist attacks. In 2002 surplus increased only 0.7 percent due to soaring underwriting losses.

- In 2006 policyholders' surplus reached a record $499.4 billion.

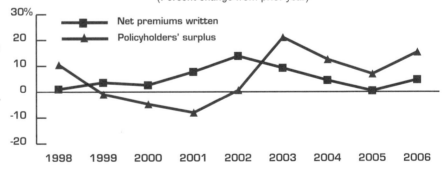

[1]After reinsurance transactions, excluding state funds.
Source: National Association of Insurance Commissioners (NAIC) Annual Statement Database, via Highline Data, LLC. Copyrighted information. No portion of this work may be copied or redistributed without the express written permission of Highline Data, LLC.

THE COMBINED RATIO

Simply put, the combined ratio represents the percentage of each premium dollar an insurer spends on claims and expenses. The following chart shows the components of the combined ratio, a measure of the industry's underwriting performance.

The combined ratio is the sum of the loss ratio and the expense ratio. The loss ratio expresses the relationship between losses and premiums in percentage terms. The expense ratio expresses the relationship between underwriting expenses and premiums.

COMPONENTS OF THE COMBINED RATIO, PROPERTY/CASUALTY INSURANCE, 1999-2006

Year	Loss ratio[1]	Expense ratio[2]	Combined ratio	Dividends to policyholders[3]	Combined ratio after dividends[4]
1999	78.5	28.0	106.5	1.2	107.7
2000	81.0	27.6	108.6	1.4	109.9
2001	88.1	26.8	114.9	0.8	115.6
2002	81.0	25.5	106.5	0.6	107.0
2003	74.7	25.0	99.7	0.5	100.2
2004	72.8	25.3	98.1	0.4	98.5
2005	74.5	25.9	100.4	0.5	100.8
2006	65.2	26.4	91.6	0.8	92.5

[1]Losses and loss adjustment expenses incurred as a percent of net premiums earned.
[2]Expenses incurred (before federal income taxes) as a percent of net premiums written.
[3]Dividends to policyholders as a percent of net premiums earned.
[4]Based on insurers' expense exhibit and are not strictly comparable with similar data shown elsewhere.

Source: National Association of Insurance Commissioners (NAIC) Annual Statement Database, via Highline Data, LLC. Copyrighted information. No portion of this work may be copied or redistributed without the express written permission of Highline Data, LLC.

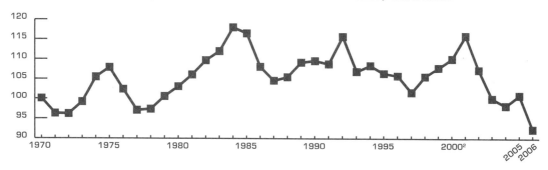

PROPERTY/CASUALTY INDUSTRY COMBINED RATIO, 1970-2006[1]

[1]Excluding state funds and residual markets. [2]Adjusted to reflect the insolvency of Reliance Insurance Company.
Source: ISO.

INVESTMENTS

Cash and invested assets of property/casualty insurance companies' totaled $1.2 trillion in 2006. This represents 83 percent of total assets, which were $1.5 trillion. Most of these assets were invested in highly liquid securities (high-quality stocks and bonds, for example, rather than real estate), which can be sold quickly to pay claims in the event of a major catastrophe.

INVESTMENTS, PROPERTY/CASUALTY INSURERS, 2002-2006
($ millions)

Investment type	Amount			Percent of total investments		
	2002	2005	2006	2002	2005	2006
Bonds	$566,259.0	$773,474.3	$823,126.3	67.12%	68.18%	67.00%
Stocks	154,193.5	208,418.3	237,303.3	18.28	18.37	19.32
Preferred	14,533.7	11,517.4	16,149.7	1.72	1.02	1.31
Common	139,659.8	196,900.9	221,153.6	16.55	17.36	18.00
Mortgage loans on real estate	2,588.6	3,241.1	3,801.7	0.31	0.29	0.31
First liens	2,528.5	3,193.9	3,787.9	0.30	0.28	0.31
Other than first liens	60.1	47.2	13.8	0.01	1	1
Real estate	9,572.0	9,323.2	9,711.3	1.13	0.82	0.79
Properties occupied by company	8,158.4	7,869.9	8,166.3	0.97	0.69	0.66
Properties held for income production	1,075.6	1,009.1	1,069.7	0.13	0.09	0.09
Properties held for sale	338.0	444.2	475.3	0.04	0.04	0.04
Cash, cash equivalent and short-term investments	71,454.0	91,497.3	98,408.3	8.47	8.06	8.01
Other invested assets	33,215.3	41,567.5	51,750.5	3.94	3.66	4.21
Receivable for securities	2,106.2	4,125.3	2,115.4	0.25	0.36	0.17
Aggregrate write-in invested assets	4,235.0	2,873.7	2,298.8	0.50	0.25	0.19
Total	**$843,623.7**	**$1,134,520.8**	**$1,228,515.5**	**100.00%**	**100.00%**	**100.00%**

[1] Less than 0.01 percent.

Source: National Association of Insurance Commissioners (NAIC) Annual Statement Database, via Highline Data, LLC. Copyrighted information. No portion of this work may be copied or redistributed without the express written permission of Highline Data, LLC.

BONDS

The asset quality of the property/casualty insurance industry's investments is unparalleled. Bonds in or near default (Class 6) accounted for less than 0.1 percent of all short- and long-term bonds and mortgage loans and other short-term investments owned by insurers at the end of 2006, according to Highline Data.

INVESTMENTS, PROPERTY/CASUALTY INSURERS, 2006

INVESTMENTS BY TYPE[1]

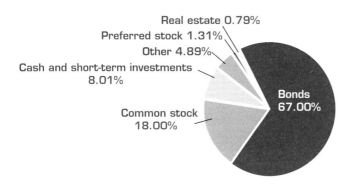

Real estate 0.79%
Preferred stock 1.31%
Other 4.89%
Cash and short-term investments 8.01%
Common stock 18.00%
Bonds 67.00%

BOND PORTFIOLIO[2]
(Represents 67.0% of total investments)

Parent, subs. and affil. 0.8%
Public utilities 2.0%
States, territories and others 12.4%
Governments 17.0%
Industrial and misc. 28.5%
Special revenue 31.8%

STOCK PORTFOLIO
(Represents 19.3% of total investments)

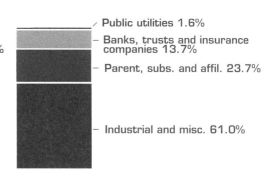

Public utilities 1.6%
Banks, trusts and insurance companies 13.7%
Parent, subs. and affil. 23.7%
Industrial and misc. 61.0%

[1]Cash and invested assets, as of December 31, 2006.
[2]Long-term bonds with maturity dates over one year.

Source: National Association of Insurance Commissioners (NAIC) Annual Statement Database, via Highline Data, LLC. Copyrighted information. No portion of this work may be copied or redistributed without the express written permission of Highline Data, LLC.

The surplus lines market exists to assume risks that licensed companies decline to insure or will only insure at a very high price, with many exclusions or with a very high deductible. To be eligible to seek coverage in the surplus lines market, a diligent effort must have been made to place insurance with an admitted company, usually defined by a certain number of "declinations," or rejections, by licensed insurers, typically three to five. Many states provide an "export list" of risks that can be insured in the surplus lines market. This obviates the diligent search requirement.

The terms applied to the surplus lines market—nonadmitted, unlicensed and unauthorized—do not mean that surplus lines companies are barred from selling insurance in a state or are unregulated. They are just less regulated. Each state has surplus lines regulations and each surplus lines company is overseen for solvency by its home state. More than half of the states maintain a list of eligible surplus lines companies and some a list of those that are not eligible to do business in that state. In addition, depending on the state, the surplus lines agent or broker, who must be licensed, is responsible for checking the eligibility of the company.

In a number of states, surplus lines companies are also monitored by surplus lines organizations, known as "Stamping Offices," which, among their many functions, assist their state's department of insurance in the regulation and oversight of surplus lines insurers. They also evaluate insurers for eligibility to do business in the state and review insurance policies obtained by surplus lines agents or brokers for their clients. Surplus lines companies thrive in hard markets, when certain kinds of coverages that are available in soft markets, such as nursing home insurance, may be more difficult to obtain.

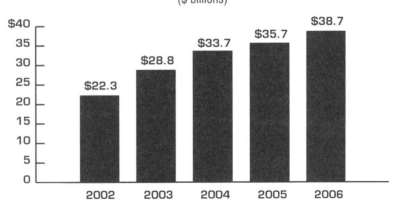

TOTAL GROSS SURPLUS LINES PREMIUMS WRITTEN, 2002-2006
($ billions)

- Surplus lines gross premiums written increased by 8 percent in 2006, following a 6 percent rise the previous year.

- Surplus lines premiums have risen by 74 percent since 2002.

2002	$22.3
2003	$28.8
2004	$33.7
2005	$35.7
2006	$38.7

Source: 2004 to 2006 premiums from Business Insurance, October 1, 2007; earlier premiums from other issues.

TOP TEN U.S.-BASED SURPLUS LINES INSURANCE COMPANIES BY NONADMITTED DIRECT WRITTEN PREMIUMS, 2006

Rank	Company	Nonadmitted direct premiums
1	Lexington Insurance Company	$6,273,352,288[1]
2	American International Specialty Lines Insurance Company	1,739,234,858
3	Steadfast Insurance Company	1,412,233,290[1]
4	Scottsdale Insurance Company	1,278,278,992[1]
5	Columbia Casualty Company	842,816,747
6	Landmark American Insurance Company	795,575,951
7	Arch Specialty Insurance Company	773,369,532
8	Evanston Insurance Company	711,214,211
9	National Fire & Marine Insurance Company	711,013,999
10	Admiral Insurance Company	602,826,555

[1]Figures provided on a pooling basis.

Source: Business Insurance, October 1, 2007.

CONCENTRATION

According to ISO, concentration in the property/casualty insurance sector increased from 229 in 1980 to 344 in 2006 on the Herfindahl scale, used to measure market concentration. The U.S. Department of Justice classifies any score under 1,000 as unconcentrated. A score over 1,800 means an industry is highly concentrated.

MARKET SHARE TRENDS BY SIZE OF INSURER, 1986-2006[1]

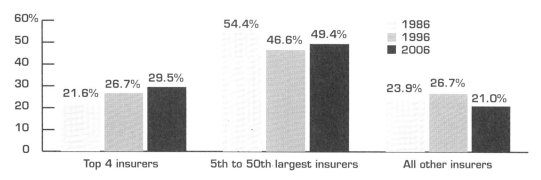

[1]Based on net premiums written, excluding state funds.

Source: ISO.

Reinsurance is essentially insurance for insurance companies. It allows primary insurers to protect against unforeseen or extraordinary losses. Reinsurance also serves to limit liability on specific risks, to increase insurers' capacity to write business, and to help insurers stabilize their business against wide swings in profit and loss margins.

REINSURANCE, 1998-2006[1]
($000)

Year	Net premiums written	Annual percent change	Combined ratio[2]	Annual point change
1998	$19,439,312	-2.5%	104.4	NA
1999	21,212,749	9.1	113.8	9.4 pts.
2000	24,853,859	17.2	114.2	0.4
2001	26,687,636	7.4	142.9	28.7
2002	29,503,920	10.6	121.3	-21.6
2003	30,630,787	3.8	101.2	-20.1
2004	28,759,085	-6.1	106.2	5.0
2005	25,330,697	-11.9	129.4	23.2
2006	25,834,026	2.0	94.9	-34.5

[1]Based on reinsurance companies responding to quarterly surveys conducted by the Reinsurance Association of America.
[2]After dividends to policyholders. NA=Data not available. Source: Reinsurance Association of America.

TOP TEN P/C REINSURERS OF U.S. BUSINESS BY GROSS PREMIUMS WRITTEN, 2006
($000)

Rank	Company	Country of parent company	Gross premiums written
1	Swiss Reinsurance America[1]	Switzerland	$6,414,868
2	National Indemnity Company (Berkshire Hathaway)	U.S.	4,606,726
3	XL Reinsurance America Inc.	Bermuda	4,388,081
4	Munich Re America Corp.[2]	Germany	3,742,663
5	Transatlantic/Putnam Reinsurance Co.	U.S.	3,659,203
6	Everest Reinsurance Company	Bermuda	3,086,844
7	OdysseyAmerica Re/Odyssey Reinsurance Corp.[3]	Canada	2,136,771
8	Berkley Insurance Co.	U.S.	1,881,347
9	General Reinsurance Corp.[4]	U.S.	1,501,527
10	Axis Reinsurance Co.[5]	Bermuda	1,151,755
	Total, all reinsurers		**$41,311,166**

[1]Represents only part of Swiss Re Group's business, including the GE Insurance Solutions business acquired from General Electric Company in June 2006. [2]Includes Munich Reinsurance America, Inc., American Alternative Insurance Corporation and The Princeton Excess and Surplus Lines Insurance Company. [3]Includes Odyssey America Reinsurance Corporation, Clearwater Insurance Company, Hudson Insurance Company, Hudson Specialty Insurance Company and Clearwater Select Insurance Company. [4]Excludes cessions to certain affiliated members of the Berkshire Hathaway Group. [5]Excludes reinsurance business of Axis Capital Holdings Ltd., written in Bermuda. Source: Reinsurance Association of America.

DIRECT PREMIUMS WRITTEN BY STATE

Direct premiums written represent premium amounts before reinsurance transactions. This contrasts with charts based on net premiums written, i.e., premium amounts after reinsurance transactions.

DIRECT PREMIUMS WRITTEN, P/C INSURANCE BY STATE, 2006[1]
($000)

State	Total, all lines	State	Total, all lines
Alabama	$6,593,510	Montana	$1,557,814
Alaska	1,525,383	Nebraska	3,171,842
Arizona	8,468,978	Nevada	4,573,605
Arkansas	3,913,012	New Hampshire	2,155,238
California	59,801,542	New Jersey	17,357,646
Colorado	7,732,157	New Mexico	2,565,279
Connecticut	7,052,258	New York	34,717,945
Delaware	2,363,454	North Carolina	11,813,383
D.C.	1,533,872	North Dakota	1,306,198
Florida	39,045,114	Ohio	13,314,181
Georgia	13,906,059	Oklahoma	5,250,419
Hawaii	2,325,192	Oregon	5,427,036
Idaho	1,853,804	Pennsylvania	19,966,389
Illinois	21,153,913	Rhode Island	1,942,407
Indiana	8,513,605	South Carolina	6,589,278
Iowa	4,572,069	South Dakota	1,456,469
Kansas	4,540,293	Tennessee	8,390,648
Kentucky	5,805,674	Texas	34,720,477
Louisiana	8,751,717	Utah	3,277,095
Maine	1,972,939	Vermont	1,111,180
Maryland	8,956,604	Virginia	10,620,969
Massachusetts	11,883,119	Washington	8,827,922
Michigan	15,320,517	West Virginia	3,082,168
Minnesota	8,670,261	Wisconsin	8,017,327
Mississippi	4,172,743	Wyoming	836,192
Missouri	9,054,590	**United States**	**$481,531,484**

- In 2006 California accounted for the largest amount of direct premiums written, followed by Florida, Texas, New York and Illinois.

- Direct premiums written in 2006 rose 2.3 percent in California, 9.6 percent in Florida, 6.2 percent in Texas, 3.9 percent in New York and 1.5 percent in Illinois. This compares with 0.6 percent growth nationally.

[1]Before reinsurance transactions, excluding state funds, territories and possessions.
Source: National Association of Insurance Commissioners (NAIC) Annual Statement Database, via Highline Data, LLC. Copyrighted information. No portion of this work may be copied or redistributed without the express written permission of Highline Data, LLC.

All insurance companies pay a state tax based on their premiums. Other payments are made to states for licenses and fees, income and property taxes, sales and use taxes, unemployment compensation taxes and franchise taxes.

PREMIUM TAXES BY STATE, PROPERTY/CASUALTY AND LIFE/HEALTH INSURANCE, 2006
($000)

- Insurance companies, including life/health and property/casualty companies, paid $15.4 billion in premium taxes to the 50 states in 2006. On a per capita basis, this works out to $51 for every person living in the United States.

- Premium taxes accounted for 2.2 percent of all taxes collected by the states in 2006.

State	Amount	State	Amount
Alabama	$273,432	Montana	$64,521
Alaska	51,912	Nebraska	37,470
Arizona	419,888	Nevada	238,334
Arkansas	127,805	New Hampshire	81,913
California	2,202,327	New Jersey	537,119
Colorado	177,783	New Mexico	103,081
Connecticut	253,430	New York	1,010,896
Delaware	85,786	North Carolina	442,301
Florida	879,079	North Dakota	29,125
Georgia	342,982	Ohio	543,977
Hawaii	92,219	Oklahoma	175,935
Idaho	86,077	Oregon	61,540
Illinois	319,805	Pennsylvania	663,997
Indiana	177,663	Rhode Island	52,860
Iowa	121,428	South Carolina	134,647
Kansas	127,819	South Dakota	58,064
Kentucky	354,148	Tennessee	379,888
Louisiana	392,035	Texas	1,233,494
Maine	93,915	Utah	120,119
Maryland	345,816	Vermont	54,722
Massachusetts	427,060	Virginia	373,781
Michigan	219,538	Washington	378,804
Minnesota	329,034	West Virginia	105,371
Mississippi	165,968	Wisconsin	150,817
Missouri	283,333	Wyoming	21,817
		United States	**$15,404,875**

Source: U.S. Department of Commerce, Bureau of the Census.

All 50 states; Washington, D.C.; Puerto Rico; and the Virgin Islands have procedures under which solvent property/casualty insurance companies cover claims against insolvent insurers. New York has a pre-assessment system, which requires the maintenance of a permanent fund to which insurance companies contribute. Estimates are made annually of how much will be needed in the coming year to fulfill the system's obligations to pay the claims of insolvent insurers. By statute, New York's pre-assessment fund balance must remain at $150 million. Some states—including New Jersey, New York and Pennsylvania—have separate pre-assessment funds for workers compensation. Florida has a post-assessment fund, which covers the claims of insolvent workers compensation insurers and self-insurers.

The lines of insurance covered by guaranty funds and the maximum amount paid on any claim vary from state to state. Assessments are used to pay claims against companies that became insolvent in the past as well as for current insolvencies.

GUARANTY FUND NET ASSESSMENTS, 1978-2005[1]

Year	Net assessment[2]	Year	Net assessment[2]
1978	$139,349,343[3]	1993	$520,215,101[4]
1979	46,222,805	1994	497,752,370[4]
1980	17,771,834	1995	66,562,926[4]
1981	49,772,896	1996	95,320,605
1982	41,109,087	1997	236,319,208
1983	30,619,239	1998	239,212,254
1984	97,435,034	1999	179,283,004
1985	292,417,521	2000	306,444,534
1986	509,409,508	2001	712,776,721
1987	903,228,359	2002	1,184,153,880[5]
1988	464,840,383	2003	874,499,309[5]
1989	713,869,682	2004	952,695,278
1990	433,562,308	2005	916,130,812
1991	434,845,812	Total	$11,351,202,780
1992	383,735,932		

- At $916.1 million, guaranty fund net assessments in 2005 were down 3.8 percent from $952.7 million in 2004, reflecting the strong financial position of the industry.

[1] Excludes New York and Workers Compensation Security Funds in New Jersey and Pennsylvania.
[2] Assessments less refunds.
[3] Includes pre-1978 net assessments.
[4] Includes separate assessments for insolvencies due to Hurricane Andrew totaling $248,542,070.
[5] Excludes data for the Louisiana Insurance Guaranty Association.

Source: National Conference of Insurance Guaranty Funds.

GUARANTY FUND NET ASSESSMENTS BY STATE, 2005[1]

State	Net assessment	State	Net assessment
Alabama	$3,397,539	Nebraska	$2,360,000
Alaska	10,758,303	Nevada	0
Arizona	0	New Hampshire	3,819,548
Arkansas	6,740,734	New Jersey	233,290,014
California	321,711,800	New Jersey Workers Compensation	15,613,640
Colorado	6,500,000	New Mexico	2,226,013
Connecticut	-15,038,354	New York	0
Delaware	504,400	North Carolina	19,978,000
D.C.	-1,437,440	North Dakota	0
Florida	0	Ohio	40,000,000
Florida Workers Compensation	114,505,450	Oklahoma	28,508,625
Georgia	19,956,662	Oregon	11,000,000
Hawaii	32,170,568	Pennsylvania[2]	-7,850,000
Idaho	0	Pennsylvania Workers Compensation	0
Illinois	-26,926,027	Rhode Island	-4,749,288
Indiana	2,500,000	South Carolina	8,185,602
Iowa	0	South Dakota	0
Kansas	0	Tennessee	17,671,355
Kentucky	0	Texas	0
Louisiana	0	Utah	0
Maine	1,997,813	Vermont	1,557,313
Maryland	0	Virginia	13,282,045
Massachusetts	-6,580,210	Washington	803,220
Michigan	12,600,720	West Virginia	0
Minnesota	0	Wisconsin	0
Mississippi	31,160,000	Wyoming	0
Missouri	7,227,710	**United States**	**$916,130,812[3]**
Montana	0		

[1]Assessments less refunds. Negative numbers represent net refunds.
[2]Excludes Workers Compensation Security Funds.
[3]Includes Puerto Rico.

Source: National Conference of Insurance Guaranty Funds.

PREMIUMS BY LINE

Premiums can be accounted for in two major ways: net premiums written, which reflect premium amounts after deductions for reinsurance, and direct premiums written, which are calculated before reinsurance transactions. Private passenger auto is the largest property/casualty line of business, based on either criteria, accounting for approximately one third of premiums written.

PREMIUMS WRITTEN BY LINE, PROPERTY/CASUALTY INSURANCE, 2006

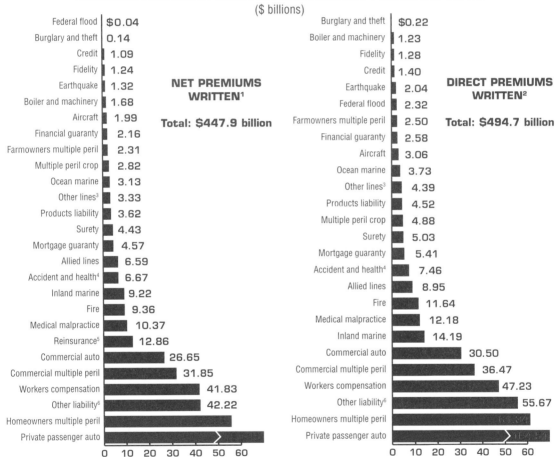

($ billions)

NET PREMIUMS WRITTEN[1]

Total: $447.9 billion

Line	Net premiums
Federal flood	$0.04
Burglary and theft	0.14
Credit	1.09
Fidelity	1.24
Earthquake	1.32
Boiler and machinery	1.68
Aircraft	1.99
Financial guaranty	2.16
Farmowners multiple peril	2.31
Multiple peril crop	2.82
Ocean marine	3.13
Other lines[3]	3.33
Products liability	3.62
Surety	4.43
Mortgage guaranty	4.57
Allied lines	6.59
Accident and health[4]	6.67
Inland marine	9.22
Fire	9.36
Medical malpractice	10.37
Reinsurance[5]	12.86
Commercial auto	26.65
Commercial multiple peril	31.85
Workers compensation	41.83
Other liability[6]	42.22
Homeowners multiple peril	
Private passenger auto	

DIRECT PREMIUMS WRITTEN[2]

Total: $494.7 billion

Line	Direct premiums
Burglary and theft	$0.22
Boiler and machinery	1.23
Fidelity	1.28
Credit	1.40
Earthquake	2.04
Federal flood	2.32
Farmowners multiple peril	2.50
Financial guaranty	2.58
Aircraft	3.06
Ocean marine	3.73
Other lines[3]	4.39
Products liability	4.52
Multiple peril crop	4.88
Surety	5.03
Mortgage guaranty	5.41
Accident and health[4]	7.46
Allied lines	8.95
Fire	11.64
Medical malpractice	12.18
Inland marine	14.19
Commercial auto	30.50
Commercial multiple peril	36.47
Workers compensation	47.23
Other liability[6]	55.67
Homeowners multiple peril	
Private passenger auto	

[1]After reinsurance transactions, excluding state funds. [2]Before reinsurance transactions, excluding state funds. May not match total premiums shown elsewhere in this book because of the use of different exhibits from Highline Data LLC. [3]Includes international and miscellaneous coverages. [4]Premiums from certain insurers that write health insurance but file financial statements with state regulators on a property/casualty basis. [5]Only includes nonproportional reinsurance, an arrangement in which a reinsurer makes payments to an insurer whose losses exceed a predetermined amount. [6]Coverages protecting against legal liability resulting from negligence, careless-ness, or failure to act.

Source: National Association of Insurance Commissioners (NAIC) Annual Statement Database, via Highline Data, LLC. Copyrighted information. No portion of this work may be copied or redistributed without the express written permission of Highline Data, LLC.

PERSONAL VS. COMMERCIAL

The property/casualty (P/C) insurance industry is divided into two main segments: personal lines and commercial lines. Personal lines includes coverage for individuals, mainly auto and home-owners. Commercial lines includes the many kinds of insurance products designed for business-es. In 2006 private passenger auto insurance was the largest line of insurance, based on net pre-miums written, making up 36 percent of all P/C insurance (commercial and personal combined) and 74 percent of personal insurance. General liability (including products liability and "other" liability) is the largest commercial line and third-largest P/C line. It accounted for 10 percent of all P/C net premiums and 20 percent of all commercial premiums.

NET PREMIUMS WRITTEN, PERSONAL AND COMMERCIAL LINES, 2006

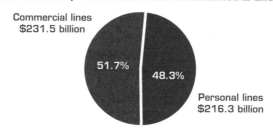

Commercial lines
$231.5 billion

51.7%

48.3%

Personal lines
$216.3 billion

Source: National Association of Insurance Commissioners (NAIC) Annual Statement Database, via Highline Data, LLC. Copyrighted information. No portion of this work may be copied or redistributed without the express written permission of Highline Data, LLC.

NET PREMIUMS WRITTEN BY LINE, PROPERTY/CASUALTY INSURANCE, 2003-2006[1]
($000)

Lines of insurance	2003	2004	2005	2006	Percent change 2003-2004	Percent change 2004-2005	Percent change 2005-2006	Percent of total 2006
Private passenger auto								
Liability	$89,284,234	$92,936,565	$94,652,534	$95,324,506	4.1%	1.8%	0.7%	21.3%
Collision and comprehensive	62,016,244	64,697,014	64,933,430	65,122,166	4.3	0.4	0.3	14.5
Total private passenger auto	151,300,478	157,633,579	159,585,964	160,446,672	4.2	1.2	0.5	35.8
Commercial auto								
Liability	18,444,917	19,569,829	19,846,866	19,702,725	6.1	1.4	-0.7	4.4
Collision and comprehensive	7,018,962	7,149,217	6,951,136	6,949,355	1.9	-2.8	0.0	1.6
Total commercial auto	25,463,879	26,719,046	26,798,002	26,652,080	4.9	0.3	-0.5	6.0
Fire	8,396,083	8,050,779	7,937,200	9,362,560	-4.1	-1.4	18.0	2.1
Allied lines	6,154,573	5,985,422	5,945,718	6,592,847	-2.7	-0.7	10.9	1.5

(table continues)

NET PREMIUMS WRITTEN BY LINE, PROPERTY/CASUALTY INSURANCE, 2003-2006[1] (Cont'd)
($000)

Lines of insurance	2003	2004	2005	2006	Percent change 2003-2004	Percent change 2004-2005	Percent change 2005-2006	Percent of total 2006
Multiple peril crop	$1,702,862	$2,203,143	$2,234,630	$2,824,769	29.4%	1.4%	26.4%	0.6%
Federal flood[2]	14,737	13,454	12,308	43,083	-8.7	-8.5	250.0	[3]
Farmowners multiple peril	2,000,834	2,118,097	2,266,920	2,310,688	5.9	7.0	1.9	0.5
Homeowners multiple peril	46,035,860	49,980,417	53,015,549	55,821,315	8.6	6.1	5.3	12.5
Commercial multiple peril	27,430,022	29,074,586	29,695,507	31,848,875	6.0	2.1	7.3	7.1
Mortgage guaranty	4,285,447	4,323,071	4,454,711	4,565,899	0.9	3.0	2.5	1.0
Ocean marine	2,588,607	2,828,685	2,948,349	3,133,418	9.3	4.2	6.3	0.7
Inland marine	7,786,214	7,940,003	8,251,432	9,215,704	2.0	3.9	11.7	2.1
Financial guaranty	2,507,763	2,133,599	2,014,467	2,163,324	-14.9	-5.6	7.4	0.5
Medical malpractice	8,753,854	9,124,240	9,734,772	10,365,836	4.2	6.7	6.5	2.3
Earthquake	1,048,714	1,098,441	1,106,378	1,315,494	4.7	0.7	18.9	0.3
Accident and health[4]	11,947,485	9,767,317	9,573,783	6,665,536	-18.2	-2.0	-30.4	1.5
Workers compensation	32,919,340	36,734,514	39,724,355	41,825,979	11.6	8.1	5.3	9.3
Products liability	2,726,599	3,401,867	3,561,223	3,623,796	24.8	4.7	1.8	0.8
Other liability[5]	36,149,829	39,752,695	39,363,222	42,220,462	10.0	-1.0	7.3	9.4
Aircraft	1,703,685	2,179,992	1,985,858	1,990,593	28.0	-8.9	0.2	0.4
Fidelity	1,192,535	1,309,344	1,216,793	1,240,822	9.8	-7.1	2.0	0.3
Surety	3,382,615	3,817,245	3,820,810	4,433,266	12.8	0.1	16.0	1.0
Burglary and theft	123,692	138,307	120,133	143,054	11.8	-13.1	19.1	[3]
Boiler and machinery	1,591,987	1,572,195	1,582,917	1,675,296	-1.2	0.7	5.8	0.4
Credit	640,580	806,381	936,108	1,090,145	25.9	16.1	16.5	0.2
International	968,819	302,599	230,366	193,622	-68.8	-23.9	-16.0	[3]
Reinsurance[6]	15,498,056	13,698,580	6,589,801	12,862,594	-11.6	-51.9	95.2	2.9
Other lines[7]	3,201,256	3,033,728	2,918,125	3,134,240	-5.2	-3.8	7.4	0.7
Total, all lines[8]	**$407,516,437**	**$425,741,326**	**$427,625,417**	**$447,761,985**	**4.5%**	**0.4%**	**4.7%**	**100.0%**

[1]After reinsurance transactions, excluding state funds. [2]Provided by FEMA through participating private insurers. [3]Less than 0.1 percent. [4]Premiums from certain insurers that write primarily health insurance but file financial statements with state regulators on a property/casualty basis. [5]Coverages protecting against legal liability resulting from negligence, carelessness or failure to act. [6]Only includes nonproportional reinsurance, an arrangement in which a reinsurer makes payments to an insurer whose losses exceed a predetermined amount. [7]Includes miscellaneous coverages. [8]May not match total premiums shown elsewhere in this book because of the use of different exhibits from Highline Data, LLC.

Source: National Association of Insurance Commissioners (NAIC) Annual Statement Database, via Highline Data, LLC. Copyrighted information. No portion of this work may be copied or redistributed without the express written permission of Highline Data, LLC.

DIRECT PREMIUMS WRITTEN, PROPERTY/CASUALTY INSURANCE BY STATE BY LINE, 2006[1]
($000)

State	Private passenger auto		Commercial auto		Homeowners multiple peril	Farmowners multiple peril
	Liability	Coll./comp.	Liability	Coll./comp.		
Alabama	$1,182,144	$1,069,526	$341,817	$122,582	$1,079,955	$52,650
Alaska	244,903	151,023	57,462	22,714	121,342	441
Arizona	1,963,398	1,604,380	412,127	143,490	1,145,558	12,382
Arkansas	794,791	611,925	181,698	91,478	505,370	13,151
California	10,981,076	8,869,924	2,341,772	844,004	6,617,181	194,799
Colorado	1,568,276	1,167,892	333,937	141,068	1,141,989	54,025
Connecticut	1,491,552	874,649	328,607	77,308	913,479	3,021
Delaware	422,770	196,437	91,313	22,800	152,384	2,449
D.C.	133,985	121,120	33,997	6,055	114,622	0
Florida	8,910,549	3,758,343	1,765,908	475,126	6,751,149	26,727
Georgia	2,804,330	2,471,875	697,626	238,709	1,678,453	78,846
Hawaii	420,623	244,907	94,675	25,890	276,658	599
Idaho	380,146	277,128	103,081	49,092	202,381	41,127
Illinois	3,156,897	2,567,129	895,536	310,273	2,282,291	99,123
Indiana	1,560,314	1,184,725	444,947	176,735	1,208,690	122,484
Iowa	663,235	602,630	237,769	120,811	454,129	94,434
Kansas	680,122	643,540	166,466	92,454	658,062	116,175
Kentucky	1,411,315	775,068	284,264	99,012	668,344	104,002
Louisiana	1,796,428	1,215,853	456,758	117,320	1,130,210	8,722
Maine	372,450	282,713	105,526	39,851	267,907	2,995
Maryland	2,113,137	1,454,984	434,103	129,250	1,166,912	20,457
Massachusetts	2,726,253	1,542,063	612,412	190,627	1,490,891	2,051
Michigan	3,296,229	2,765,439	528,946	283,951	2,131,961	104,147
Minnesota	1,627,520	1,142,623	343,638	171,771	1,175,252	80,272
Mississippi	788,121	620,397	247,097	78,529	616,829	14,125
Missouri	1,540,102	1,227,893	461,192	165,067	1,126,790	96,968
Montana	299,628	212,186	89,997	50,602	173,937	43,035
Nebraska	473,565	377,021	136,019	80,128	374,502	103,374
Nevada	1,101,087	613,937	211,666	52,303	464,975	6,174
New Hampshire	391,486	329,198	103,404	38,616	271,073	1,299
New Jersey	3,840,908	2,074,249	1,088,220	202,240	1,696,424	2,739
New Mexico	621,495	398,656	133,559	50,503	306,833	18,930
New York	6,704,813	3,289,212	1,770,875	317,400	3,627,091	33,066
North Carolina	2,368,706	1,834,908	582,513	199,714	1,534,798	42,807
North Dakota	147,430	162,168	50,935	34,099	109,348	54,040
Ohio	3,023,797	2,182,980	701,473	246,145	1,817,514	102,534
Oklahoma	1,015,493	743,260	258,394	102,470	860,834	93,302
Oregon	1,270,318	663,078	253,865	82,700	538,649	47,961
Pennsylvania	4,194,079	2,828,358	954,846	333,684	2,285,391	78,016
Rhode Island	470,016	233,128	92,454	22,100	241,675	146
South Carolina	1,469,357	937,260	301,929	104,096	1,018,190	5,034
South Dakota	188,812	171,538	58,779	38,417	123,440	61,175
Tennessee	1,510,552	1,245,626	394,492	159,713	1,115,802	94,302
Texas	6,508,129	5,255,175	1,648,557	512,127	4,842,699	115,385
Utah	704,323	467,478	172,581	79,900	315,603	7,458
Vermont	169,352	153,280	49,568	21,880	146,643	10,490
Virginia	2,331,146	1,719,988	494,282	170,069	1,375,473	42,466
Washington	2,304,783	1,209,852	396,423	135,660	1,112,151	48,291
West Virginia	643,864	408,688	126,436	48,418	306,888	10,229
Wisconsin	1,245,925	991,869	388,670	166,610	837,173	107,575
Wyoming	149,571	143,645	53,456	31,329	104,913	21,495
United States	**96,179,300**	**66,090,923**	**22,516,070**	**7,516,890**	**60,680,808**	**2,497,494**

[1]Excludes state funds. Source: National Association of Insurance Commissioners (NAIC) Annual Statement Database, via Highline Data, LLC.
Copyrighted information. No portion of this work may be copied or redistributed without the express written permission of Highline Data, LLC.

DIRECT PREMIUMS WRITTEN, PROPERTY/CASUALTY INSURANCE BY STATE BY LINE, 2006[1]
($000)

Commercial multiple peril	Workers compensation	Medical malpractice	Products liability	Other liability	Fire	Allied lines	Inland marine
$550,500	$382,194	$173,593	$51,744	$587,908	$170,306	$143,564	$213,500
110,141	345,202	25,692	7,416	130,509	30,560	15,891	97,716
598,307	345,794	297,567	91,087	895,787	118,022	81,355	215,733
264,891	303,880	87,425	23,635	381,047	135,056	97,486	144,575
4,710,414	7,586,120	972,706	750,080	7,647,164	1,293,034	722,709	1,943,649
644,526	378,808	212,100	90,830	1,005,094	108,743	99,984	212,067
581,031	731,741	222,511	54,596	875,877	103,629	98,349	209,174
280,789	246,666	46,862	13,933	254,935	21,821	19,894	46,930
141,728	171,752	44,577	7,012	334,521	35,867	25,299	50,342
2,295,063	3,736,915	847,260	293,480	3,302,057	1,132,363	1,296,918	1,086,630
854,283	1,345,652	372,619	106,383	1,365,893	292,940	200,539	396,126
148,916	356,161	36,849	23,311	285,247	74,290	71,556	44,080
183,820	124,234	47,598	13,168	165,398	25,705	26,379	56,909
1,581,160	2,596,732	729,368	183,823	3,535,928	373,284	274,458	523,670
721,831	817,877	135,301	66,255	733,242	168,528	113,717	271,635
306,703	531,152	100,093	37,054	450,637	70,922	119,826	154,080
321,234	415,270	98,320	31,129	342,054	71,678	112,041	133,030
424,816	681,732	172,664	31,410	396,677	115,108	82,297	212,705
473,431	860,759	104,426	49,252	729,632	245,053	222,288	306,883
208,457	242,088	58,708	8,118	144,752	36,789	24,197	49,475
604,745	686,933	337,326	61,522	902,736	155,407	94,105	217,543
1,021,616	1,124,566	296,397	115,189	1,463,212	256,263	160,289	277,655
1,099,188	1,130,835	253,828	102,775	1,262,632	315,148	149,540	310,129
651,629	872,739	100,054	104,975	895,251	136,051	197,724	204,057
297,207	338,125	56,212	24,006	298,014	134,717	151,830	147,518
658,568	1,002,698	238,513	69,596	995,858	185,978	137,820	244,308
141,941	107,362	44,541	8,046	120,626	19,665	25,317	38,199
259,244	351,101	37,644	17,396	250,727	44,360	91,976	89,606
310,125	497,714	108,721	59,070	553,432	76,199	58,527	113,958
210,959	304,720	43,683	17,019	234,498	26,737	21,727	47,628
1,314,336	2,004,260	592,844	219,938	2,331,897	324,053	216,633	410,067
209,962	278,502	47,439	14,005	192,614	31,188	33,042	65,507
3,180,652	2,431,693	1,524,545	317,657	6,029,738	806,746	468,609	913,226
838,920	1,385,661	317,271	105,504	970,936	253,561	207,810	334,966
86,475	1,131	17,696	7,472	74,174	17,532	70,970	29,657
1,169,178	39,643	530,250	124,806	1,493,766	307,128	187,116	358,014
379,824	423,885	145,271	41,810	456,743	104,086	101,100	162,677
444,387	766,705	126,348	57,060	476,355	104,165	54,345	132,488
1,550,324	2,272,869	741,717	179,623	2,354,928	372,799	242,233	374,238
144,611	201,150	39,568	11,041	206,611	35,801	28,319	46,695
446,804	748,964	61,878	49,470	406,530	185,685	176,161	191,348
104,007	130,980	26,059	8,974	89,409	17,463	28,336	40,138
591,731	947,781	344,578	61,586	727,437	213,194	129,049	250,934
1,858,481	2,813,269	487,663	285,124	3,848,761	1,325,725	915,325	1,132,810
222,884	488,114	72,872	39,980	303,122	50,847	37,726	90,230
110,587	205,403	27,922	6,843	101,498	22,445	12,518	26,443
730,674	977,025	299,559	75,817	1,065,462	187,336	131,320	265,002
730,478	45,876	254,759	97,465	1,056,274	169,562	109,057	283,289
179,040	771,979	110,870	15,669	188,843	56,077	30,531	53,349
618,070	1,664,416	112,109	79,146	751,221	119,850	100,273	199,278
78,953	5,195	23,955	8,091	82,402	13,680	12,019	37,318
35,647,644	**47,222,024**	**12,208,329**	**4,320,392**	**53,750,067**	**10,693,145**	**8,230,093**	**13,457,182**

[1]Excludes state funds. Source: National Association of Insurance Commissioners (NAIC) Annual Statement Database, via Highline Data, LLC. Copyrighted information. No portion of this work may be copied or redistributed without the express written permission of Highline Data, LLC.

DIRECT PREMIUMS WRITTEN, PROPERTY/CASUALTY INSURANCE BY STATE BY LINE, 2006[1] (Cont'd)
($000)

State	Ocean marine	Surety	Fidelity	Burglary and theft	Boiler and machinery	Financial guaranty
Alabama	$33,462	$65,149	$13,862	$2,030	$21,497	$33,659
Alaska	26,666	24,418	2,054	215	5,052	8,670
Arizona	11,555	106,696	12,271	2,111	15,359	49,644
Arkansas	14,627	33,967	8,220	2,389	13,004	4,517
California	297,170	714,826	124,079	21,823	105,838	296,414
Colorado	9,555	97,170	16,170	3,200	17,009	52,453
Connecticut	52,335	66,406	41,360	4,188	14,584	23,579
Delaware	6,837	15,557	11,187	950	3,052	94,493
D.C.	4,333	67,619	13,448	1,772	3,735	21,221
Florida	301,392	385,276	54,012	12,346	52,211	152,019
Georgia	78,662	149,989	30,414	6,746	28,195	24,997
Hawaii	14,525	41,637	4,827	281	3,052	13,350
Idaho	2,675	20,011	2,820	561	6,079	1,803
Illinois	77,990	156,863	75,630	8,358	51,958	88,949
Indiana	16,218	71,945	16,740	3,126	26,379	27,446
Iowa	6,349	35,968	10,768	1,525	19,268	9,240
Kansas	5,396	40,367	9,782	1,372	15,191	5,076
Kentucky	19,237	59,159	9,643	1,249	19,799	11,182
Louisiana	256,655	114,195	11,126	1,929	19,149	55,133
Maine	23,015	13,366	3,636	566	7,282	2,611
Maryland	86,978	129,462	21,632	3,312	16,000	36,616
Massachusetts	98,577	99,966	34,435	4,277	26,502	51,524
Michigan	41,332	77,693	30,658	6,128	40,363	91,593
Minnesota	25,937	70,450	26,344	4,079	24,486	41,253
Mississippi	17,564	58,347	7,535	1,337	11,132	9,268
Missouri	39,346	75,848	20,401	4,496	20,934	32,586
Montana	1,527	17,752	2,568	305	3,339	6,993
Nebraska	3,883	26,217	7,041	2,218	11,612	5,756
Nevada	8,244	91,822	6,651	1,022	8,103	22,668
New Hampshire	13,343	15,373	2,956	623	4,852	2,602
New Jersey	117,068	164,924	44,447	8,715	35,347	64,669
New Mexico	1,355	36,000	3,713	516	5,490	6,690
New York	599,118	309,510	151,683	26,744	82,534	1,164,454
North Carolina	38,736	113,283	27,351	3,808	28,835	39,969
North Dakota	975	11,687	2,339	262	5,356	2,290
Ohio	37,688	124,912	43,861	7,980	47,910	52,749
Oklahoma	17,234	45,493	7,615	3,208	12,825	7,733
Oregon	28,249	60,098	8,578	1,722	13,511	8,929
Pennsylvania	51,325	205,400	54,038	9,038	52,815	122,167
Rhode Island	29,073	14,184	3,738	891	3,807	13,976
South Carolina	28,591	55,931	8,605	1,791	15,189	19,621
South Dakota	496	11,576	2,930	406	4,281	2,111
Tennessee	42,466	75,899	18,972	3,253	20,952	21,469
Texas	315,524	396,075	59,388	23,820	81,873	95,263
Utah	5,237	35,487	5,889	924	6,742	5,199
Vermont	3,897	6,681	1,554	408	2,703	4,705
Virginia	58,885	143,114	26,594	4,050	24,766	12,179
Washington	124,041	129,967	17,717	3,102	23,356	37,972
West Virginia	3,158	33,999	4,127	480	5,652	8,517
Wisconsin	24,302	42,688	19,447	3,197	32,013	13,905
Wyoming	626	18,003	1,472	205	4,246	716
United States	**3,123,427**	**4,978,423**	**1,146,327**	**209,056**	**1,125,219**	**2,982,600**

[1]Excludes state funds. Source: National Association of Insurance Commissioners (NAIC) Annual Statement Database, via Highline Data, LLC.

DIRECT PREMIUMS WRITTEN, PROPERTY/CASUALTY INSURANCE BY STATE BY LINE, 2006[1]

($000)

Aircraft	Earthquake	Federal flood	Credit	Accident and health	Multiple peril crop	Mortgage guaranty	Misc.
$24,574	$7,875	$22,950	$23,274	$47,497	$35,969	$82,058	$57,672
42,281	16,396	1,524	342	14,905	36	16,183	5,632
78,765	7,201	15,123	10,961	53,880	8,902	130,057	41,467
24,205	17,399	6,888	8,037	38,727	49,777	39,343	15,505
227,866	1,062,083	149,024	106,939	320,846	190,197	405,386	304,419
42,370	8,730	10,187	6,732	76,723	109,498	96,329	26,695
42,412	5,867	25,163	75,166	35,713	3,828	53,518	42,616
13,753	1,352	10,736	17,278	300,574	5,592	55,172	6,938
11,525	2,287	507	888	111,859	0	71,200	2,602
167,301	33,929	780,907	67,017	267,064	144,728	472,654	475,772
90,769	15,523	42,739	29,394	118,198	91,361	205,111	89,687
18,078	7,583	19,704	3,482	21,217	1,308	64,241	8,146
14,389	2,617	3,094	1,253	25,229	42,061	27,014	8,030
95,745	46,052	25,308	79,893	284,509	423,427	250,741	378,821
30,513	31,154	14,912	21,941	177,151	194,648	126,651	28,501
13,641	3,290	5,968	4,994	78,181	370,281	51,090	18,031
20,945	4,859	4,633	6,357	65,609	336,371	50,131	92,625
11,226	35,719	10,825	10,514	50,314	40,768	45,284	21,340
59,981	6,369	223,116	14,509	56,354	39,318	72,368	104,499
4,811	1,464	4,893	4,567	25,256	5,164	18,189	14,093
24,953	8,723	24,783	17,085	66,107	17,659	95,604	28,529
24,554	16,700	31,216	25,055	63,726	2,646	91,801	32,653
46,829	7,368	13,273	58,242	144,040	79,962	173,693	774,596
50,757	3,931	4,620	19,398	137,228	322,225	205,758	30,239
14,454	15,942	26,574	9,467	73,054	45,813	37,771	31,759
35,102	78,431	12,685	18,907	271,558	131,322	96,532	65,092
11,675	3,012	1,650	1,272	11,298	100,012	12,096	9,232
11,905	2,778	5,569	5,642	57,963	301,874	28,125	14,594
33,763	12,855	6,920	31,624	17,964	765	72,490	30,825
10,395	1,949	4,216	4,076	14,267	334	27,931	10,278
71,492	15,731	129,421	49,964	110,860	3,539	152,866	69,793
11,331	2,175	6,759	2,905	19,826	14,478	29,718	22,088
118,297	37,786	82,245	63,544	310,566	19,088	207,284	129,766
49,498	10,170	63,303	36,566	94,602	91,946	184,348	52,893
6,471	239	2,529	761	14,338	387,133	6,725	1,964
58,871	29,452	19,136	19,554	169,035	130,175	191,832	96,683
21,864	4,579	6,170	13,086	59,233	79,485	50,322	32,423
30,690	52,176	15,079	24,414	48,605	24,022	51,188	41,351
52,269	14,057	38,117	26,569	252,520	32,916	249,259	42,795
14,099	2,318	11,341	4,473	41,809	64	17,440	11,882
17,544	29,069	90,439	15,243	55,727	33,352	94,544	20,923
6,499	476	1,651	665	35,468	287,336	10,250	4,799
40,716	57,818	9,761	44,551	94,605	36,078	93,510	43,822
214,867	28,825	233,756	272,804	378,385	451,248	362,972	256,445
26,927	24,562	1,794	2,626	47,180	2,391	50,576	8,444
2,276	1,191	2,218	933	4,675	971	10,448	3,648
33,662	10,901	48,183	18,549	88,432	27,812	207,472	50,750
68,471	117,912	17,243	12,793	78,796	53,924	114,255	74,451
4,416	1,554	10,360	1,507	23,460	10,738	16,104	7,216
30,171	3,815	6,573	37,992	188,798	93,528	89,309	49,404
4,989	2,276	1,294	773	11,152	10,522	12,023	1,873
2,184,955	**1,916,523**	**2,307,077**	**1,334,576**	**5,155,086**	**4,886,591**	**5,376,965**	**3,794,299**

[1]Excludes state funds. Source: National Association of Insurance Commissioners (NAIC) Annual Statement Database, via Highline Data, LLC.
Copyrighted information. No portion of this work may be copied or redistributed without the express written permission of Highline Data, LLC.

TOTAL AUTO PREMIUMS BY SECTOR, 2006
(\$ billions, net premiums written)

Private passenger auto $160.4 — 85.8%
Commercial auto $26.7 — 14.2%

Liability $115.0 — 61.5%
Collision/comprehensive $72.1 — 38.5%

AUTO SHARE OF P/C INDUSTRY, 2006
(\$ billions, net premiums written)

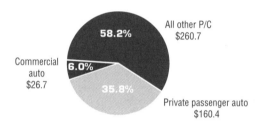

All other P/C $260.7 — 58.2%
Commercial auto $26.7 — 6.0%
Private passenger auto $160.4 — 35.8%

Source: National Association of Insurance Commissioners (NAIC) Annual Statement Database, via Highline Data, LLC. Copyrighted information. No portion of this work may be copied or redistributed without the express written permission of Highline Data, LLC.

PRIVATE PASSENGER AUTOMOBILE INSURANCE, 1999-2006
(\$000)

Year	Liability				Collision and comprehensive			
	Net premiums written[1]	Annual percent change	Combined ratio[2]	Annual point change	Net premiums written[1]	Annual percent change	Combined ratio[2]	Annual point change
1999	$69,789,333	-1.7%	106.6	NA	$52,894,885	12.9%	95.2	NA
2000	69,450,796	-0.5	111.9	5.3 pts.	50,534,284	-4.5	107.5	12.3 pts.
2001	74,447,481	7.2	111.4	-0.5	53,567,928	6.0	101.6	-5.9
2002	82,014,633	10.2	109.7	-1.7	57,567,169	7.5	95.4	-6.2
2003	89,284,234	8.9	102.6	-7.1	62,016,244	7.7	91.5	-3.8
2004	92,936,565	4.1	98.4	-4.2	64,697,014	4.3	86.5	-5.1
2005	94,652,534	1.8	98.0	-0.4	64,933,430	0.4	90.2	3.7
2006	95,324,506	0.7	97.4	-0.6	65,122,166	0.3	89.9	-0.2

[1]After reinsurance transactions, excluding state funds. [2]After dividends to policyholders. A drop in the combined ratio represents an improvement; an increase represents a deterioration. See also Glossary. NA=Data not available.

Source: National Association of Insurance Commissioners (NAIC) Annual Statement Database, via Highline Data, LLC. Copyrighted information. No portion of this work may be copied or redistributed without the express written permission of Highline Data, LLC.

PRIVATE PASSENGER AUTO
NET PREMIUMS WRITTEN, PERCENT CHANGE FROM PRIOR YEAR, 1999-2006

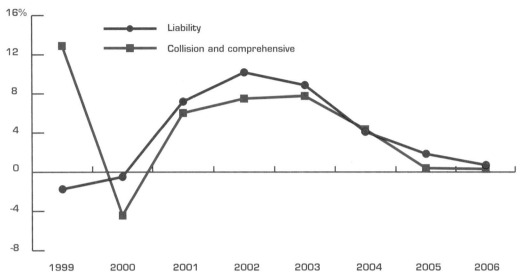

Source: National Association of Insurance Commissioners (NAIC) Annual Statement Database, via Highline Data, LLC. Copyrighted information. No portion of this work may be copied or redistributed without the express written permission of Highline Data, LLC.

LEADING WRITERS OF PRIVATE PASSENGER AUTO INSURANCE
BY DIRECT PREMIUMS WRITTEN, 2006
($000)

Rank	Company/Group	Direct premiums written[1]	Market share
1	State Farm Mutual Group	$29,582,026	18.0%
2	Allstate Insurance Co. Group	18,293,861	11.1
3	Progressive Casualty Group	12,077,096	7.3
4	National Indemnity Co. Group (Berkshire Hathaway)	11,105,001	6.7
5	Farmers Insurance Group	8,109,760	4.9
6	Nationwide Group	7,489,998	4.5
7	United Services Automobile Association Group	5,964,245	3.6
8	American International Group	5,002,978	3.0
9	Liberty Mutual Group	4,251,008	2.6
10	American Family Insurance Group	3,536,914	2.1

[1]Before reinsurance transactions, excluding state funds.

Source: National Association of Insurance Commissioners (NAIC) Annual Statement Database, via Highline Data, LLC. Copyrighted information. No portion of this work may be copied or redistributed without the express written permission of Highline Data, LLC.

COMMERCIAL AUTOMOBILE INSURANCE, 1999-2006
($000)

Year	Liability				Collision and comprehensive			
	Net premiums written[1]	Annual percent change	Combined ratio[2]	Annual point change	Net premiums written[1]	Annual percent change	Combined ratio[2]	Annual point change
1999	$12,979,182	-2.1%	120.5	NA	$5,381,430	5.4%	111.5	NA
2000	13,734,120	5.8	122.0	1.5 pts.	6,070,862	12.8	104.8	-6.7 pts.
2001	15,270,917	11.2	122.8	0.8	6,459,093	6.4	101.7	-3.1
2002	17,232,258	12.8	108.1	-14.7	7,322,301	13.4	93.6	-8.1
2003	18,444,917	7.0	99.5	-8.6	7,018,962	-4.1	83.7	-9.9
2004	19,569,829	6.1	96.8	-2.6	7,149,217	1.9	82.9	-0.8
2005	19,846,866	1.4	91.8	-5.0	6,951,136	-2.8	88.0	5.2
2006	19,702,725	-0.7	95.5	3.7	6,949,355	0.0	88.4	0.4

[1]After reinsurance transactions, excluding state funds. [2]After dividends to policyholders. A drop in the combined ratio represents an improvement; an increase represents a deterioration. See also Glossary. NA=Data not available.

Source: National Association of Insurance Commissioners (NAIC) Annual Statement Database, via Highline Data, LLC. Copyrighted information. No portion of this work may be copied or redistributed without the express written permission of Highline Data, LLC.

LEADING WRITERS OF COMMERCIAL AUTO INSURANCE BY DIRECT PREMIUMS WRITTEN, 2006
($000)

Rank	Company/Group	Direct premiums written[1]	Market share
1	Travelers Group	$2,091,419	6.8%
2	Zurich Insurance Group	2,011,032	6.6
3	Progressive Group	1,980,784	6.5
4	American International Group	1,441,652	4.7
5	Liberty Mutual Insurance Group	1,316,040	4.3
6	State Farm IL Group	1,254,478	4.1
7	Nationwide Group	1,164,411	3.8
8	Old Republic Group	792,805	2.6
9	CNA Insurance Group	789,492	2.6
10	Hartford Fire & Casualty Group	717,040	2.3

[1]Before reinsurance transactions, excluding state funds.

Source: National Association of Insurance Commissioners (NAIC) Annual Statement Database, via Highline Data, LLC. Copyrighted information. No portion of this work may be copied or redistributed without the express written permission of Highline Data, LLC.

AUTO: COSTS/EXPENDITURES

The average cost of automobile insurance declined by 1.3 percent in 2005, according to a September 2007 report from the National Association of Insurance Commissioners (NAIC). New Jersey had the highest average expenditure ($1,184), followed by the District of Columbia ($1,182), New York ($1,122), Massachusetts ($1,113) and Louisiana ($1,076).

AVERAGE EXPENDITURES FOR AUTO INSURANCE, UNITED STATES, 1996-2005

Year	Average expenditure	Percent change	Year	Average expenditure	Percent change
1996	$691	3.4%	2001	$726	5.2%
1997	705	2.0	2002	781	7.6
1998	703	-0.3	2003	824	5.5
1999	685	-2.6	2004	840	1.9
2000	690	0.7	2005	829	-1.3

Source: © 2007 National Association of Insurance Commissioners.

- 77 percent of insured drivers purchase comprehensive coverage in addition to liability insurance, and 72 percent buy collision coverage, based on 2005 NAIC data.

AUTO INSURANCE EXPENDITURES, BY STATE

The table on the following pages shows estimated average expenditures for private passenger automobile insurance by state for 2001 to 2005, providing approximate measures of the relative cost of automobile insurance to consumers in each state. To calculate average expenditures the National Association of Insurance Commissioners (NAIC) assumes that all insured vehicles carry liability coverage but not necessarily collision or comprehensive coverage. The average expenditure measures what consumers actually spend for insurance on each vehicle. It does not equal the sum of liability, collision and comprehensive expenditures because not all policyholders purchase all three coverages.

Expenditures are affected by the coverages purchased as well as other factors. In states where the economy is healthy, people are more likely to purchase new cars. Since new car owners are more likely to purchase physical damage coverages, these states will have a higher average expenditure. The NAIC notes that urban population, traffic density and per capita income have a significant impact on premiums. The latest report shows that high premium states tend also to be highly urban, with higher wage and price levels and greater traffic density. Tort liability and other auto laws, labor costs, liability coverage requirements, theft rates and other factors can also affect auto insurance prices.

AVERAGE EXPENDITURES FOR AUTO INSURANCE BY STATE, 2001-2005

State	2005 Liability	Collision	Comprehensive	Average expenditure	Rank[1]
Alabama	$367	$316	$134	$678	37
Alaska	596	390	165	962	11
Arizona	511	310	242	926	14
Arkansas	391	297	165	693	34
California[2]	487	365	117	845	18
Colorado	471	304	198	827	21
Connecticut	626	343	127	991	9
Delaware	713	294	113	1,028	8
D.C.	627	446	270	1,182	2
Florida	757	280	111	1,063	6
Georgia	420	372	168	784	24
Hawaii	547	298	114	843	19
Idaho	339	236	133	583	48
Illinois	410	300	121	743	28
Indiana	372	266	120	657	41
Iowa	290	205	169	555	50
Kansas	301	244	205	590	47
Kentucky	489	272	137	750	26
Louisiana	665	358	208	1,076	5
Maine	368	273	111	644	42
Maryland	556	331	149	945	12
Massachusetts	724	339	139	1,113	4
Michigan	487	436	166	931	13
Minnesota	460	237	190	791	23
Mississippi	419	304	171	745	27
Missouri	381	271	152	685	35
Montana	409	250	207	685	36
Nebraska	337	226	208	621	44
Nevada	636	336	146	983	10
New Hampshire	431	305	114	792	22
New Jersey	751	403	183	1,184	1
New Mexico	449	293	167	727	30
New York	765	338	159	1,122	3
North Carolina	336	269	125	602	46
North Dakota	259	209	254	554	51
Ohio	390	255	110	669	39
Oklahoma	395	277	174	678	38
Oregon	484	235	110	737	29
Pennsylvania	508	316	131	849	16
Rhode Island	714	380	130	1,059	7
South Carolina	471	253	151	753	25
South Dakota	298	211	214	565	49
Tennessee	363	298	126	659	40
Texas[3]	476	315	155	845	17
Utah	427	270	122	706	31
Vermont	368	306	134	699	32
Virginia	398	271	127	698	33
Washington	541	265	132	840	20
West Virginia	532	303	193	857	15
Wisconsin	339	215	133	615	45
Wyoming	336	263	224	639	43
United States	$496	$309	$143	$829	

[1]Ranked by average expenditure. [2]Preliminary. [3]Due to the exclusion of county mutuals, which had 44 percent of the market in 2005, Texas results are not comparable with results from other states. Note: Average expenditure=Total written premium/liability car years.

AVERAGE EXPENDITURES FOR AUTO INSURANCE BY STATE, 2001-2005

2004		Average expenditure percent change 2004-2005	Average expenditure[1]			State
Average expenditure	Rank		2003	2002	2001	
$677	39	0.1%	$657	$627	$605	Alabama
974	11	-1.2	938	884	826	Alaska
931	14	-0.5	921	887	822	Arizona
708	32	-2.0	698	672	621	Arkansas
847	17	0.3	837	778	723	California[2]
850	16	-2.6	923	921	808	Colorado
991	9	0.0	988	970	912	Connecticut
1,022	8	0.6	977	900	851	Delaware
1,185	2	-0.2	1,135	1,044	1,012	D.C.
1,062	6	0.1	1,018	934	850	Florida
779	24	0.6	759	739	703	Georgia
817	22	3.1	776	739	705	Hawaii
590	48	-1.2	586	563	523	Idaho
760	26	-2.3	762	729	683	Illinois
671	40	-2.0	671	648	615	Indiana
580	50	-4.3	581	548	513	Iowa
603	46	-2.2	611	587	556	Kansas
758	27	-1.1	739	688	645	Kentucky
1,062	5	1.3	1,015	928	839	Louisiana
650	42	-0.9	633	587	546	Maine
947	12	-0.3	893	840	784	Maryland
1,113	4	0.0	1,052	984	936	Massachusetts
980	10	-5.1	950	887	735	Michigan
829	21	-4.6	837	801	735	Minnesota
749	29	-0.6	710	681	638	Mississippi
702	33	-2.4	702	669	634	Missouri
683	37	0.3	675	628	572	Montana
637	43	-2.6	624	590	554	Nebraska
939	13	4.7	914	896	851	Nevada
798	23	-0.8	779	733	686	New Hampshire
1,221	1	-3.1	1,193	1,125	1,028	New Jersey
728	30	0.0	732	706	662	New Mexico
1,172	3	-4.2	1,168	1,100	1,015	New York
597	47	0.9	605	588	565	North Carolina
562	51	-1.4	537	505	498	North Dakota
680	38	-1.6	672	642	614	Ohio
690	36	-1.8	689	654	610	Oklahoma
753	28	-2.2	736	682	643	Oregon
843	19	0.8	813	777	726	Pennsylvania
1,034	7	2.4	997	939	880	Rhode Island
763	25	-1.4	745	703	636	South Carolina
587	49	-3.7	564	542	510	South Dakota
666	41	-1.1	650	632	611	Tennessee
847	18	-0.2	837	791	735	Texas[3]
722	31	-2.3	733	703	640	Utah
693	35	0.9	683	650	603	Vermont
702	34	-0.6	658	626	610	Virginia
839	20	0.2	825	791	750	Washington
875	15	-2.1	844	778	707	West Virginia
636	44	-3.2	621	611	573	Wisconsin
629	45	1.6	618	585	528	Wyoming
$840		**-1.3**	**$824**	**$781**	**$726**	**United States**

A car year is equal to 365 days of insured coverage for a single vehicle. The NAIC does not rank state average expenditures and does not endorse any conclusion drawn from these data. Source: © 2007 National Association of Insurance Commissioners.

TOP TEN MOST EXPENSIVE AND LEAST EXPENSIVE STATES FOR AUTOMOBILE INSURANCE, 2005[1]

Rank	Most expensive states	Average expenditure	Rank	Least expensive states	Average expenditure
1	New Jersey	$1,184	1	North Dakota	$554
2	D.C.	1,182	2	Iowa	555
3	New York	1,122	3	South Dakota	565
4	Massachusetts	1,113	4	Idaho	583
5	Louisiana	1,076	5	Kansas	590
6	Florida	1,063	6	North Carolina	602
7	Rhode Island	1,059	7	Wisconsin	615
8	Delaware	1,028	8	Nebraska	621
9	Connecticut	991	9	Wyoming	639
10	Nevada	983	10	Maine	644

[1]Based on average automobile insurance expenditures.

Source: © 2007 National Association of Insurance Commissioners.

TOP FIVE MOST EXPENSIVE AND LEAST EXPENSIVE CITIES FOR AUTOMOBILE INSURANCE, 2007[1]

- Auto insurance is more expensive in urban areas because of the higher density of traffic, increased likelihood of theft and vandalism, and greater incidence of fraud.

Rank	Most expensive cities	Average annual auto premiums	Rank	Least expensive cities	Average annual auto premiums
1	Detroit, MI	$5,072	1	Eau Claire, WI	$869
2	Philadelphia, PA	3,779	2	Norfolk, VA	954
3	Newark, NJ	3,381	3	Raleigh, NC	966
4	Los Angeles, CA	3,027	4	Bismarck, ND	989
5	Hempstead, NY	2,764	5	Burlington, VT	1,001

[1]As of June 2007. Assumes $100,000/$300,000/$50,000 liability limits, collision and comprehensive with $500 deductibles, and $100,000/$300,000 uninsured motorist coverage.

Source: Runzheimer International.

WHERE THE PREMIUM DOLLAR GOES, PRIVATE PASSENGER AUTO INSURANCE, 2006

PREMIUMS EARNED:		**$100**
CLAIMS:		
Payments to injured persons:		
Medical	$9	
Wage loss and other economic payments	2	
Pain and suffering and other noneconomic awards	5	
Lawyers' fees	11	
Costs of settling claims	1	
Subtotal		$28
Payments for damage to cars[1]:		
Property damage liability	$15	
Collision claims	16	
Comprehensive claims	7	
Costs of settling claims	1	
Subtotal		$39
Total claims		**$67**
EXPENSES:		
Commissions and other selling expenses	$17	
General expenses (costs of company operations)	6	
State premium taxes, licenses and fees	2	
Dividends to policyholders	1	
Total expenses		**$26**
Claims and expense total		**$93**
BOTTOM LINE:		
Investment gain[2]		$7
Pretax income ($100 - $93 + $7)		14
Tax		-5
Income after taxes		**$9**

[1]Includes theft and damage to other property, e.g., road signs.
[2]Includes interest, dividends and realized capital gains.

Source: Insurance Information Institute estimate based on data from ISO; National Association of Insurance Commissioners (NAIC) Annual Statement Database, via Highline Data, LLC. Copyrighted information. No portion of this work may be copied or redistributed without the express written permission of Highline Data, LLC.; Insurance Research Council; A.M. Best Company, Inc.

- In 2006 claims accounted for $67 of every $100 earned in private passenger auto insurance premiums in the United States.

- Lawyers' fees accounted for $11 out of every $100 in premiums. Half of the fees went to plaintiffs' attorneys and the remainder to defendants' attorneys.

- Theft accounted for about 25 percent of the dollars that go to pay comprehensive claims, or 2 percent of premiums earned for private passenger auto insurance.

WHERE THE REVENUE DOLLAR GOES, 2006
(Premiums and investments)

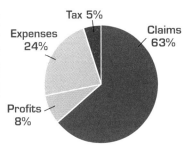

Tax 5%
Expenses 24%
Claims 63%
Profits 8%

PRIVATE PASSENGER AUTO INSURANCE LOSSES, 1997-2006[1]

| | Liability | | | | Physical damage | | | |
| | Bodily injury[2] | | Property damage[3] | | Collision[4] | | Comprehensive[4,5] | |
Year	Claim frequency[6]	Claim severity[7]	Claim frequency[6]	Claim severity[7]	Claim frequency[6]	Claim severity[7]	Claim frequency[6]	Claim severity[7]
1997	1.31	$9,517	4.03	$2,183	5.44	$2,234	2.68	$1,152
1998	1.26	9,437	3.97	2,240	5.39	2,273	2.93	1,078
1999	1.23	9,646	4.00	2,294	5.73	2,352	2.80	1,116
2000	1.20	9,807	3.98	2,393	5.61	2,480	2.89	1,125
2001	1.17	10,032	3.98	2,461	5.53	2,525	3.11	1,152
2002	1.17	10,289	3.94	2,539	5.42	2,551	2.90	1,210
2003	1.17	10,510	3.89	2,590	5.35	2,633	2.73	1,229
2004	1.15	10,915	3.80	2,612	5.19	2,683	2.43	1,293
2005	1.11	11,213	3.70	2,684	5.17	2,733	2.29	1,356
2006	1.05	11,847	3.52	2,801	5.03	2,790	2.28	1,444

[1]For all limits combined. Includes all loss adjustment expenses.
[2]Excludes Massachusetts and most states with no-fault automobile insurance laws.
[3]Excludes Massachusetts, Michigan and New Jersey.
[4]Based on coverage with a $500 deductible.
[5]Excludes wind and water losses.
[6]Claim frequency is claims per 100 earned car years. A car year is equal to 365 days of insured coverage for a single vehicle.
[7]Claim severity is the size of the loss, measured by the average amount paid for each claim.

Source: ISO.

INCURRED LOSSES FOR AUTO INSURANCE, 2002-2006[1]
($000)

	2002	2003	2004	2005	2006
Private passenger liability	$58,847,771	$59,888,192	$59,462,599	$60,162,287	$58,001,992
Private passenger physical damage	36,796,195	37,275,789	35,340,643	38,058,732	37,249,977
Commercial auto liability	13,518,027	12,935,514	12,465,305	12,246,997	12,017,532
Commercial auto physical damage	3,900,759	3,623,862	3,615,720	3,865,846	3,903,000
Total	$113,062,752	$113,723,357	$110,884,267	$114,333,862	$111,172,501

[1]Losses occurring within a fixed period, whether or not adjusted or paid during the same period, on a direct basis before reinsurance.

Source: National Association of Insurance Commissioners (NAIC) Annual Statement Database, via Highline Data, LLC. Copyrighted information. No portion of this work may be copied or redistributed without the express written permission of Highline Data, LLC.

AUTO: HIGH-RISK MARKETS

UNINSURED MOTORISTS

About 14.6 percent of motorists were uninsured in 2004, according to a 2006 survey by the Insurance Research Council.

STATES WITH LOWEST AND HIGHEST PERCENTAGE OF UNINSURED MOTORISTS, 2004

Lowest	Percent	Highest	Percent
Maine	4%	Mississippi	26%
Massachusetts	6	Alabama	25
Vermont	6	California	25
New York	7	New Mexico	24
Nebraska	8	Arizona	22

Source: Insurance Research Council.

THE SHARED/RESIDUAL MARKET AND NONSTANDARD MARKETS

All states and the District of Columbia use special systems to guarantee that auto insurance is available to those who cannot obtain it in the private market. Each type of system is commonly known as an assigned risk plan, although the term technically applies to only one type of plan. The assigned risk and other plans are known in the insurance industry as the shared, or residual, market. Policyholders in assigned risk plans are, as the name suggests, assigned to various insurance companies doing business in the state. Hence the term voluntary (regular) market, where auto insurers are free to select policyholders rather than have them assigned.

The percentage of vehicles insured in the shared market is dropping, in part because of growth in the nonstandard sector of the voluntary market. The nonstandard market is a niche market for drivers who have a worse than average driving record or drive specialized cars such as high-powered sports cars and custom-built cars. It is made up of small specialty companies, whose only business is the nonstandard market, and well-known auto insurance companies with nonstandard divisions.

Until the mid-1960s, most drivers who did not meet an insurance company's "standard" or "preferred risk" underwriting criteria could only find coverage in the shared market, where prices are generally much higher and insurers pool or share the profits and losses. With advancements in computer technology that made it easier to set appropriate prices for smaller and smaller risk categories, some insurers began to specialize in insuring drivers with marginally bad driving records. By the late 1990s the nonstandard market accounted for about one-fifth of the total private passenger auto insurance market.

PRIVATE PASSENGER CARS INSURED IN THE SHARED AND VOLUNTARY MARKETS, 2005

- In 2005, 1.3 percent of vehicles were insured in the shared market, compared with 3.6 percent in 1995.

- The number of vehicles in the shared market nationwide fell 11.8 percent in 2005.

- North Carolina has the highest percentage of cars in the shared market, 23 percent, followed by Massachusetts with 6 percent and Rhode Island with 5 percent.

State	Voluntary	Shared market	Total	Shared market as a percent of total
Alabama	3,176,976	39	3,177,015	0.001%
Alaska	391,726	936	392,662	0.238
Arizona	3,661,357	224	3,661,581	0.006
Arkansas	1,951,114	10	1,951,124	0.001
California	24,493,775	29,349	24,523,124	0.120
Colorado	3,345,472	5	3,345,477	1
Connecticut	2,400,289	3,473	2,403,762	0.144
Delaware	589,067	210	589,277	0.036
D.C.	214,919	1,298	216,217	0.600
Florida	10,879,337	238	10,879,575	0.002
Georgia	6,412,105	41	6,412,146	0.001
Hawaii	764,912	5,563	770,475	0.722
Idaho	1,099,670	106	1,099,776	0.010
Illinois	7,660,096	3,085	7,663,181	0.040
Indiana	4,266,377	19	4,266,396	1
Iowa	2,313,665	34	2,313,699	0.001
Kansas	2,265,849	2,061	2,267,910	0.091
Kentucky	2,870,315	708	2,871,023	0.025
Louisiana	2,664,598	349	2,664,947	0.013
Maine	1,022,983	345	1,023,328	0.034
Maryland	3,678,817	100,465	3,779,282	2.658
Massachusetts	3,899,990	246,772	4,146,762	5.951
Michigan	6,319,595	3,692	6,323,287	0.058
Minnesota	3,580,638	NA	3,580,634	NA
Mississippi	1,696,577	385	1,696,962	0.023
Missouri	3,984,312	148	3,984,460	0.004
Montana	728,196	425	728,621	0.058
Nebraska	1,426,135	11	1,426,146	0.001
Nevada	1,631,359	42	1,631,401	0.003
New Hampshire	879,213	2,087	881,300	0.237
New Jersey	5,043,694	88,921	5,132,615	1.732
New Mexico	1,328,702	149	1,328,851	0.011

(table continues)

PRIVATE PASSENGER CARS INSURED
IN THE SHARED AND VOLUNTARY MARKETS, 2005 (Cont'd)

State	Voluntary	Shared market	Total	Shared market as a percent of total
New York	8,887,213	213,655	9,100,868	2.348%
North Carolina	5,083,738	1,546,437	6,630,175	23.324
North Dakota	562,102	1	562,103	[1]
Ohio	7,936,071	0	7,936,071	[1]
Oklahoma	2,552,269	277	2,552,546	0.011
Oregon	2,575,410	28	2,575,438	0.001
Pennsylvania	8,230,275	50,757	8,281,032	0.613
Rhode Island	641,028	32,331	673,359	4.801
South Carolina	3,040,916	2	3,040,918	[1]
South Dakota	642,607	0	642,607	[1]
Tennessee	3,999,819	96	3,999,915	0.002
Texas	NA	NA	NA	NA
Utah	1,620,366	3	1,620,369	[1]
Vermont	464,849	1,708	466,557	0.366
Virginia	5,795,282	7,490	5,802,772	0.129
Washington	4,225,103	3	4,225,106	[1]
West Virginia	1,236,758	579	1,237,337	0.047
Wisconsin	3,618,968	0	3,618,968	[1]
Wyoming	460,658	1	460,659	[1]
United States	**178,215,262**	**2,344,554**	**180,559,816**	**1.298%**

[1]Less than 0.001 percent.
NA=Data not available.

Source: Automobile Insurance Plans Service Office.

• While North Carolina, Massachusetts and New York have the most vehicles in shared market plans, the number of cars in each of the states' plans fell in 2005—by 37.8 percent in New York, 8.4 percent in Massachusetts and 0.5 percent in North Carolina.

AUTOMOBILE FINANCIAL RESPONSIBILITY LAWS

Most states require car owners to buy a minimum amount of bodily injury and property damage liability insurance before they can legally drive their cars. All states have financial responsibility laws. This means that people involved in an automobile accident will be required to furnish proof of financial responsibility up to certain minimum dollar limits. To comply with financial responsibility laws, most drivers purchase automobile liability insurance. The insurance industry and consumer groups generally recommend a minimum of $100,000 of bodily injury protection per person and $300,000 per accident since accidents may cost far more than the minimum limits mandated by most states.

The chart below shows mandatory requirements for bodily injury **(BI)**, physical damage **(PD)** liability, no-fault personal injury protection **(PIP)**, and uninsured **(UM)** and underinsured **(UIM)** motorists coverage. It also indicates which states only have financial responsibility **(FR)** laws.

AUTOMOBILE FINANCIAL RESPONSIBILITY LIMITS BY STATE

State	Insurance required	Minimum liability limits[1]
Alabama	BI & PD Liab	20/40/10
Alaska	BI & PD Liab	50/100/25
Arizona	BI & PD Liab	15/30/10
Arkansas	BI & PD Liab, PIP	25/50/25
California	BI & PD Liab	15/30/5[2]
Colorado	BI & PD Liab	25/50/15
Connecticut	BI & PD Liab, UM, UIM	20/40/10
Delaware	BI & PD Liab, PIP	15/30/10
D.C.	BI & PD Liab, UM	25/50/10
Florida	PD Liab, PIP*	10/20/10[3]
Georgia	BI & PD Liab	25/50/25
Hawaii	BI & PD Liab, PIP	20/40/10
Idaho	BI & PD Liab	25/50/15
Illinois	BI & PD Liab, UM	20/40/15
Indiana	BI & PD Liab	25/50/10
Iowa	BI & PD Liab	20/40/15
Kansas	BI & PD Liab, PIP, UM	25/50/10
Kentucky	BI & PD Liab, PIP	25/50/10
Louisiana	BI & PD Liab	10/20/10
Maine	BI & PD Liab, UM, UIM	50/100/25[4]
Maryland	BI & PD Liab, PIP[5], UM	20/40/15
Massachusetts	BI & PD Liab, PIP, UM	20/40/5
Michigan	BI & PD Liab, PIP	20/40/10
Minnesota	BI & PD Liab, PIP, UM, UIM	30/60/10
Mississippi	BI & PD Liab	25/50/25
Missouri	BI & PD Liab, UM	25/50/10
Montana	BI & PD Liab	25/50/10

(table continues)

AUTOMOBILE FINANCIAL RESPONSIBILITY LIMITS BY STATE

State	Insurance required	Minimum liability limits[1]
Nebraska	BI & PD Liab	25/50/25
Nevada	BI & PD Liab	15/30/10
New Hampshire	FR only, UM	25/50/25
New Jersey	BI & PD Liab, PIP, UM	15/30/5[6]
New Mexico	BI & PD Liab	25/50/10
New York	BI & PD Liab, PIP, UM	25/50/10[7]
North Carolina	BI & PD Liab	30/60/25
North Dakota	BI & PD Liab, PIP, UM	25/50/25
Ohio	BI & PD Liab	12.5/25/7.5
Oklahoma	BI & PD Liab	25/50/25
Oregon	BI & PD Liab, PIP, UM	25/50/10
Pennsylvania	BI & PD Liab, PIP	15/30/5
Rhode Island	BI & PD Liab, UM	25/50/25[3]
South Carolina	BI & PD Liab, UM	25/50/25
South Dakota	BI & PD Liab, UM	25/50/25
Tennessee	BI & PD Liab	25/50/10[3]
Texas	BI & PD Liab	20/40/15**
Utah	BI & PD Liab, PIP	25/50/15[3]
Vermont	BI & PD Liab, UM, UIM	25/50/10
Virginia	BI & PD Liab, UM	25/50/20
Washington	BI & PD Liab	25/50/10
West Virginia	BI & PD Liab, UM	20/40/10
Wisconsin	FR only, UM	25/50/10
Wyoming	BI & PD Liab	25/50/20

[1]The first two numbers refer to bodily injury liability limits and the third number to property liability. For example, 20/40/10 means coverage up to $40,000 for all persons injured in an accident, subject to a limit of $20,000 for one individual, and $10,000 coverage for property damage. [2]Low-cost policy limits for low-income drivers in the California Automobile Assigned Risk Plan are 10/20/3. [3]Instead of policy limits, policyholders can satisfy the requirement with a combined single limit policy. Amounts vary by state. [4]In addition, policyholders must also carry at least $1,000 for medical payments. [5]May be waived for the policyholder but is compulsory for passengers. [6]Basic policy (optional) limits are 10/10/5. Uninsured and underinsured motorist coverge not available under the basic policy but uninsured motorist coverage is required under the standard policy. [7]In addition, policyholders must have 50/100 for wrongful death coverage. *Florida's no-fault law not in effect from October 1, 2007 to December 31, 2007. **Minimum coverage requirements will increase to 25/50/25 on April 1, 2008 and to 30/60/30 on January 1, 2011.

Source: Property Casualty Insurers Association of America; state departments of insurance.

STATE AUTO INSURANCE LAWS GOVERNING LIABILITY COVERAGE

State auto insurance laws governing liability coverage fall into four broad categories: no-fault, choice no-fault, tort liability and add-on. The major differences are whether there are restrictions on the right to sue and whether the policyholder's own insurer pays first-party benefits, up to the state maximum amount, regardless of who is at fault in the accident.

- **No-fault:** The no-fault system is intended to lower the cost of auto insurance by taking small claims out of the courts. Each insurance company compensates its own policyholders for the cost of minor injuries regardless of who was at fault in the accident. These first-party benefits, known as personal injury protection (PIP) which are a mandatory coverage, vary by state. In states with the most comprehensive benefits, a policyholder receives compensation for medical fees, lost wages, funeral costs and other out-of-pocket expenses. The term "no-fault" can be confusing because it is often used to denote any auto insurance system in which each driver's own insurance company pays for certain losses, regardless of fault. In its strict form, the term no-fault applies only to states where insurance companies pay first-party benefits and where there are restrictions on the right to sue.

  Drivers in no-fault states may sue for severe injuries if the case meets certain conditions. These conditions are known as the tort liability threshold, and may be expressed in verbal terms such as death or significant disfigurement (verbal threshold) or in dollar amounts of medical bills (monetary threshold).

- **Choice no-fault:** In choice no-fault states, drivers may select one of two options: a no-fault auto insurance policy, usually with a verbal threshold, or a traditional tort liability policy.

- **Tort liability:** In traditional tort liability states, there are no restrictions on lawsuits. A policyholder at fault in a car crash can be sued by the other driver and by the other driver's passengers for the pain and suffering the accident caused as well as for out-of-pocket expenses such as medical costs.

- **Add-on:** In add-on states, drivers receive compensation from their own insurance company as they do in no-fault states but there are no restrictions on lawsuits. The term "add-on" is used because in these states first-party benefits have been added on to the traditional tort liability system. In add-on states, first-party coverage may not be mandatory and the benefits may be lower than in true no-fault states.

STATE AUTO INSURANCE LAWS GOVERNING LIABILITY COVERAGE

"True" no-fault	First-party benefits		Restrictions on lawsuits		Thresholds for lawsuits	
	Compulsory	Optional	Yes	No	Monetary	Verbal
Florida*	X		X			X
Hawaii	X		X		X	
Kansas	X	.	X		X	
Kentucky	X		X	X[1]	X[1]	
Massachusetts	X		X		X	
Michigan	X		X			X
Minnesota	X		X		X	
New Jersey	X		X	X[1]		X[1,2]
New York	X		X			X
North Dakota	X		X		X	
Pennsylvania	X		X	X[1]		X[1]
Utah	X		X		X	
Puerto Rico	X		X		X	
Add-on						
Arkansas		X		X		
Delaware	X			X		
D.C.		X	X[3]	X[3]		
Maryland	X			X		
New Hampshire		X		X		
Oregon	X			X		
South Dakota		X		X		
Texas		X		X		
Virginia		X		X		
Washington		X		X		
Wisconsin		X		X		

- In the following 28 states auto liability is based on the traditional tort liability system. In these states, there are no restrictions on lawsuits:

  Alabama
  Alaska
  Arizona
  California
  Colorado
  Connecticut
  Georgia
  Idaho
  Illinois
  Indiana
  Iowa
  Louisiana
  Maine
  Mississippi
  Missouri
  Montana
  Nebraska
  Nevada
  New Mexico
  North Carolina
  Ohio
  Oklahoma
  Rhode Island
  South Carolina
  Tennessee
  Vermont
  West Virginia
  Wyoming

[1]"Choice" no-fault state. Policyholder can choose a policy based on the no-fault system or traditional tort liability. [2]Verbal threshold for the Basic Liability Policy, the Special Policy and the Standard Policy where the policyholder chooses no-fault. The Basic and Special Policies contain lower amounts of coverage. [3]The District of Columbia is neither a true no-fault nor add-on state. Drivers are offered the option of no-fault or fault-based coverage, but in the event of an accident a driver who originally chose no-fault benefits has 60 days to decide whether to receive those benefits or file a claim against the other party. *Florida's no-fault law not in effect from October 1, 2007 until December 31, 2007.

Source: American Insurance Association.

SEAT-BELT LAWS

Only 26 states and the District of Columbia have a primary seat-belt enforcement law, which allows law enforcement officers to stop a car for noncompliance with seat-belt laws. The other states have secondary laws; officials can only issue seat-belt violations if they stop motorists for other infractions. New Hampshire is the only state that does not have a seat-belt law that applies to adults.

Seat-belt use reached 82 percent nationwide in 2007, a slight gain from 81 percent use in 2006. States with primary seat-belt laws had an average 87 percent usage rate, versus 73 percent in states with secondary laws.

STATE SEAT-BELT USE LAWS

State	2006 usage rate[1]	Primary/ secondary enforcement[2]	Requirements	Maximum fine, first offense	Damages reduced[3]
Alabama	82.9%	P	15+ yrs. in front seat	$25	
Alaska	83.2	P	16+ yrs. in all seats	15	X
Arizona	NA	S	5+ yrs. in front seat; 5-15 in all seats	10	X
Arkansas	69.3	S	15+ yrs. in front seat	25	
California	93.4	P	16+ yrs. in all seats	20	X
Colorado	80.3	S	16+ yrs. in front seat	15	X
Connecticut	83.5	P	7+ yrs. in front seat	15	
Delaware	86.1	P	16+ yrs. in all seats	25	
D.C.	85.4	P	16+ yrs. in all seats	50	
Florida	NA	S	6+ yrs. in front seat; 6-17 yrs. in all seats	30	X
Georgia	NA	P	6-17 yrs. in all seats; 18+ yrs. in front seat	15	
Hawaii	92.5	P	8-17 yrs. in all seats; 18+ yrs. in front seat	45	
Idaho	79.8	S	7+ yrs. in all seats	25	
Illinois	87.8	P	16+ yrs. in front seat; 18 and younger in all seats if driver is younger than 18 yrs.	25	
Indiana	84.3	P	16+ yrs. in all seats	25	
Iowa	89.6	P	11+ yrs. in front seat	25	X
Kansas	73.5	4	14-17 yrs. in all seats; 18+ yrs. in front seat	30	X
Kentucky	67.2	P	more than 40 in. in all seats	25	
Louisiana	74.8	P	13+ yrs. in front seat	25	
Maine	77.2	P	18+ yrs. in all seats	50	
Maryland	NA	P	16+ yrs. in front seat	25	
Massachusetts	66.9	S	12+ yrs. in all seats	25	
Michigan	94.3	P	4+ yrs. in front seat; 4-15 yrs. in all seats	25	X
Minnesota	83.3	S	all in front seat; 3-10 yrs. in all seats	25	
Mississippi	73.6	P	4-7 yrs. in all seats; 8+ yrs. in front seat	25	

(table continues)

STATE SEAT-BELT USE LAWS (Cont'd)

State	2006 usage rate[1]	Primary/ secondary enforcement[2]	Requirements	Maximum fine, first offense	Damages reduced[3]
Missouri	75.2%	4	16+ yrs. in front seat	$10	X
Montana	79.0	S	6+ yrs. in all seats	20	
Nebraska	76.0	S	18+ yrs. in front seat	25	X
Nevada	NA	S	6+ yrs. in all seats	25	
New Hampshire	NA	S			
New Jersey	90.0	P	7 yrs. and younger but more than 80 lbs.; 8-17 yrs. in all seats; 18+ yrs. in front seat	20	X
New Mexico	89.6	P	18+ yrs. in all seats	25	
New York	83.0	P	16+ yrs. in front seat	50	X
North Carolina	88.5	P	16+ yrs. in all seats	25	
North Dakota	79.0	S	18+ yrs. in front seat	20	X
Ohio	81.7	S	4-14 yrs. in all seats; 15+ yrs. in front seat	30 driver/ 20 passenger	X
Oklahoma	83.7	P	13+ yrs. in front seat	20	
Oregon	94.1	P	16+ yrs. in all seats	75	X
Pennsylvania	NA	S	8-17 yrs. in all seats; 18+ yrs. in front seat	10	
Rhode Island	NA	4	13+ yrs. in all seats	57	
South Carolina	72.5	P	6+ yrs. in front seat; 6+ yrs. in rear seat with shoulder belt	25	
South Dakota	71.3	S	18+ yrs. in front seat	20	
Tennessee	78.6	P	16+ yrs. in front seat	50	
Texas	90.4	P	4 yrs. and younger but 36 inches or more; 5-16 yrs. in all seats; 17+ yrs. in front seat	200	
Utah	88.6	4	16+ yrs. in all seats	45	
Vermont	82.4	S	16+ yrs. in all seats	25	
Virginia	78.7	S	16+ yrs. in front seat	25	
Washington	96.3	P	16+ yrs. in all seats	37	
West Virginia	NA	S	8+ yrs. in front seat; 8-17 yrs. in all seats	25	X
Wisconsin	75.4	S	8+ yrs. in all seats	10	X
Wyoming	63.5	S	9+ yrs. in all seats	25 driver/ 10 passenger	
United States	**81.0%**				

[1]Surveys used by states must be actual observation of shoulder-belt use by drivers and front seat passengers. [2]Primary enforcement means police may stop a vehicle and issue a fine for noncompliance with seat-belt laws. Secondary enforcement means that police may issue a fine for not wearing a seat-belt only if the vehicle has been stopped for other traffic violations. [3]Court awards for compensation for injury may be reduced if seat-belt laws were violated. [4]Primary enforcement for children; ages vary. NA=Data not available.

Source: National Highway Traffic Safety Administration, U.S. Department of Transportation; Insurance Institute for Highway Safety.

DRUNK DRIVING LAWS

As of 2004 every state and the District of Columbia had lowered the limit defining drunk driving from 0.10 BAC (blood-alcohol content) to 0.08.

- All states and the District of Columbia have adopted 21 as the legal drinking age.

- All states have more stringent restrictions for drivers under the age of 21, ranging from zero tolerance to a limit of 0.02 BAC.

- A death is considered alcohol-related when any person involved in the accident had some measure of alcohol in his or her blood, even if it was below the legal limit.

- There is an alcohol-related traffic death in the United States every 30 minutes and an injury every 2 minutes.

- In 2006, 17,602 traffic deaths were alcohol-related, up slightly from 17,590 in 2005.

- In 2006, 41 percent of all traffic fatalities were alcohol-related, up from 40 percent in 2005.

STATE LAWS CURBING DRUNK DRIVING

State	License revocation		Open container law[3]	Prelim. breath test permitted by law	DWI plea bargaining prohibited
	Admin. license rev./ susp.[1]	Mandatory 90-day license rev./ susp.[2]			
Alabama	X	X	X		
Alaska	X	X	X[4]	X	
Arizona	X	X	X	X	X
Arkansas	X	X			X
California	X	X	X	X	X
Colorado	X	X	X	X	X
Connecticut	X	X			
Delaware	X	X		X	
D.C.	X	X	X	X	
Florida	X	X	X	X	X[5]
Georgia	X	X	X		
Hawaii	X	X	X	X[5]	
Idaho	X	X	X		
Illinois	X	X	X	X	
Indiana	X	X	X	X[5]	
Iowa	X	X	X	X	
Kansas	X		X[4]	X	X
Kentucky			X	X	X[5]
Louisiana	X	X	X		
Maine	X	X	X		
Maryland	X		X	X	
Massachusetts	X	X	X		
Michigan			X	X	X[5]
Minnesota	X	X	X	X	
Mississippi	X	X		X	X
Missouri	X			X	
Montana			X	X	
Nebraska	X	X	X	X	
Nevada	X	X	X	X	X

(table continues)

STATE LAWS CURBING DRUNK DRIVING (Cont'd)

State	License revocation		Open container law[3]	Prelim. breath test permitted by law	DWI plea bargaining prohibited
	Admin. license rev./ susp.[1]	Mandatory 90-day license rev./ susp.[2]			
New Hampshire	X	X	X	X	
New Jersey			X		X[6]
New Mexico	X	X	X		X[5]
New York	[7]		X	X	X
North Carolina	X		X	X[5]	
North Dakota	X	X	X	X	
Ohio	X	X	X		
Oklahoma	X	X	X[4]		
Oregon	X	X	X		X
Pennsylvania			X	X	X[5]
Rhode Island			X[4]	X	
South Carolina	X		X		
South Dakota			X	X	
Tennessee			X[4]		
Texas	X	X	X		
Utah	X	X	X		X[5]
Vermont	X	X	X	X	
Virginia	X			X	
Washington	X	X	X		
West Virginia	X	X		X	
Wisconsin	X	X	X	X	
Wyoming	X	X	X[4]		X

[1]On-the-spot drivers license suspension or revocation if BAC is over the legal limit or the driver refuses to take a BAC test. [2]Mandatory penalty for violation of the implied consent law, which means that drivers who refuse to take a breath alcohol test when stopped or arrested for drunk driving will have their license revoked or suspended. [3]Prohibits unsealed alcohol containers in motor vehicle passenger compartments for all occupants. Arresting officer not required to witness consumption. [4]Applies only to the driver. [5]With limitations or conditions. [6]Not specifically for drunk driving; Attorney General has established a no plea bargain policy. [7]Administrative license suspension lasts until prosecution is complete.

Source: U.S. Department of Transportation, National Highway Traffic Safety Administration; Insurance Institute for Highway Safety; Property Casualty Insurers Association of America; Insurance Information Institute.

- A major factor in the long-term downward trend in alcohol-related fatalities is the enactment, beginning in the 1980s, of state laws designed to deter drunk driving such as:

  - Requiring persons to be at least 21 years old before they can purchase alcohol

  - Mandatory drivers license revocation when a driver's BAC level is above the state's legal limit

  - Lowering the legal BAC level to 0.08

  - Prohibiting open containers of alcoholic beverages in motor vehicles

  - Increasing measures to prevent underage drivers from obtaining alcohol

  - Canceling the vehicle registration of drivers who have had their licenses suspended or revoked due to alcohol-related offenses

  - Instituting sobriety checkpoints

ALCOHOL SERVER LIABILITY LAWS

Many states have enacted liquor liability laws, which hold businesses and people who serve liquor liable for the damage a drunk driver causes.

STATUTES OR COURT CASES HOLDING ALCOHOLIC BEVERAGE SERVERS LIABLE

State	Commercial servers Statute[1]	Court[2]	Social hosts Statute[3]	Court	State	Commercial servers Statute[1]	Court[2]	Social hosts Statute[3]	Court
Alabama	X			X[4]	Montana	X	X	X[4]	
Alaska	X		X		Nebraska	X*		X*	
Arizona	X	X	X[4]	X[4]	Nevada			X[5]	
Arkansas	X[4]	X			New Hampshire	X		X	X
California	X[4]				New Jersey	X		X	X
Colorado	X	X	X[4]		New Mexico	X		X	X
Connecticut	X	X		X	New York	X		X[4]	
Delaware					North Carolina	X	X		X
D.C.		X			North Dakota	X		X	
Florida	X[4]			X[4]	Ohio	X	X	X	X[4]
Georgia	X[4]		X[4]		Oklahoma	X	X		
Hawaii		X			Oregon	X		X[4]	
Idaho	X	X	X[4]		Pennsylvania	X	X		X[4]
Illinois	X[4]		X		Rhode Island	X			X
Indiana	X	X	X	X	South Carolina		X		X[5]
Iowa	X	X	X[4]		South Dakota				
Kansas					Tennessee	X			
Kentucky	X	X			Texas	X[4]	X	X	X[4]
Louisiana	X[4]	X[4]	X	X[4]	Utah	X[4]			X[4]
Maine	X		X[4]		Vermont	X		X	X[4]
Maryland					Virginia				
Massachusetts	X	X	X	X	Washington	X	X	X	X[4]
Michigan	X			X[4]	West Virginia		X		
Minnesota	X		X[4]	X[4]	Wisconsin	X[4]	X[4]	X[4]	X[4]
Mississippi	X	X	X[4]	X[4]	Wyoming	X[4]		X[4]	
Missouri	X								

[1]Indicates some form of liability is permitted by statute. [2]States where common-law liability has not been specifically overruled by statute or where common-law actions are specifically recognized in addition to statutory liability. [3]Indicates that language is capable of being read broadly enough to include noncommercial servers. [4]With limitations or conditions. [5]For guests under the age of 21. *Effective January 1, 2008.

Source: U.S. Department of Transportation, National Highway Traffic Safety Administration; Property Casualty Insurers Association of America.

OLDER DRIVERS

"Older" drivers (age 70 and above) have higher rates of fatal crashes, based on estimated annual travel, than any other group except drivers under the age of 21, according to the U.S. Department of Transportation, in part because they are less likely to survive the trauma of an accident. Recognizing the higher fatality rates and the need for older drivers to retain their mobility and independence, some states issue restricted licenses. Depending on ability, older drivers may be limited to driving during daylight hours or on nonfreeway types of roads. In most states, restrictions such as these can be placed on anyone's drivers license, regardless of age, if his or her medical condition warrants it.

STATE DRIVERS LICENSE RENEWAL LAWS INCLUDING REQUIREMENTS FOR OLDER DRIVERS

State	Require retest for renewals at all ages[1]			Age at which states require older drivers to pass tests				Require doctors to report medical conditions[2]	Age limits on mail renewal
	Vision	Road	Knowledge	Vision	Road	Knowledge	Medical		
Alabama									
Alaska	X	[3]	X						69
Arizona	X	[3]		65					70
Arkansas	X								
California	X	[3]	X					X [4]	70
Colorado	X	[3]	[3]						61
Connecticut				65					65
Delaware		[3]	[3]	[3]	[3]	[3]	[3]	X	
D.C.				70	75	75	70		
Florida	X	[3]	[3]	80					[5]
Georgia	X							X	64
Hawaii	X	[3]			[3]	[3]	[3]		
Idaho	X	[3]							
Illinois	X		X	75					
Indiana							[3]		
Iowa		[3]	[3]						
Kansas	X	[3]	X						
Kentucky		[3]							
Louisiana	X	[3]	X	70					70
Maine				40, 62					
Maryland	X	[3]	[3]	40			[3]		
Massahusetts									
Michigan	X	[3]	X						
Minnesota	X		X						

(table continues)

PROPERTY/CASUALTY INSURANCE BY LINE

AUTO: LAWS

STATE DRIVERS LICENSE RENEWAL LAWS INCLUDING REQUIREMENTS FOR OLDER DRIVERS
(Cont'd)

State	Require retest for renewals at all ages[1]			Age at which states require older drivers to pass tests				Require doctors to report medical conditions[2]	Age limits on mail renewal
	Vision	Road	Knowledge	Vision	Road	Knowledge	Medical		
Mississippi		3	3						
Missouri	X								
Montana	X	3							5
Nebraska	X	3	3						
Nevada	X	3	3	65			70	X	6
New Hampshire	X				75				
New Jersey	X							X	
New Mexico									
New York		3	3						
North Carolina	X	3	X						
North Dakota	X	3	3						
Ohio	X	3	3						
Oklahoma	X								
Oregon				50				X	
Pennsylvania				45			45	X	
Rhode Island	X	3							
South Carolina	X	3	3	65					
South Dakota	X								
Tennessee									
Texas	X			85					79
Utah	X	3	3	65				X	
Vermont									
Virginia	X		3	80					
Washington	X	3	3						
West Virginia								X	
Wisconsin		3							
Wyoming	X	3	3						

[1]Periodic retests. Some states will waive vision retests for mail renewal or clean-record drivers. Most states require medical tests at application and renewal for certain medical conditions or after a certain number of accidents. [2]Physicians must report physical conditions that might impair driving skills. [3]Retesting only for cause, e.g., after specific number of accidents or other points and infractions, for specific physical conditions; sometimes at examiner's discretion. [4]Specifically requires doctors to report a diagnosis of dementia. [5]Only two successive renewals may be made electronically or by mail, regardless of age. [6]All drivers must renew in person every 8 years.

Source: U.S. Department of Transportation, Federal Highway Administration; AARP; American Automobile Association; American Association of Motor Vehicle Administrators; Insurance Institute for Highway Safety.

CELL PHONE/DRIVER DISTRACTION LAWS

A 2006 study by the Virginia Tech Transportation Institute and the National Highway Traffic Safety Administration found that almost 80 percent of crashes and 65 percent of near-crashes involved some form of driver inattention within three seconds of the event, with the most prevalent distraction being cell phones, followed by drowsiness. A number of states have passed laws to address the cell-phone problem. In July 2008 California will be the sixth jurisdiction to have a law banning the use of hand-held cell phones while driving, joining Connecticut, New Jersey, New York, Washington State and the District of Columbia. Washington State is the first state to ban the practice of "texting" with a cell phone while driving. By October 2007, 15 states had passed laws banning or restricting young drivers from using cell phones while driving.

YOUNG DRIVER LAWS

Young drivers account for a disproportionate number of motor vehicle crashes. States are increasingly adopting laws to help lower the crash rate. One approach has been to lower blood alcohol content (BAC) limits so those young drivers who drink even small amounts of alcohol will be penalized. Another has been to require a more rigorous learning period before granting young drivers the privilege of a drivers license. This requires young drivers between the ages of 15 and 18 to apply for a graduated drivers license (GDL) to help them improve their driving skills and habits before receiving full driving privileges.

- Motor vehicle crashes are the leading cause of death among 15- to 20-year olds.

- Among licensed drivers, motorists between the ages of 15 and 20 have the highest rate of fatal crashes relative to other age groups, including the elderly.

Graduated licensing as defined by the National Highway Traffic Safety Administration consists of three stages. Some of the requirements and recommendations included in Stage 1 (learners permit) are a vision test, a road knowledge test, driving accompanied by a licensed adult, safety-belt use by all vehicle occupants, a zero BAC level, and six months with no crashes or convictions for traffic violations. Stage 2 (intermediate license) includes the completion of Stage 1, a behind-the-wheel road test, advanced driver education training, driving accompanied by a licensed adult at night, and 12 consecutive months with no crashes or convictions for traffic offenses before reaching Stage 3 (full license).

STATE YOUNG DRIVER LAWS[1]

State	Graduated licensing[2]		Restrictions on night driving[3]	Passenger restrictions[4]	Driver may not operate a cell phone in learner and intermediate stages
	Learners permit required for a minimum period	Intermediate or provisional license required			
Alabama	6 months	X	X	X	
Alaska	6 months	X	X	X	
Arizona	6 months*	X*	X*	X*	
Arkansas	6 months	X			
California	6 months	X	X	X	X[5]*
Colorado	12 months	X	X	X	X
Connecticut	6 months	X	X	X	X[5]
Delaware	6 months	X	X	X	X
D.C.	6 months	X	X	X	X[5]
Florida	12 months	X	X		
Georgia	12 months	X	X	X	
Hawaii	6 months	X	X	X	
Idaho	6 months	X	X	X	
Illinois	9 months**	X	X	X	X
Indiana	2 months	X	X	X	
Iowa	6 months	X	X		
Kansas	6 months				
Kentucky	6 months	X	X	X	
Louisiana	6 months	X	X		
Maine	6 months	X	X	X	X
Maryland	6 months	X	X	X	X[6]
Massachusetts	6 months	X	X	X	
Michigan	6 months	X	X		
Minnesota	6 months	X			X
Mississippi	6 months	X	X		
Missouri	6 months	X	X	X	
Montana	6 months	X	X	X	
Nebraska	6 months**	X	X	X**	X**
Nevada	6 months	X	X	X	
New Hampshire	3 months[7]	X	X	X	

(table continues)

STATE YOUNG DRIVER LAWS[1] (Cont'd)

State	Graduated licensing[2] Learners permit required for a minimum period	Intermediate or provisional license required	Restrictions on night driving[3]	Passenger restrictions[4]	Driver may not operate a cell phone in learner and intermediate stages
New Jersey	6 months	X	X	X	X[5]
New Mexico	6 months	X	X	X	
New York	6 months[8]	X	X	X	X[6]
North Carolina	12 months	X	X	X	X[8]
North Dakota	6 months				
Ohio	6 months	X	X	X	
Oklahoma	6 months	X	X	X	
Oregon	6 months	X	X	X	X**
Pennsylvania	6 months	X	X		
Rhode Island	6 months	X	X	X	X[6]
South Carolina	6 months	X	X	X	
South Dakota	6 months[8]	X	X		
Tennessee	6 months	X	X	X	X
Texas	6 months	X	X	X	X
Utah	6 months	X	X	X	
Vermont	12 months	X		X	
Virginia	9 months	X	X	X	X
Washington	6 months	X	X	X	X[5]**
West Virginia	6 months	X	X	X	X
Wisconsin	6 months	X	X	X	
Wyoming	10 days	X	X	X	

[1]Designed to aid young novice drivers between the ages of 15 and 18 gain driving experience. To date they apply only to drivers under the age of 18. All states have lower blood alcohol content laws for under-21 drivers which range from none to 0.02, in contrast with 0.08 for drivers over the age of 21 in all states. [2]Graduated licensing as defined by the National Highway Traffic Safety Administration. [3]Vary by state with regard to age of driver, night hours that driving is restricted, and who must accompany driver during night hours. Exceptions may be made for work, school or religious activities and emergencies. [4]Limits the number of teenage passengers a young driver may have in the vehicle. [5]Laws ban all drivers from using handheld cell phones. [6]For drivers younger than 18. [7]New Hampshire does not issue learner's permits. The minimum holding period refers to the intermediate license for 16- and 17-year-olds for the first 3 months only. [8]Minimum holding period applies to the limited junior driver license for permit holders who pass a road test and certify 20 or more hours of practice; with some restrictions. *Effective July 1, 2008. **Effective January 1, 2008.

Source: Insurance Institute for Highway Safety; U.S. Department of Transportation, National Highway Traffic Safety Administration; National Conference of State Legislatures; Insurance Information Institute.

HOMEOWNERS PREMIUMS AS A PERCENT OF ALL P/C PREMIUMS, 2006

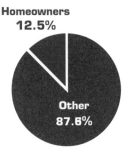

Homeowners
12.5%

Other
87.6%

Source: National Association of Insurance Commissioners (NAIC) Annual Statement Database, via Highline Data, LLC. Copyrighted information. No portion of this work may be copied or redistributed without the express written permission of Highline Data, LLC.

HOMEOWNERS INSURANCE

Homeowners insurance accounts for 12.5 percent of all property/casualty insurance premiums and 26 percent of personal lines insurance.

Homeowners insurance is a "package" policy, providing both property and personal liability insurance. The typical policy covers the house, garage and other structures on the property—as well as personal property inside the house—against a wide variety of perils, such as fire, windstorm, vandalism and accidental water damage. The typical homeowners policy includes theft coverage on personal property anywhere in the world and liability coverage for accidental harm caused to others. It also reimburses the policyholder for the additional cost of living elsewhere while his or her house is being repaired or rebuilt after a fire or other disaster.

Earthquake damage and flood damage caused by external flooding are not covered by standard homeowners policies but can be purchased separately. Flood coverage is provided by the federal government's National Flood Insurance Program.

HOMEOWNERS MULTIPLE PERIL INSURANCE, 1999-2006
($000)

Year	Net premiums written[1]	Annual percent change	Combined ratio[2]	Annual point change
1999	$30,814,719	5.4%	107.9	NA
2000	32,729,981	6.2	110.4	2.5 pts.
2001	35,364,334	8.0	120.6	10.2
2002	40,238,172	13.8	108.6	-12.0
2003	46,035,860	14.4	98.0	-10.6
2004	49,980,417	8.6	95.8	-2.2
2005	53,015,549	6.1	104.7	8.9
2006	55,821,315	5.3	89.2	-15.5

[1]After reinsurance transactions, excluding state funds.
[2]After dividends to policyholders. A drop in the combined ratio represents an improvement; an increase represents a deterioration. See also Glossary.
NA=Data not available.

Source: National Association of Insurance Commissioners (NAIC) Annual Statement Database, via Highline Data, LLC. Copyrighted information. No portion of this work may be copied or redistributed without the express written permission of Highline Data, LLC.

LEADING WRITERS OF HOMEOWNERS INSURANCE BY DIRECT PREMIUMS WRITTEN, 2006
($000)

Rank	Company/Group	Direct premiums written[1]	Market share
1	State Farm Mutual Group	$13,580,291	22.2%
2	Allstate Insurance Group	7,309,829	11.9
3	Zurich Insurance Group	4,280,574	7.0
4	Nationwide Group	2,853,602	4.7
5	Travelers Group	2,660,259	4.3
6	USAA Group	2,504,863	4.1
7	Liberty Mutual Insurance Group	1,889,463	3.1
8	Chubb & Son Group	1,745,025	2.9
9	American Family Insurance Group	1,431,085	2.3
10	Hartford Fire & Casualty Group	1,047,858	1.7

[1]Before reinsurance transactions, excluding state funds.

Source: National Association of Insurance Commissioners (NAIC) Annual Statement Database, via Highline Data, LLC. Copyrighted information. No portion of this work may be copied or redistributed without the express written permission of Highline Data, LLC.

HIGH-RISK MARKETS

LEADING STATES IN COASTAL POPULATION GROWTH, 1980-2003[1]

	Total change			Percent change	
Rank	State	By change in number (millions of people)	Rank	State	By percent change
1	California	9.9	1	Florida	75%
2	Florida	7.1	2	Alaska	63
3	Texas	2.5	3	Washington	54
4	Washington	1.7	4	Texas	52
5	Virginia	1.6	5	Virginia	48
6	New York	1.6	6	California	47
7	New Jersey	1.2	7	New Hampshire	46
8	Maryland	1.2	8	Delaware	38
9	Michigan	0.8	9	Georgia	35
10	Massachusetts	0.7	10	South Carolina	33

- In 2003, 53 percent of the nation's population, or 153 million people, lived in the 673 U.S. coastal counties, an increase of 33 million people since 1980, according to the National Oceanic and Atmospheric Administration. Coastal counties account for 17 percent of U.S. land area.

[1]Includes coastal states in the Northeast, Southeast, Gulf of Mexico, Pacific and Great Lakes regions. Note: Latest data available.

Source: U.S. Department of Commerce, Census Bureau.

- In 2004 the value of insured coastal properties in the 18 East Coast and Gulf states exposed to hurricanes totaled $6.9 trillion, or 16 percent of insurers' total exposure to loss in the United States (see footnote 2 on the chart), according to AIR Worldwide.

- AIR estimates that property values in coastal areas of the United States have doubled over the last decade.

- The percentage of homes that are undervalued, relative to what it would cost to rebuild, dropped from 73 percent in 2002 to 58 percent in 2006, according to a Marshall & Swift/Boechk survey. Homes were undervalued by an average of 21 percent in 2006, down from 35 percent in 2002.

VALUE OF INSURED COASTAL PROPERTIES VULNERABLE TO HURRICANES BY STATE, 2004[1]
($ billions)

State	Coastal	Total exposure[2]	Coastal as a percent of total
Florida	$1,937.4	$2,443.5	79%
New York	1,901.6	3,123.6	61
Texas	740.0	2,895.3	26
Massachusetts	662.4	1,223.0	54
New Jersey	505.8	1,504.8	34
Connecticut	404.9	641.3	63
Louisiana	209.3	551.7	38
South Carolina	148.8	581.2	26
Virginia	129.7	1,140.2	11
Maine	117.2	202.4	58
North Carolina	105.3	1,189.3	9
Alabama	75.9	631.3	12
Georgia	73.0	1,235.7	6
Delaware	46.4	140.1	33
New Hampshire	45.6	196.0	23
Mississippi	44.7	331.4	13
Rhode Island	43.8	156.6	28
Maryland	12.1	853.6	1
Coastal states	**$6,863.0**	**$19,041.1**	**36%**

[1]Includes residential and commercial properties. Ranked by value of insured coastal property.
[2]Total exposure is an estimate of the actual total value of all property in the state that is insured or can be insured, including the full replacement value of structures and their contents and the time value of business interruption coverage.
Note: Latest data available.

Source: AIR Worldwide.

INSURANCE THROUGH FAIR PLANS

Fair Access to Insurance Requirements (FAIR) Plans were created in the late 1960s after the era of urban riots, to make property insurance more readily available to those who had difficulty obtaining it in certain areas because of abnormal exposure to risks over which they had no control. The plans, operated by the insurance industry, make insurance available to properties meeting established standards, regardless of location or exposure. All FAIR Plan policies insure for losses from fire, vandalism, riot and windstorm. About a dozen states offer some form of homeowners insurance, which includes liability coverage. In California, the FAIR Plan also covers areas prone to brush fires.

INSURANCE PROVIDED BY FAIR PLANS, 1997-2006[1]

| Year | Number of | | Exposure[2] ($000) | Direct written premiums ($000) |
	Habitational policies	Commercial policies		
1997	1,035,941	57,932	$124,410,722	$391,561
1998	1,466,626	52,173	169,994,265	576,296
1999	1,068,525	44,893	140,281,262	415,749
2000	919,703	38,868	113,333,445	376,456
2001	912,829	36,748	143,459,479	438,241
2002	1,422,990	81,887	269,566,059	1,202,010
2003	1,510,665	65,532	345,909,146	1,770,353
2004	1,907,337	138,163	400,413,034	2,164,546
2005	1,928,292	117,942	387,780,124	2,234,493
2006	2,389,299	172,070	601,859,916	4,063,324

[1]Data from 2002 to 2005 include Florida's Citizens Property Insurance Corporation, which includes FAIR and Beach Plans; data after 2002 includes the Texas Fair plan; data after 2004 include Louisiana's Citizen's Property Insurance Corporation.
[2]Exposure is the estimate of the aggregate value of all insurance in force in all FAIR Plans in all lines (except liability, where applicable, and crime) for 12 months ending September through December.

Source: Property Insurance Plans Service Office (PIPSO).

INSURANCE PROVIDED BY FAIR PLANS BY STATE, 2006[1]

State	Number of Habitational policies	Number of Commercial policies	Exposure ($000)	Direct written premiums ($000)
California	193,615	12,509	$50,577,001	$82,268
Connecticut	4,682	297	768,728	4,717
Delaware	2,963	122	295,795	793
Florida (CPIC)[2]	1,409,587	137,691	408,837,779	3,400,400
Georgia[3]	28,167	1,531	3,114,897	16,625
Illinois	9,970	206	769,000	7,393
Indiana	3,633	128	300,953	2,210
Iowa	1,425	65	94,079	861
Kansas	9,659	251	416,676	4,300
Kentucky	14,040	926	141,533	7,872
Massachusetts	216,074	982	68,607,352	235,997
Michigan	73,952	2,018	10,186,674	72,684
Minnesota	8,600	3	1,839,520	6,870
Mississippi	12,080	[4]	661,360	7,626
Missouri	8,928	556	421,162	3,613
New Jersey	41,974	1,631	5,440,130	21,595
New Mexico	12,687	394	671,920	3,774
New York[3]	60,797	7,172	12,927,080	35,857
Ohio	59,983	1,386	11,309,456	30,267
Oregon	4,225	175	322,196	1,402
Pennsylvania	37,386	2,625	2,079,026	13,030
Rhode Island	21,708	173	4,728,942	23,776
Texas	109,461	[4]	13,320,285	59,873
Virginia	37,058	871	3,944,094	16,424
Washington	90	58	33,346	187
West Virginia	1,364	117	50,932	795
Wisconsin	5,191	183	NA	2,297
Total	**2,389,299**	**172,070**	**$601,859,916**	**$4,063,324**

[1]Does not include the FAIR Plans of Arkansas, Washington D.C., Hawaii, Maryland, North Carolina and Louisiana Citizens. [2]Citizens Property Insurance Corporation, which combined the FAIR and Beach Plans. [3]Includes a wind and hail option for any dwelling including those in coastal communities. [4]The Mississippi and Texas FAIR Plans do not offer a commercial policy. NA=Data not available.

Source: Property Insurance Plans Service Office (PIPSO).

INSURANCE PROVIDED BY BEACH AND WINDSTORM PLANS

Beach and Windstorm Insurance Plans ensure that insurance is available against damage from hurricanes and other windstorms. In Georgia, Massachusetts and New York, FAIR Plans provide wind and hail coverage for certain coastal communities. These states do not have Beach and Windstorm Plans. New Jersey does not have a Beach Plan but its WindMap operates in the voluntary market to help homeowners in coastal areas obtain homeowners insurance.

INSURANCE PROVIDED BY BEACH AND WINDSTORM PLANS, 2006[1]

State	Habitational policies	Commercial policies	Exposure[2] ($000)	Direct written premiums ($000)
Mississippi	28,880	2,082	$5,369,509	$48,813
South Carolina	27,082	2,992	11,179,099	67,309
Texas	140,375	17,858	38,313,022	196,833
Total	196,337	22,932	$54,861,630	$312,955

[1]Does not include the FAIR Plans of Alabama and North Carolina and the Florida and Louisiana Citizens.
[2]Exposure is the estimate of the aggregate value of all insurance in force in each state's Beach and Windstorm Plan in all lines (except liability, where applicable, and crime) for 12 months ending September through December.

Source: Property Insurance Plans Service Office (PIPSO).

COSTS/EXPENDITURES

AVERAGE PREMIUMS FOR HOMEOWNERS AND RENTERS INSURANCE, UNITED STATES, 1998-2004

Year	Homeowners[1]	Percent change	Renters[2]	Percent change
1998	$481	5.7%	$170	0.6%
1999	488	1.5	171	0.6
2000	508	4.1	175	2.3
2001	536	5.5	178	1.7
2002	593	10.6	186	4.5
2003	668	12.6	192	3.2
2004	729	9.1	195	1.6

- A 2006 Insurance Research Council poll found that 96 percent of homeowners had homeowners insurance while 43 percent of renters had renters insurance.

[1]Based on the HO-3 homeowner package policy for owner-occupied dwellings, 1 to 4 family units. Provides "all risks" coverage (except those specifically excluded in the policy) on buildings, broad named-peril coverage on personal property, and is the most common package written. [2]Based on the HO-4 renters insurance policy for tenants. Includes broad named-peril coverage for the personal property of tenants.

Source: © 2007 National Association of Insurance Commissioners. Reprinted with permission. Further reprint or distribution strictly prohibited without written permission of NAIC.

AVERAGE PREMIUMS FOR HOMEOWNERS AND RENTERS INSURANCE, BY STATE, 2004

State	Homeowners Average premium[1]	Rank	Renters Average premium[2]	Rank	State	Homeowners Average premium[2]	Rank	Renters Average premium[1]	Rank
Alabama	$793	11	$226	8	Montana	$661	25	$163	36
Alaska	810	10	191	19	Nebraska	730	19	153	43
Arizona	642	29	227	7	Nevada	632	33	217	10
Arkansas	768	15	229	6	New Hampshire	599	40	162	37
California[3]	835	7	265	2	New Jersey	641	30	181	27
Colorado	811	9	181	25	New Mexico	585	43	203	15
Connecticut	777	13	201	16	New York	785	12	220	9
Delaware	488	48	163	35	North Carolina	623	34	155	42
D.C.	894	6	189	21	North Dakota	704	22	130	49
Florida	929	4	199	17	Ohio	523	45	169	32
Georgia	635	32	215	11	Oklahoma	991	3	257	4
Hawaii	726	20	209	14	Oregon	492	47	174	31
Idaho	448	51	159	39	Pennsylvania	593	41	150	46
Illinois	659	26	186	22	Rhode Island	769	14	194	18
Indiana	636	31	181	26	South Carolina	768	16	190	20
Iowa	575	44	144	48	South Dakota	601	39	127	51
Kansas	833	8	180	28	Tennessee	681	24	212	13
Kentucky	615	37	165	33	Texas[4]	1,362	1	277	1
Louisiana	1,074	2	253	5	Utah	473	50	151	45
Maine	513	46	145	47	Vermont	608	38	157	40
Maryland	652	27	160	38	Virginia	616	35	153	44
Massachusetts	759	18	215	12	Washington	590	42	177	29
Michigan	726	21	184	23	West Virginia	616	36	175	30
Minnesota	767	17	156	41	Wisconsin	483	49	128	50
Mississippi	907	5	262	3	Wyoming	650	28	164	34
Missouri	689	23	182	24	**United States**	**$729**		**$195**	

[1]Based on the HO-3 homeowner package policy for owner-occupied dwellings, 1 to 4 family units. Provides "all risks" coverage (except those specifically excluded in the policy) on buildings, broad named-peril coverage on personal property, and is the most common package written. [2]Based on the HO-4 renters insurance policy for tenants. Includes broad named-peril coverage for the personal property of tenants. [3]California data were provided by the California Department of Insurance. [4]The Texas Department of Insurance developed home insurance policy forms that are similar but not identical to the standard forms. Note: Average premium=premiums/exposure per house years. A house year is equal to 365 days of insured coverage for a single dwelling. The NAIC does not rank State Average Expenditures and does not endorse any conclusions drawn from this data.

WHERE THE PREMIUM DOLLAR GOES, HOMEOWNERS INSURANCE, 2005

PREMIUMS EARNED:	**$100**
CLAIMS:	
Property damage:	
Fire and lightning	$16
Wind and hail	30
Water damage and freezing	11
All other property damage[1]	4
Theft	2
Subtotal	$63
Liability:	
Bodily injury and property damage	$2
Medical payments and other	1
Subtotal	$3
Costs of settling claims	9
Total claims	**$75**
EXPENSES:	
Commissions and other selling expenses	$21
General expenses (costs of company operations)	5
State premium taxes, licenses and fees	3
Dividends to policyholders	1
Total expenses	**$30**
Claims and expense total	**$105**
BOTTOM LINE:	
Investment gain[2]	$8
Pretax income ($100 - $105 + $8)	3
Tax	1
Income after taxes	**$2**

[1]Includes vandalism and malicious mischief.

[2]Includes interest, dividends, and realized capital gains.

Source: Insurance Information Institute estimate based on data from ISO; National Association of Insurance Commissioners (NAIC) Annual Statement Database, via Highline Data, LLC. Copyrighted information. No portion of this work may be copied or redistributed without the express written permission of Highline Data, LLC; A.M. Best Company, Inc.

- In 2005 claims accounted for $75 of every $100 of homeowners insurance premiums earned, up from $67 in 2004.

- Property damage and theft claims accounted for 84 percent of all claims payments. Liability claims accounted for 4 percent. The cost of settling these claims accounted for the remaining 12 percent of total claim costs.

- Expenses—including commissions, general overhead expenses, state premium taxes, licenses, fees and dividends to policyholders—accounted for $30 of every $100 of premium earned.

WHERE THE REVENUE DOLLAR GOES, 2005
(Premiums and investments)

Tax 1%
Expenses 28%
Claims 70%
Profits 1%

CAUSES OF HOMEOWNERS INSURANCE LOSSES

Each year about 7 percent of insured homes have damage that results in a claim, according to ISO. Changes in the percentage of each type of homeowners loss from one year to another are partially influenced by large fluctuations in the number and severity of weather-related events such as hurricanes and winter storms. There are two ways of looking at losses: by the average number of claims filed per 100 policies (frequency) and by the average amount paid for each claim (severity). The loss category "water damage and freezing" includes damage caused by mold. Every state except Arkansas, New York, North Carolina and Virginia has adopted an ISO mold limitation for homeowners insurance coverage, which allows insurers to exclude the coverage unless the condition results from a covered peril.

HOMEOWNERS INSURANCE LOSSES BY CAUSE, 2001-2005[1]
(Percent of losses incurred)

Cause of loss	2001	2002	2003	2004	2005
Property damage					
Fire, lightning and debris removal	30.8%	32.6%	31.8%	20.5%	25.1%
Wind and hail	21.7	20.7	25.5	51.2	45.0
Water damage and freezing	22.3	21.5	21.9	15.7	16.8
Theft	4.7	4.5	3.3	2.2	2.6
All other property damage[2]	13.2	12.3	10.7	6.1	6.5
Liability					
Bodily injury and property damage	6.5	7.3	5.8	3.7	3.3
Medical payments and other	0.7	0.8	0.8	0.7	0.7
Credit card and other[3]	0.2	0.3	0.2	0.1	0.1

[1]Data exclude tenants and condominium owners insurance.
[2]Includes vandalism and malicious mischief.
[3]Includes coverage for unauthorized use of fund transfer cards, and forgery and counterfeit currency.

Source: ISO.

HOMEOWNERS INSURANCE CLAIMS AND PAYOUT FOR LIGHTNING LOSSES

	2004	2005	2006	Percent change 2004-2006
Number of paid claims	278,000	265,700	256,000	-7.9%
Insured losses ($ millions)	$735.5	$819.6	$882.2	20.0
Average cost per claim	$2,646	$3,084	$3,446	30.3

Source: Insurance Information Institute.

- Lightning caused an estimated $1 billion in losses in 2007, according to the Insurance Information Institute.

HOMEOWNERS INSURANCE LOSSES, 2001-2005[1]

Year	Water damage and freezing		Total homeowner losses	
	Claim frequency[2]	Claim severity[3]	Claim frequency[2]	Claim severity[3]
2001	2.08	$3,627	7.91	$4,273
2002	1.66	4,160	6.89	4,652
2003	1.79	4,625	7.10	5,324
2004	1.62	5,229	6.72	8,064
2005	1.43	5,477	5.81	8,074
Average[4]	1.71	4,562	6.87	5,974

[1]For homeowners multiple peril policies. Excludes tenants and condominium policies. [2]Claims per 100 house years (policies). [3]Accident year incurred losses, excluding loss adjustment expenses, i.e., indemnity costs per accident year incurred claims. [4]Weighted average.

Source: ISO.

- Incurred homeowners losses decreased by 32.1 percent from $41.8 billion in 2005 to $28.4 billion in 2006, on a direct basis before reinsurance, according to the National Association of Insurance Commissioners.

FLOOD INSURANCE

NATIONAL FLOOD INSURANCE PROGRAM

In 1968 Congress created the National Flood Insurance Program (NFIP) in response to the rising cost of taxpayer-funded disaster relief for flood victims and the increasing amount of damage caused by floods. The NFIP makes federally backed flood insurance available in communities that agree to adopt and enforce floodplain management ordinances to reduce future flood damage. The NFIP is self-supporting for the average historical loss year. This means that unless there is a widespread disaster, operating expenses and flood insurance claims are financed through premiums collected.

- 101 insurance companies participate in the "Write-Your-Own" Program, a program started in 1983 in which insurers issue policies and adjust flood claims on behalf of the federal government

- The 2004 Flood Insurance Reform Act addressed the issue of repetitive loss properties, which represented 1 percent of all properties insured but 25 to 30 percent of claims losses. The 2004 reforms provide for a pilot program to mitigate repetitive losses.

- Loss payments totaled $553 million in 2006. In 2005 loss payments totaled $17.4 billion, the highest amount on record, including losses from hurricanes Katrina, Rita and Wilma.

- In 2006 the average amount of flood coverage was $190,849 and the average premium was $474.

- The average flood claim in 2006 was $25,675, down from $82,952 in 2005.

A growing number of private insurers have begun offering "excess flood" policies, intended to provide more extensive water damage protection to homeowners than the coverage provided by NFIP policies alone. In addition, some insurers have introduced special policies for high value properties. These high-end policies may cover homes in noncoastal areas and/or provide enhancements to traditional flood coverage.

According to a Rand Corporation study conducted for the NFIP, nationwide about 49 percent of single family homes in special flood hazard areas (SFHAs) were covered by flood insurance in 2004. In the South and West the percentage was about 60 percent. Only about 1 percent of homeowners in non-SFHAs purchase the coverage.

NATIONAL FLOOD INSURANCE PROGRAM, 1980-2006

Year	Policies in force at end of year	Losses paid Number	Losses paid Amount ($000)
1980	2,103,851	41,918	$230,414.3
1985	2,016,785	38,676	368,238.8
1990	2,477,861	14,766	167,919.6
1995	3,476,829	62,441	1,295,581.5
1996	3,693,076	52,679	828,040.3
1997	4,102,416	30,338	519,511.9
1998	4,235,138	57,344	886,247.7
1999	4,329,985	47,246	754,874.3
2000	4,369,087	16,360	251,559.3
2001	4,458,470	43,550	1,276,965.8
2002	4,519,799	25,274	433,329.7
2003	4,565,491	36,619	776,537.5
2004	4,667,446	55,375	2,189,617.7
2005	4,962,011	209,801	17,403,355.7
2006	5,517,089	21,547	553,208.9

Source: U.S. Department of Homeland Security, Federal Emergency Management Agency.

FLOOD INSURANCE IN THE UNITED STATES, 2006[1]

State	Direct NFIP business		WYO business		Total NFIP/WYO	
	Number of policies	Insurance in force[2] ($000)	Number of policies	Insurance in force[2] ($000)	Number of policies	Insurance in force[2] ($000)
Alabama	5,716	$719,899	46,592	$8,218,812	52,308	$8,938,711
Alaska	119	22,839	2,498	483,089	2,617	505,928
Arizona	792	136,788	33,247	6,598,465	34,039	6,735,253
Arkansas	1,060	95,066	15,328	1,598,068	16,388	1,693,133
California	10,994	2,162,329	260,180	57,992,669	271,174	60,154,998
Colorado	787	145,636	15,824	3,176,766	16,611	3,322,402
Connecticut	2,695	480,403	31,811	6,532,589	34,506	7,012,992
Delaware	632	119,921	22,203	4,627,924	22,835	4,747,844
D.C.	8	2,514	1,494	192,274	1,502	194,788
Florida	15,285	2,396,910	2,159,347	423,965,440	2,174,632	426,362,350
Georgia	1,349	239,595	84,103	17,652,442	85,452	17,892,037
Hawaii	481	88,649	54,613	8,480,105	55,094	8,568,755
Idaho	386	81,949	6,793	1,389,053	7,179	1,471,002
Illinois	5,155	634,297	41,816	5,877,218	46,971	6,511,514
Indiana	2,759	292,118	25,398	3,191,747	28,157	3,483,866
Iowa	885	88,204	9,503	1,173,663	10,388	1,261,867
Kansas	1,684	178,385	8,682	1,056,672	10,366	1,235,057
Kentucky	1,261	128,381	20,319	2,313,097	21,580	2,441,478
Louisiana	48,302	2,951,709	446,068	82,773,994	494,370	85,725,703
Maine	551	103,874	7,434	1,329,045	7,985	1,432,919
Maryland	1,950	275,143	61,320	11,308,768	63,270	11,583,910
Massachusetts	8,961	1,626,040	39,282	7,876,838	48,243	9,502,879
Michigan	2,483	337,405	23,915	3,379,700	26,398	3,717,105
Minnesota	634	78,814	7,788	1,318,748	8,422	1,397,561
Mississippi	6,248	281,450	69,967	12,692,255	76,215	12,973,705
Missouri	2,504	311,083	20,537	2,734,879	23,041	3,045,962
Montana	194	27,196	3,266	488,923	3,460	516,119
Nebraska	941	100,401	10,821	1,440,324	11,762	1,540,725
Nevada	224	58,505	16,006	3,636,567	16,230	3,695,072
New Hampshire	502	84,807	7,104	1,165,770	7,606	1,250,577
New Jersey	10,889	1,915,658	203,135	40,027,229	214,024	41,942,887
New Mexico	391	52,736	14,428	2,001,003	14,819	2,053,739

(table continues)

FLOOD INSURANCE IN THE UNITED STATES, 2006[1] (Cont'd)

State	Direct NFIP business		WYO business		Total NFIP/WYO	
	Number of policies	Insurance in force[2] ($000)	Number of policies	Insurance in force[2] ($000)	Number of policies	Insurance in force[2] ($000)
New York	10,715	$1,830,824	121,797	$25,841,294	132,512	$27,672,118
North Carolina	4,491	890,058	125,058	25,561,220	129,549	26,451,278
North Dakota	447	57,416	4,646	708,699	5,093	766,116
Ohio	4,846	472,639	34,360	4,489,910	39,206	4,962,549
Oklahoma	1,509	172,217	12,643	1,577,778	14,152	1,749,996
Oregon	1,149	229,421	29,395	5,586,927	30,544	5,816,348
Pennsylvania	7,587	795,275	59,271	9,327,897	66,858	10,123,172
Rhode Island	1,019	200,846	13,770	2,930,166	14,789	3,131,012
South Carolina	782	161,970	187,360	39,481,194	188,142	39,643,164
South Dakota	322	36,560	2,882	397,975	3,204	434,535
Tennessee	1,353	188,723	18,523	3,059,475	19,876	3,248,198
Texas	7,655	1,248,985	609,352	126,542,282	617,007	127,791,266
Utah	412	27,558	3,698	787,034	4,110	814,592
Vermont	317	42,379	2,871	454,303	3,188	496,682
Virginia	1,818	306,830	98,978	20,622,828	100,796	20,929,658
Washington	1,712	299,946	31,388	5,878,570	33,100	6,178,517
West Virginia	3,755	237,365	18,607	1,882,978	22,362	2,120,343
Wisconsin	1,284	163,493	11,861	1,630,442	13,145	1,793,935
Wyoming	174	25,163	2,296	397,958	2,470	423,122
American Samoa	1	46	0	0	1	46
Guam	196	29,430	60	10,626	256	40,057
N. Mariana Islands	18	463	0	0	18	463
Puerto Rico	3,820	118,941	50,795	4,618,420	54,615	4,737,360
Trust Territory of the Pacific	1	73	1	108	2	181
Virgin Islands	444	73,335	1,845	261,064	2,289	334,399
Unknown areas	24	626	0	0	24	626
United States	**192,673**	**$23,829,285**	**5,212,279**	**$1,008,743,283**	**5,404,952**	**$1,032,572,568**

[1]Direct and WYO business may not add to total due to rounding. [2]Total limits of liability for all policies in force.

Source: U.S. Department of Homeland Security, Federal Emergency Management Agency.

EARTHQUAKE INSURANCE

Standard homeowners, renters and business insurance policies do not cover damage from earthquakes. Coverage is available either in the form of an endorsement or as a separate policy. Earthquake insurance provides protection from the shaking and cracking that can destroy buildings and personal possessions. Coverage for other kinds of damage that may result from earthquakes, such as fire and water damage due to burst gas and water pipes, is provided by standard home and business insurance policies. Unlike flood insurance, earthquake coverage is available from private insurance companies rather than from the government. In California, homeowners can also get coverage from the California Earthquake Authority (CEA), a privately funded, publicly managed organization. A 2006 A.M. Best study estimates that 12 percent of California homeowners bought earthquake insurance in 2005, compared with 10 to 15 percent of homeowners nationwide.

EARTHQUAKE INSURANCE, 1999-2006
($000)

Year	Net premiums written[1]	Annual percent change	Combined ratio[2]	Annual point change
1999	$730,494	NA	64.5	NA
2000	762,443	4.4%	77.7	13.2 pts.
2001	857,562	12.5	108.9	31.2
2002	999,455	16.5	86.6	-22.3
2003	1,048,714	4.9	55.7	-31.0
2004	1,098,441	4.7	48.4	-7.3
2005	1,106,378	0.7	50.7	2.3
2006	1,315,494	18.9	40.1	-10.6

[1]After reinsurance transactions, excluding state funds.
[2]After dividends to policyholders. A drop in the combined ratio represents an improvement; an increase represents a deterioration. See also Glossary.
NA=Data not available.

Source: National Association of Insurance Commissioners (NAIC) Annual Statement Database, via Highline Data, LLC. Copyrighted information. No portion of this work may be copied or redistributed without the express written permission of Highline Data, LLC.

- The state-run California Earthquake Authority (CEA), the largest provider of earthquake insurance in California, is not included in this chart. The CEA accounted for $454.5 million in premiums written in 2006, down 9.7 percent from $503.4 million in 2005. At the end of 2006 the CEA had about 755,000 policies in force in the state, about the same as the previous year.

LEADING WRITERS OF COMMERCIAL LINES INSURANCE BY DIRECT PREMIUMS WRITTEN, 2006
($000)

Rank	Company/Group	Direct premiums written[1]	Market share
1	American International Group	$28,192,567	11.7%
2	Travelers Group	14,771,701	6.1
3	Zurich Insurance Group	14,667,924	6.1
4	Liberty Mutual Insurance Group	11,759,948	4.9
5	CNA Insurance Group	8,245,121	3.4
6	Hartford Fire & Casualty Group	7,732,773	3.2
7	ACE Ltd. Group	7,503,088	3.1
8	Chubb & Son Group	7,093,470	2.9
9	Nationwide Group	5,475,111	2.3
10	State Farm IL Group	5,328,671	2.2

[1]Before reinsurance transactions, excluding state funds. Includes all lines except private passenger auto and homeowners.

Source: National Association of Insurance Commissioners (NAIC) Annual Statement Database, via Highline Data, LLC. Copyrighted information. No portion of this work may be copied or redistributed without the express written permission of Highline Data, LLC.

TOP TEN COMMERCIAL INSURANCE BROKERS OF U.S. BUSINESS BY REVENUES, 2006[1]
($ millions)

Rank	Company	Brokerage revenues[1]
1	Marsh & McLennan Cos. Inc.	$5,341.7
2	Aon Corp.	2,750.7
3	Arthur J. Gallagher & Co.	1,250.9
4	Willis Group Holdings Ltd.	1,100.3
5	Wells Fargo Insurance Services Inc.	1,008.7
6	Brown & Brown Inc.	864.7
7	BB&T Insurance Services Inc.	842.3
8	Hilb Rogal & Hobbs Co.	682.8
9	USI Holdings Corp.	546.3
10	Lockton Cos. LLC	453.4[2]

[1]Companies that derive more than 20 percent of revenues generated by U.S.-based clients, from commercial retail brokerage.
[2]Fiscal year ending April 30.

Source: Business Insurance, July 16, 2007.

WORKERS COMPENSATION INSURANCE

Workers compensation insurance provides for the cost of medical care and rehabilitation for injured workers. It also provides for lost wages and death benefits for the dependents of persons killed in work-related accidents. Workers compensation systems vary from state to state.

Workers compensation combined ratios are expressed in two ways. Calendar year results reflect claim payments and changes in reserves for accidents that happened in that year or earlier. Accident year results only include losses from a particular year and may present a better picture of the industry's performance at a given point in time.

WORKERS COMPENSATION INSURANCE, 1999-2006

| Year | Net premiums written[1] ($000) | Annual percent change | Combined ratio[2] | | | |
			Calendar year[3]	Annual point change	Accident year[3]	Annual point change
1999	$23,090,325	-4.7%	120.0	NA	140	9 pts.
2000	26,185,928	13.4	114.9	-5.1 pts.	135	-5
2001	27,123,299	3.6	117.3	2.4	123	-12
2002	30,612,127	12.9	108.7	-8.6	104	-19
2003	32,919,340	7.5	108.9	0.2	96	-8
2004	36,734,514	11.6	105.5	-3.4	88	-8
2005	39,724,355	8.1	100.5	-5.0	87	-1
2006	41,825,979	5.3	93.8	-6.7	87[4]	0

[1]After reinsurance transactions, excluding state funds.
[2]After dividends to policyholders. A drop in the combined ratio represents an improvement; an increase represents a deterioration. See also Glossary.
[3]Calendar year data are from National Association of Insurance Commissioners (NAIC) Annual Statement Database, via Highline Data, LLC. Accident year data are from the National Council on Compensation Insurance.
[4]Preliminary.
NA=Data not available.

Source: National Association of Insurance Commissioners (NAIC) Annual Statement Database, via Highline Data, LLC. Copyrighted information. No portion of this work may be copied or redistributed without the express written permission of Highline Data, LLC; National Council on Compensation Insurance.

WORKERS COMPENSATION MEDICAL COSTS, 1997-2006

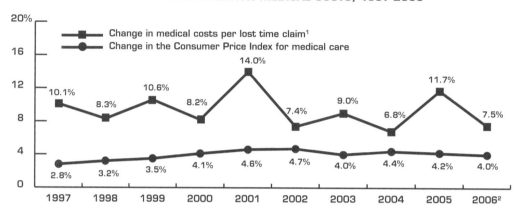

[1]Based on states where the National Council on Compensation Insurance provides ratemaking services. Represents costs for injuries that resulted in time off from work.
[2]Change in medical costs per lost time claim is preliminary.

Source: U.S. Bureau of Labor Statistics; National Council on Compensation Insurance.

COMPARISON OF WORKERS COMPENSATION BENEFITS, COVERAGE AND COSTS, 2004-2005

	2004	2005	Percent change
Covered workers (000)	125,863	128,141	1.8%
Covered wages ($ billions)	$4,953	$5,212	5.2
Workers compensation benefits paid ($ billions)	56.1	55.3	-1.4
Medical benefits	26.4	26.2	-0.5
Cash benefits	29.7	29.1	-2.1
Employer costs for workers compensation ($ billions)	86.8	88.8	2.3

Source: National Academy of Social Insurance.

GENERAL LIABILITY INSURANCE

General liability insurance covers the liability risks of a business arising from injuries or property damage that is caused by its products, completed jobs, premises and operations. It consists of two lines of insurance: "products liability" and "other liability."

GENERAL LIABILITY INSURANCE, 1999-2006

Total ($000)

Year	Net premiums written[1]	Annual percent change	Year	Net premiums written[1]	Annual percent change
1999	$19,163,683	-1.0%	2003	38,876,428	24.9%
2000	20,127,095	5.0	2004	43,154,562	11.0
2001	23,451,789	16.5	2005	42,924,445	-0.5
2002	31,129,659	32.7	2006	45,844,258	6.8

Products Liability ($000)

Year	Net premiums written[1]	Annual percent change	Combined ratio[2]	Annual point change
1999	$1,586,915	-2.4%	159.1	NA
2000	1,413,984	-10.9	130.7	-28.4 pts.
2001	2,035,893	44.0	213.8	83.1
2002	1,787,544	-12.2	355.0	141.2
2003	2,726,599	52.5	165.8	-189.2
2004	3,401,867	24.8	152.4	-13.4
2005	3,561,223	4.7	130.9	-21.5
2006	3,623,796	1.8	77.6	-53.3

Other Liability ($000)

Year	Net premiums written[1]	Annual percent change	Combined ratio[2]	Annual point change
1999	$17,576,768	-0.9%	106.2	NA
2000	18,713,111	6.5	110.5	4.3 pts.
2001	21,415,896	14.4	120.4	9.9
2002	29,342,115	37.0	124.6	4.2
2003	36,149,829	23.2	112.1	-12.5
2004	39,752,695	10.0	114.0	1.9
2005	39,363,222	-1.0	110.4	-3.6
2006	42,220,462	7.3	94.6	-15.8

[1]After reinsurance transactions, excluding state funds. [2]After dividends to policyholders. A drop in the combined ratio represents an improvement; an increase represents a deterioration. See also Glossary. NA=Data not available.

Source: National Association of Insurance Commissioners (NAIC) Annual Statement Database, via Highline Data, LLC. Copyrighted information. No portion of this work may be copied or redistributed without the express written permission of Highline Data, LLC.

COMMERCIAL AND FARMOWNERS MULTIPLE PERIL INSURANCE

Commercial multiple peril insurance is a package policy that includes property, boiler and machinery, crime and general liability coverages. Farmowners multiple peril insurance, similar to homeowners insurance, provides coverage to farmowners and ranchowners against a number of named perils and liabilities. It covers a dwelling and its contents, as well as barns, stables and other structures.

COMMERCIAL MULTIPLE PERIL INSURANCE, 1999-2006

Total
($000)

Year	Net premiums written[1]	Annual percent change	Year	Net premiums written[1]	Annual percent change
1999	$18,983,821	-2.4%	2003	$27,430,022	7.9%
2000	20,072,151	5.7	2004	29,074,586	6.0
2001	22,230,355	10.8	2005	29,695,507	2.1
2002	25,421,072	14.4	2006	31,848,875	7.3

Nonliability Portion
($000)

Year	Net premiums written[1]	Annual percent change	Combined ratio[2]	Annual point change
1999	$10,293,766	-1.4%	121.7	NA
2000	11,706,119	13.7	114.8	-6.9 pts.
2001	13,010,431	11.1	117.2	2.4
2002	15,251,130	17.2	96.1	-21.1
2003	16,352,256	7.2	88.1	-8.0
2004	16,971,835	3.8	96.7	8.6
2005	17,705,984	4.3	93.8	-2.9
2006	18,245,136	3.0	86.9	-6.9

(table continues)

COMMERCIAL MULTIPLE PERIL INSURANCE, 1999-2006 (Cont'd)

Liability Portion
($000)

Year	Net premiums written[1]	Annual percent change	Combined ratio[2]	Annual point change
1999	$8,690,055	-3.6%	113.4	NA
2000	8,366,032	-3.7	115.4	2.0 pts.
2001	9,219,924	10.2	121.3	5.9
2002	10,169,942	10.3	113.9	-7.4
2003	11,077,766	8.9	115.0	1.1
2004	12,102,751	9.3	105.4	-9.6
2005	11,989,523	-0.9	102.7	-2.7
2006	13,603,739	13.5	97.8	-4.9

[1]After reinsurance transactions, excluding state funds.
[2]After dividends to policyholders. A drop in the combined ratio represents an improvement; an increase represents a deterioration. See also Glossary.
NA=Data not available.

Source: National Association of Insurance Commissioners (NAIC) Annual Statement Database, via Highline Data, LLC. Copyrighted information. No portion of this work may be copied or redistributed without the express written permission of Highline Data, LLC.

FARMOWNERS MULTIPLE PERIL INSURANCE, 1999-2006
($000)

Year	Net premiums written[1]	Annual percent change	Combined ratio[2]	Annual point change
1999	$1,478,142	2.7%	111.4	NA
2000	1,524,233	3.1	108.9	-2.5 pts.
2001	1,640,592	7.6	113.5	4.6
2002	1,779,336	8.5	106.7	-6.8
2003	2,000,834	12.4	99.1	-7.6
2004	2,118,097	5.9	91.7	-7.4
2005	2,266,920	7.0	94.6	2.9
2006	2,310,688	1.9	122.8	28.2

[1]After reinsurance transactions, excluding state funds.
[2]After dividends to policyholders. A drop in the combined ratio represents an improvement; an increase represents a deterioration. See also Glossary.
NA=Data not available.

Source: National Association of Insurance Commissioners (NAIC) Annual Statement Database, via Highline Data, LLC. Copyrighted information. No portion of this work may be copied or redistributed without the express written permission of Highline Data, LLC.

MEDICAL MALPRACTICE INSURANCE

Medical malpractice insurance covers doctors and other professionals in the medical field for liability claims arising from their treatment of patients.

MEDICAL MALPRACTICE INSURANCE, 1999-2006
($000)

Year	Net premiums written[1]	Annual percent change	Combined ratio[2]	Annual point change
1999	$5,181,729	3.1%	128.6	NA
2000	5,726,696	10.5	127.9	-0.7 pts.
2001	6,256,399	9.2	150.4	22.5
2002	7,440,970	18.9	138.0	-12.4
2003	8,753,854	17.6	138.8	0.8
2004	9,124,240	4.2	108.6	-30.2
2005	9,734,772	6.7	100.1	-8.5
2006	10,365,836	6.5	89.5	-10.6

[1]After reinsurance transactions, excluding state funds.
[2]After dividends to policyholders. A drop in the combined ratio represents an improvement; an increase represents a deterioration. See also Glossary.
NA=Data not available.

Source: National Association of Insurance Commissioners (NAIC) Annual Statement Database, via Highline Data, LLC. Copyrighted information. No portion of this work may be copied or redistributed without the express written permission of Highline Data, LLC.

FIRE AND ALLIED LINES INSURANCE

Fire insurance provides coverage against losses caused by fire and lightning. It is usually sold as part of a package policy such as commercial multiple peril.

Allied lines insurance includes property insurance that is usually bought in conjunction with a fire insurance policy. Allied lines includes coverage for wind and water damage and vandalism.

FIRE INSURANCE, 1999-2006
($000)

Year	Net premiums written[1]	Annual percent change	Combined ratio[2]	Annual point change
1999	$4,773,647	1.4%	104.0	NA
2000	4,740,558	-0.7	110.9	6.9 pts.
2001	5,097,592	7.5	117.5	6.6
2002	7,365,861	44.5	84.0	-33.5
2003	8,396,083	14.0	79.6	-4.4
2004	8,050,779	-4.1	73.1	-6.5
2005	7,937,200	-1.4	83.2	10.1
2006	9,362,560	18.0	77.9	-5.3

[1]After reinsurance transactions, excluding state funds. [2]After dividends to policyholders. A drop in the combined ratio represents an improvement; an increase represents a deterioration. See also Glossary. NA=Data not available.

Source: National Association of Insurance Commissioners (NAIC) Annual Statement Database, via Highline Data, LLC. Copyrighted information. No portion of this work may be copied or redistributed without the express written permission of Highline Data, LLC.

ALLIED LINES INSURANCE, 1999-2006
($000)

Year	Net premiums written[1]	Annual percent change	Combined ratio[2]	Annual point change
1999	$2,815,608	-4.8%	123.7	NA
2000	2,933,047	4.2	115.6	-8.1 pts.
2001	3,732,266	27.2	151.1	35.5
2002	4,838,138	29.6	86.3	-64.8
2003	6,154,573	27.2	77.9	-8.4
2004	5,985,422	-2.7	119.8	41.9
2005	5,945,718	-0.7	152.9	33.1
2006	6,592,847	10.9	94.4	-58.5

[1]After reinsurance transactions, excluding state funds. [2]After dividends to policyholders. A drop in the combined ratio represents an improvement; an increase represents a deterioration. See also Glossary. NA=Data not available.

Source: National Association of Insurance Commissioners (NAIC) Annual Statement Database, via Highline Data, LLC. Copyrighted information. No portion of this work may be copied or redistributed without the express written permission of Highline Data, LLC.

INLAND MARINE AND OCEAN MARINE INSURANCE

Inland marine insurance covers bridges and tunnels, goods in transit, movable equipment, unusual property, and communications-related structures as well as expensive personal property. Ocean marine insurance provides coverage on all types of vessels, for property damage to the vessels and cargo, as well as associated liabilities.

INLAND MARINE INSURANCE, 1999-2006
($000)

Year	Net premiums written[1]	Annual percent change	Combined ratio[2]	Annual point change
1999	$6,063,160	2.8%	101.2	NA
2000	6,577,227	8.5	92.0	-9.2 pts.
2001	6,686,003	1.7	98.7	6.7
2002	6,987,446	4.5	85.7	-13.0
2003	7,786,214	11.4	80.1	-5.6
2004	7,940,003	2.0	84.1	4.0
2005	8,251,432	3.9	90.3	6.2
2006	9,215,704	11.7	72.6	-17.7

[1]After reinsurance transactions, excluding state funds. [2]After dividends to policyholders. A drop in the combined ratio represents an improvement; an increase represents a deterioration. See also Glossary. NA=Data not available.

Source: National Association of Insurance Commissioners (NAIC) Annual Statement Database, via Highline Data, LLC. Copyrighted information. No portion of this work may be copied or redistributed without the express written permission of Highline Data, LLC.

OCEAN MARINE INSURANCE, 1999-2006
($000)

Year	Net premiums written[1]	Annual percent change	Combined ratio[2]	Annual point change
1999	$1,756,781	-5.5%	115.5	NA
2000	1,738,796	-1.0	102.6	-12.9 pts.
2001	1,979,205	13.8	104.1	1.5
2002	2,442,039	23.4	100.9	-3.2
2003	2,588,607	6.0	103.1	2.2
2004	2,828,685	9.3	95.4	-7.7
2005	2,948,349	4.2	114.5	19.1
2006	3,133,418	6.3	97.3	-17.2

[1]After reinsurance transactions, excluding state funds.
[2]After dividends to policyholders. A drop in the combined ratio represents an improvement; an increase represents a deterioration. See also Glossary. NA=Data not available.

Source: National Association of Insurance Commissioners (NAIC) Annual Statement Database, via Highline Data, LLC. Copyrighted information. No portion of this work may be copied or redistributed without the express written permission of Highline Data, LLC.

SURETY AND FIDELITY

Surety bonds provide monetary compensation in the event that a policyholder fails to perform certain acts such as the proper fulfillment of a construction contract within a stated period. Surety bonds are usually purchased by the party which has contracted to complete a project. They are required for public projects in order to protect taxpayers.

Fidelity bonds, which are usually purchased by an employer, protect against losses caused by employee fraud or dishonesty.

SURETY BONDS, 1999-2006
($000)

Year	Net premiums written[1]	Annual percent change	Combined ratio[2]	Annual point change
1999	$3,273,926	7.2%	83.6	NA
2000	3,362,627	2.7	86.7	3.1 pts.
2001	3,039,761	-9.6	121.6	34.9
2002	3,260,415	7.3	110.3	-11.3
2003	3,382,615	3.7	119.9	9.6
2004	3,817,245	12.8	119.5	-0.4
2005	3,820,810	0.1	101.4	-18.1
2006	4,433,266	16.0	80.6	-20.8

[1]After reinsurance transactions, excluding state funds. [2]After dividends to policyholders. A drop in the combined ratio represents an improvement; an increase represents a deterioration. See also Glossary. NA=Data not available.

Source: National Association of Insurance Commissioners (NAIC) Annual Statement Database, via Highline Data, LLC. Copyrighted information. No portion of this work may be copied or redistributed without the express written permission of Highline Data, LLC.

FIDELITY BONDS, 1999-2006
($000)

Year	Net premiums written[1]	Annual percent change	Combined ratio[2]	Annual point change
1999	$871,365	11.8%	90.4	NA
2000	815,007	-6.5	93.3	2.9 pts.
2001	842,428	3.4	93.2	-0.1
2002	1,024,107	21.6	104.7	11.5
2003	1,192,535	16.4	70.9	-33.8
2004	1,309,344	9.8	79.7	8.8
2005	1,216,793	-7.1	85.1	5.4
2006	1,240,822	2.0	87.2	2.1

[1]After reinsurance transactions, excluding state funds. [2]After dividends to policyholders. A drop in the combined ratio represents an improvement; an increase represents a deterioration. See also Glossary. NA=Data not available.

Source: National Association of Insurance Commissioners (NAIC) Annual Statement Database, via Highline Data, LLC. Copyrighted information. No portion of this work may be copied or redistributed without the express written permission of Highline Data, LLC.

MORTGAGE GUARANTY INSURANCE

Private mortgage insurance (PMI), known as mortgage guaranty insurance, guarantees that, in the event of a default, the insurer will pay the mortgage lender for any loss resulting from a property foreclosure up to a specific amount. PMI, which is purchased by the borrower but protects the lender, is sometimes confused with mortgage insurance, a life insurance product that pays off the mortgage if the borrower dies before the loan is repaid. Banks generally require PMI for all borrowers with down payments of less than 20 percent.

MORTGAGE GUARANTY INSURANCE, 1999-2006
($000)

Year	Net premiums written[1]	Annual percent change	Combined ratio[2]	Annual point change
1999	$3,095,621	3.9%	56.2	NA
2000	3,411,356	10.2	47.3	-8.9 pts.
2001	3,738,058	9.6	52.1	4.8
2002	3,987,772	6.7	58.2	6.1
2003	4,285,447	7.5	67.6	9.4
2004	4,323,071	0.9	75.6	8.0
2005	4,454,711	3.0	75.2	-0.4
2006	4,565,899	2.5	71.0	-4.2

[1]After reinsurance transactions, excluding state funds.
[2]After dividends to policyholders. A drop in the combined ratio represents an improvement; an increase represents a deterioration. See also Glossary.
NA=Data not available.

Source: National Association of Insurance Commissioners (NAIC) Annual Statement Database, via Highline Data, LLC. Copyrighted information. No portion of this work may be copied or redistributed without the express written permission of Highline Data, LLC.

BURGLARY AND THEFT AND BOILER AND MACHINERY INSURANCE

Burglary and theft insurance covers the loss of property, money and securities due to burglary, robbery or larceny.

Boiler and machinery insurance is also known as mechanical breakdown, equipment breakdown or systems breakdown coverage. Among the types of equipment covered by this insurance are heating, cooling, electrical, telephone/communications and computer equipment.

BURGLARY AND THEFT INSURANCE, 1999-2006
($000)

Year	Net premiums written[1]	Annual percent change	Combined ratio[2]	Annual point change
1999	$111,059	1.4%	82.3	NA
2000	116,885	5.2	60.3	-22.0 pts.
2001	121,629	4.1	71.3	11.0
2002	114,299	-6.0	53.4	-17.9
2003	123,692	8.2	66.8	13.4
2004	138,307	11.8	68.3	1.5
2005	120,133	-13.1	63.5	-4.8
2006	143,054	19.1	64.2	0.7

[1]After reinsurance transactions, excluding state funds. [2]After dividends to policyholders. A drop in the combined ratio represents an improvement; an increase represents a deterioration. See also Glossary. NA=Data not available.

Source: National Association of Insurance Commissioners (NAIC) Annual Statement Database, via Highline Data, LLC. Copyrighted information. No portion of this work may be copied or redistributed without the express written permission of Highline Data, LLC.

BOILER AND MACHINERY INSURANCE, 1999-2006
($000)

Year	Net premiums written[1]	Annual percent change	Combined ratio[2]	Annual point change
1999	$760,055	-1.8%	117.8	NA
2000	1,144,068	50.5	89.9	-27.9 pts.
2001	1,119,295	-2.2	88.2	-1.7
2002	1,410,316	26.0	73.6	-14.6
2003	1,591,987	12.9	68.4	-5.2
2004	1,572,195	-1.2	67.1	-1.3
2005	1,582,917	0.7	60.2	-6.9
2006	1,675,296	5.8	73.1	12.9

[1]After reinsurance transactions, excluding state funds. [2]After dividends to policyholders. A drop in the combined ratio represents an improvement; an increase represents a deterioration. See also Glossary. NA=Data not available.

Source: National Association of Insurance Commissioners (NAIC) Annual Statement Database, via Highline Data, LLC. Copyrighted information. No portion of this work may be copied or redistributed without the express written permission of Highline Data, LLC.

CROP INSURANCE

There are two kinds of crop insurance: crop-hail, which is provided by the private market and covers just hail, fire and wind, and federally sponsored multiple peril, which is sold and serviced by the private market but subsidized and reinsured by the federal government.

CROP-HAIL INSURANCE, 1997-2006
($000)

Year	Direct premiums written[1]	Annual percent change	Loss ratio[2]	Annual point change
1997	$594,464	-5.8%	57	-15 pts.
1998	576,464	-3.0	83	26
1999	508,108	-11.9	76	-7
2000	468,405	-7.8	68	-8
2001	433,743	-7.4	69	1
2002	405,003	-6.6	70	1
2003	422,137	4.2	56	-14
2004	427,567	1.3	58	2
2005	434,711	1.7	44	-14
2006	405,268	6.8	50	6

[1]Before reinsurance transactions, total for all policyholders of crop-hail insurance. [2]The percentage of each premium dollar spent on claims and associated costs. A drop in the loss ratio represents an improvement; an increase represents a deterioration. See also Glossary.
Source: National Crop Insurance Services.

MULTIPLE PERIL CROP INSURANCE, 1999-2006
($000)

Year	Net premiums written[1]	Annual percent change	Combined ratio[2]	Annual point change
1999	$725,821	1.8%	98.2	NA
2000	938,840	29.3	90.4	-7.8 pts.
2001	1,321,820	40.8	96.0	5.6
2002	2,003,443	51.6	124.4	28.4
2003	1,702,862	-15.0	109.8	-14.6
2004	2,203,143	29.4	76.1	-33.7
2005	2,234,630	1.4	91.3	15.2
2006	2,824,769	26.4	77.9	-13.4

[1]After reinsurance transactions, excluding state funds. [2]After dividends to policyholders. A drop in the combined ratio represents an improvement; an increase represents a deterioration. See also Glossary. NA=Data not available.
Source: National Association of Insurance Commissioners (NAIC) Annual Statement Database, via Highline Data, LLC. Copyrighted information. No portion of this work may be copied or redistributed without the express written permission of Highline Data, LLC.

WORLD INSURANCE LOSSES

Insured losses span a wide range of catastrophes from weather-related events such as windstorms and floods to man-made disasters such as riots and satellite failures. Outside the United States, natural disaster losses are less likely to be insured.

THE 15 MOST COSTLY WORLD INSURANCE LOSSES, 2006[1]
($ millions)

Rank	Date	Location	Event	Insured loss in U.S. dollars
1	Apr. 13	U.S.	Tornado, storms with winds up to 240 km/h, hail	$1,850
2	Apr. 6	U.S.	42 tornadoes with winds up to 274 km/h, hail	1,282
3	Sep. 15	Japan, Sea of Japan	Typhoon Shanshan/No. 13 with winds up to 126 km/h	1,024
4	Mar. 11	U.S.	Tornadoes with winds up to 202 km/h; floods	920
5	Aug. 23	U.S.	Storms, tornadoes, hail, floods	560
6	Apr. 2	U.S.	Thunderstorms, tornadoes, hail; damage to buildings	500
7	Aug. 1	India	Floods caused by monsoon rains	407
8	Jun. 25	U.S.	Thunderstorms, heavy rain, floods, landslides	401
9	Apr. 23	U.S.	Hail and tornadoes	355
10	Mar. 20	Australia, South Pacific Ocean	Tropical cyclone Larry with winds up to 290 km/h	335
11	May 1	U.S.	Hail, thunderstorms with winds up to 110 km/h	315
12	Feb. 7	Austria, Germany	Heavy snowfall	290
13	Aug. 27	Caribbean Sea, U.S., Cuba et al.	Tropical storm Ernesto with winds up to 113 km/h	245
14	Dec. 14	U.S.	Heavy storms, snow, power outages	220
15	Jan. 22	Brazil	System breakdown at iron works	NA

[1]Property and business interruption losses, excluding life and liability losses.

Note: Loss data shown here may differ from figures shown elsewhere for the same event due to revisions in loss estimates.

NA=Data not available.

Source: Swiss Re, *sigma*, No. 2/2007; ISO, insured losses for natural catastrophes in the United States.

THE TEN MOST COSTLY WORLD INSURANCE LOSSES, 1970-2006[1]
($ millions)

Rank	Date	Country	Event	Insured loss in 2006 U.S. dollars[2]
1	Aug. 25, 2005	U.S., Gulf of Mexico, Bahamas, North Atlantic	Hurricane Katrina; floods, dams burst, damage to oil rigs	$66,311
2	Aug. 23, 1992	U.S., Bahamas	Hurricane Andrew; flooding	22,987
3	Sep. 11, 2001	U.S.	Terrorist attacks on WTC, Pentagon and other buildings	21,379
4	Jan. 17, 1994	U.S.	Northridge earthquake (magnitude 6.6)	19,040
5	Sep. 2, 2004	U.S., Caribbean: Barbados, et al.	Hurricane Ivan; damage to oil rigs	13,651
6	Oct. 19, 2005	U.S., Mexico, Jamaica, Haiti, et al.	Hurricane Wilma; torrential rain and floods	12,953
7	Sep. 20, 2005	U.S., Gulf of Mexico, Cuba	Hurricane Rita; floods, damage to oil rigs	10,382
8	Aug. 11, 2004	U.S., Cuba, Jamaica, et al.	Hurricane Charley	8,590
9	Sep. 27, 1991	Japan	Typhoon Mireille/No. 19	8,357
10	Sep. 15, 1989	U.S., Puerto Rico, et al.	Hurricane Hugo	7,434

[1]Property and business interruption losses, excluding life and liability losses. Includes flood losses in the United States insured via the National Flood Insurance Program.
[2]Adjusted to 2006 dollars by Swiss Re.
Note: Loss data shown here may differ from figures shown elsewhere for the same event due to differences in the date of publication, the geographical area covered and other criteria used by organizations collecting the data.
Source: Swiss Re, *sigma*, No. 2/2007.

WORLD INSURED CATASTROPHE LOSSES, 1997-2006[1]
(U.S. $ millions)

Year	In 2006 dollars	Year	In 2006 dollars
1997	$10,745	2002	$16,241
1998	23,971	2003	20,964
1999	41,857	2004	51,175
2000	14,582	2005	110,369
2001	40,635	2006	15,881

[1]In order to maintain comparability of the data over the course of time, the minimum threshold for losses was adjusted annually to compensate for inflation in the United States. Adjusted to 2006 dollars by Swiss Re.
Source: Swiss Re, *sigma*, 2/2007.

THE TEN DEADLIEST WORLD CATASTROPHES, 2006[1]

Rank	Date	Country	Event	Victims
1	May 27	Indonesia	Earthquake (magnitude 6.3); Bantul almost completely destroyed	5,778
2	Jun. 1	Netherlands, Belgium, France	Heat wave in Europe	1,900
3	Nov. 26	Philippines, Viet Nam	Typhoon Durian/No. 21; mud flows on slopes of Mayon volcano	1,363
4	Jan. 15	Ukraine, Poland, et al.	Cold wave in Eastern Europe; power shortage	1,333
5	Feb. 2	Red Sea, Egypt	Egyptian Ferry al-Salam 98 sinks about 80 km off coast	1,026
6	Feb. 12	Philippines	Flash floods, landslides caused by persistent rain	1,000
7	Jul. 11	China, Philippines, et al.	Typhoon Bilis/No. 4, floods; homes, crops destroyed	847
8	Jul. 17	Indonesia	Earthquake (magnitude 7.7) triggers tsunami	802
9	Aug. 15	Ethiopia, Sudan	Floods along the Blue Nile caused by heavy rain	620
10	Aug. 26	Nepal	Floods and mudslides caused by heavy monsoon rain	605

[1]Dead and missing.

Source: Swiss Re, *sigma*, No. 2/2007.

THE TEN DEADLIEST WORLD CATASTROPHES, 1970-2006[1]

Rank	Date	Country	Event	Victims
1	Nov. 14, 1970	Bangladesh	Storm and flood	300,000
2	Jul. 28, 1976	China	Earthquake (magnitude 7.5)	255,000
3	Dec. 26, 2004	Indonesia, Thailand, et al.	Earthquake (magnitude 9); tsunami in Indian Ocean	220,000
4	Apr. 29, 1991	Bangladesh	Tropical cyclone Gorky	138,000
5	Oct. 8, 2005	Pakistan, India, et al.	Earthquake (magnitude 7.6); aftershocks, landslides	73,300
6	May 31, 1970	Peru	Earthquake (magnitude 7.7); rock slides	66,000
7	Jun. 21, 1990	Iran	Earthquake (magnitude 7.7); landslides	40,000
8	Jun. 1, 2003	France, Italy, Germany, et al.	Heat wave and drought in Europe	35,000
9	Dec. 26, 2003	Iran	Earthquake (magnitude 6.5) destroys 85 percent of Bam	26,271
10	Dec. 7, 1988	Armenia, ex-USSR	Earthquake (magnitude 6.9)	25,000

[1]Dead and missing.

Source: Swiss Re, *sigma*, No. 2/2007.

AVIAN FLU

Since late 2003 the H5N1 influenza virus, a highly lethal virus that now mostly affects birds, has caused 204 human deaths in 12 countries. Indonesia, with 89 deaths, recorded the most fatalities, followed by Viet Nam (46 deaths), Thailand (17) and China (16).

CONFIRMED HUMAN CASES OF AVIAN FLU, 2003-2007[1]

Country	2003-2004		2005		2006		2007		Total	
	Cases	Deaths	Cases	Deaths	Cases	Deaths	Cases	Deaths	Cases	Deaths
Azerbaijan	0	0	0	0	8	5	0	0	8	5
Cambodia	0	0	4	4	2	2	1	1	7	7
China	1	1	8	5	13	8	3	2	25	16
Djibouti	0	0	0	0	1	0	0	0	1	0
Egypt	0	0	0	0	18	10	20	5	38	15
Indonesia	0	0	19	12	56	46	36	31	111	89
Iraq	0	0	0	0	3	2	0	0	3	2
Lao People's Democratic Republic	0	0	0	0	0	0	2	2	2	2
Nigeria	0	0	0	0	0	0	1	1	1	1
Thailand	17	12	5	2	3	3	0	0	25	17
Turkey	0	0	0	0	12	4	0	0	12	4
Viet Nam	32	23	61	19	0	0	7	4	100	46
Total	**50**	**36**	**97**	**42**	**116**	**80**	**70**	**46**	**333**	**204**

[1] As of October 31, 2007. Includes only laboratory-confirmed deaths.

Source: World Health Organization.

CATASTROPHES IN THE UNITED STATES

ISO defines a catastrophe as an event that causes $25 million or more in insured property losses and affects a significant number of property/casualty policyholders and insurers. The estimates in the following chart represent anticipated insured losses from catastrophes on an industry-wide basis, reflecting the total net insurance payment for personal and commercial property lines of insurance covering fixed property, vehicles, boats, related-property items, business inter-ruption and additional living expenses. They exclude loss-adjustment expenses. Losses from catastrophic events declined sharply in 2006 but were nonetheless at their sixth-highest level since 1997. The number of catastrophes, 33 events, was the second-highest level in a decade.

MAJOR U.S. CATASTROPHES, 2006
($ millions)

Date	Catastrophes	States	Estimated insured loss
First quarter			
Jan. 14-15	Winter storm	CT, NY, NY, PA	$105
Jan. 18-19	Winter storm	CT, MA, NJ, NY, PA	125
Feb. 3-4	Wind, thunderstorm	OR, WA	55
Feb. 17-18	Winter storm	MA, NH, NY	85
Mar. 8-10	Tornado	AL, AR, KY, MS, TN, TX	140
Mar. 11-13	Tornado	AR, IN, KS, MO, OK	920
Mar. 19-20	Wind, thunderstorm	TX	50
Total first quarter losses			**1,480**
Total second quarter losses[1]			**5,042**
Third quarter			
Aug. 23-25	Severe weather	IL, IN, MN, WI	560
Aug. 29-Sep. 3	Tropical storm Ernesto	DE, FL, MD, NC, NJ, NY, SC, VA	245
Total third quarter losses[2]			**1,251**
Total fourth quarter losses[3]			**1,395**
Total losses (full year)			**$9,168**[4]

[1]Includes 13 events.
[2]Includes seven events.
[3]Includes six events.
[4]Calculated from rounded loss figures.
Note: Catastrophes are assigned serial numbers by ISO's Property Claim Services unit when the insured loss to the industry resulting from an occurrence reaches at least $25 million and affects a significant number of policyholders and insurers.

Source: ISO's Property Claim Services unit.

THE TEN MOST COSTLY CATASTROPHES, UNITED STATES[1]

Rank	Date	Event	Insured loss ($ millions)	
			Dollars when occurred	In 2006 dollars[2]
1	Aug. 2005	Hurricane Katrina	$41,100	$42,426
2	Aug. 1992	Hurricane Andrew	15,500	22,272
3	Sep. 2001	World Trade Center, Pentagon terrorist attacks	18,800	21,401
4	Jan. 1994	Northridge, CA earthquake	12,500	17,004
5	Oct. 2005	Hurricane Wilma	10,300	10,632
6	Aug. 2004	Hurricane Charley	7,475	7,978
7	Sep. 2004	Hurricane Ivan	7,110	7,588
8	Sep. 1989	Hurricane Hugo	4,195	6,820
9	Sep. 2005	Hurricane Rita	5,627	5,809
10	Sep. 2004	Hurricane Frances	4,595	4,904

[1]Property coverage only.
[2]Adjusted to 2006 dollars by ISO and the Insurance Information Institute.

Source: ISO's Property Claim Services unit; Insurance Information Institute.

INSURED LOSSES, U.S. CATASTROPHES, 1997-2006[1]

Year	Number of catastrophes	Number of claims (millions)	Dollars when occurred ($ billions)	In 2006 dollars[2] ($ billions)
1997	25	1.6	$2.6	$3.3
1998	37	3.6	10.1	12.5
1999	27	3.2	8.3	10.0
2000	24	1.5	4.6	5.4
2001	20	1.5	26.5	30.2
2002	25	1.8	5.9	6.6
2003	21	2.7	12.9	14.1
2004	22	3.4	27.5	29.3
2005	24	4.4	62.3	64.3
2006	33	2.3	9.2	9.2

[1]Includes catastrophes causing insured losses to the industry of at least $25 million and affecting a significant number of policyholders and insurers.
[2]Adjusted to 2006 dollars by the Insurance Information Institute.

Source: ISO's Property Claim Services unit; Insurance Information Institute.

INFLATION-ADJUSTED U.S. CATASTROPHE LOSSES BY CAUSE OF LOSS, 1987-2006[1]
(2006 $ billions)

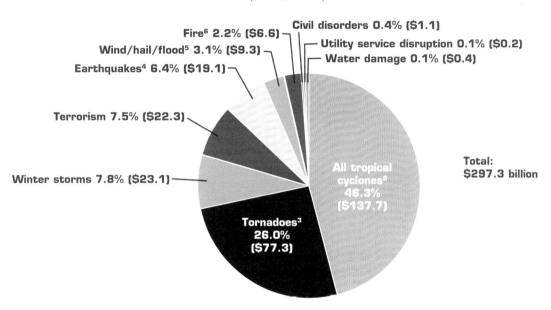

Fire[6] 2.2% ($6.6)
Civil disorders 0.4% ($1.1)
Wind/hail/flood[5] 3.1% ($9.3)
Utility service disruption 0.1% ($0.2)
Earthquakes[4] 6.4% ($19.1)
Water damage 0.1% ($0.4)
Terrorism 7.5% ($22.3)
Winter storms 7.8% ($23.1)
All tropical cyclones[2] 46.3% ($137.7)
Tornadoes[3] 26.0% ($77.3)

Total: $297.3 billion

[1]Catastrophes are all events causing direct insured losses to property of $25 million or more in 2006 dollars. Adjusted for inflation by ISO. [2]Includes hurricanes and tropical storms. [3]Excludes snow. [4]Includes other geologic events such as volcanic eruptions and other earth movement. [5]Does not include flood damage covered by the federally administered National Flood Insurance Program. [6]Includes wildland fires.

Source: ISO's Property Claim Services unit.

HURRICANES

Hurricanes are tropical cyclones. A hurricane's winds revolve around a center of low pressure, expressed in millibars (mb) or inches of mercury. Hurricanes are categorized on the Saffir/Simpson intensity scale, which ranges from 1 to 5, reflecting a hurricane's wind and ocean-surge intensity.

THE SAFFIR/SIMPSON CLASSIFICATION SYSTEM FOR HURRICANES

Category	Wind speeds	Pressures	Storm surge	Damage
1	74-95 mph	Greater than 980 mb	4-5 ft.	Light
2	96-110 mph	965-979 mb	6-8 ft.	Moderate
3	111-130 mph	945-964 mb	9-12 ft.	Extensive
4	131-155 mph	920-944 mb	13-18 ft.	Extreme
5	More than 155 mph	Less than 920 mb	Greater than 18 ft.	Catastrophic

Source: U.S. Department of Commerce, National Oceanic and Atmospheric Administration, National Hurricane Center.

HURRICANES AND RELATED DEATHS IN THE UNITED STATES, 1987-2006

Year	Made landfall as hurricane in the U.S.	Hurricanes	Deaths[1]	Year	Made landfall as hurricane in the U.S.	Hurricanes	Deaths[1]
1987	1	1	0	1997	1	1	6
1988	1	2	1	1998	3	10	23
1989	3	6	56	1999	2	8	60
1990	0	1	0	2000	0	8	4
1991	1	1	18	2001	0	9	42
1992	1	4	27	2002	1	4	5
1993	1	1	3	2003	2	7	24
1994	0	1	8	2004	6[2]	9	59
1995	3	3	29	2005	7	15	1,518
1996	2	3	59	2006	0	5	0

[1]Includes fatalities from high winds of less than hurricane force from tropical storms.
[2]One hurricane (Alex) is considered a strike but not technically a landfall.

Source: Insurance Information Institute from data supplied by the U.S. Department of Commerce, National Oceanic and Atmospheric Administration, National Hurricane Center; ISO.

DEADLIEST MAINLAND U.S. HURRICANES[1]

Rank	Hurricane	Year	Category	Deaths
1	Texas (Galveston)	1900	4	8,000[2]
2	Florida (Southeast; Lake Okeechobee)	1928	4	2,500[3]
3	Hurricane Katrina (Southeast Louisiana; Mississippi)	2005	3	1,500
4	Louisiana (Cheniere Caminanda)	1893	4	1,100-1,400[4]
5	South Carolina; Georgia (Sea Islands)	1893	3	1,000-2,000
6	Georgia; South Carolina	1881	2	700
7	Hurricane Audrey (Southwest Louisiana; North Texas)	1957	4	416
8	Florida (Keys)	1935	5	408
9	Louisiana (Last Island)	1856	4	400[5]
10	Florida (Miami, Pensacola); Mississippi; Alabama	1926	4	372

[1]Based on a National Hurricane Center analysis of mainland U.S. tropical cyclones from 1851-2006.
[2]Could be as high as 12,000.
[3]Could be as high as 3,000.
[4]Total including offshore losses is near 2,000.
[5]Total including offshore losses is 600.

Source: National Weather Service, National Hurricane Center, National Oceanic and Atmospheric Administration.

TOP TEN MOST COSTLY HURRICANES IN THE UNITED STATES
($ millions)

Rank	Date	Location	Hurricane	Estimated insured loss[1]	
				Dollars when occurred	In 2006 dollars[2]
1	Aug. 25-30, 2005	AL, FL, GA, LA, MS, TN	Katrina	$41,100	$42,426
2	Aug. 24-26, 1992	FL, LA	Andrew	15,500	22,272
3	Oct. 24, 2005	FL	Wilma	10,300	10,632
4	Aug. 13-14, 2004	FL, NC, SC	Charley	7,475	7,978
5	Sep. 15-21, 2004	AL, DE, FL, GA, LA, MD, MS, NJ, NY, NC, OH, PA, TN, VA, WV	Ivan	7,110	7,588
6	Sep. 17-22, 1989	GA, NC, PR, SC, VA, U.S. Virgin Islands	Hugo	4,195	6,820
7	Sep. 20-26, 2005	AL, AR, FL, LA, MS, TN, TX	Rita	5,627	5,809
8	Sep. 3-9, 2004	FL, GA, NC, NY, SC	Frances	4,595	4,904
9	Sep. 15-29, 2004	DE, FL, GA, MD, NJ, NY, NC, PA, PR, SC, VA	Jeanne	3,655	3,901
10	Sep. 21-28, 1998	AL, FL, LA, MS, PR, U.S. Virgin Islands	Georges	2,955	3,655

[1]Property coverage only.
[2]Adjusted to 2006 dollars by ISO.

Source: ISO's Property Claim Services unit; Insurance Information Institute.

THE 2006 AND 2007 ATLANTIC HURRICANE SEASONS

In contrast with the 2005 Atlantic hurricane season, which was the most active since record keeping began in 1851 with 28 named storms, the 2006 hurricane season was close to average, with nine named storms (the average is 11). Five of those storms became hurricanes (the average is six). None of the hurricanes struck the United States, the first time since 2001. However, three named storms made landfall as tropical storms. Tropical Storm Ernesto, which made landfall twice in Florida and then in North Carolina, caused an estimated $245 million in insured losses in eight states in late August and early September, according to PCS.

The 2007 hurricane season, as of November, had produced 14 named storms, five of which became hurricanes. Only one hurricane, Humberto, hit the United States, the first to strike the country since Hurricane Wilma in October 2005. Humberto struck Texas and Louisiana on September 13 and caused wind and rain damage in Texas but below catastrophe loss levels as defined by ISO. In addition, Tropical Storm Gabrielle made landfall in North Carolina on September 9.

CATASTROPHIC HURRICANE CLAIMS AND LOSSES IN THE UNITED STATES, 1998-2006[1]

	1998	1999	2002	2003	2004	2005	2006
Frequency	2	5	1	2	5	6	0
Claims	729,450	695,850	133,700	527,800	2,259,150	3,315,550	NA
Personal[2]	72.8%	73.9%	83.8%	82.3%	73.6%	70.0%	NA
Commercial[2]	15.7%	17.2%	3.0%	4.1%	13.4%	9.3%	NA
Vehicles	11.5%	9.0%	13.2%	13.5%	12.9%	20.7%	NA
Losses ($ millions)	$3,315	$2,315	$430	$1,775	$22,900	$58,337	NA
Personal[2]	34.9%	39.4%	66.5%	74.9%	65.7%	49.8%	NA
Commercial[2]	59.8%	55.6%	26.7%	14.0%	29.6%	44.7%	NA
Vehicles	5.4%	5.0%	6.7%	11.1%	4.6%	5.5%	NA
Average claim severity							
Personal[2]	$2,176	$1,773	$2,554	$3,061	$9,049	$12,515	NA
Commercial[2]	$17,331	$10,769	$28,750	$11,376	$22,337	$84,953	NA
Vehicles	$2,124	$1,856	$1,638	$2,755	$3,626	$4,698	NA

[1]ISO's Property Claim Services unit currently defines catastrophes as events causing at least $25 million in direct insured losses to property and affecting significant numbers of insurers and insureds. There were no catastrophic hurricanes in 2000, 2001 or 2006.
[2]Property losses excluding vehicle losses.
Note: Data are as of August 2007 and may differ from similar data shown elsewhere. NA=Not applicable.
Source: ISO's Property Claim Services unit.

CATASTROPHIC HURRICANE LOSSES IN THE UNITED STATES, 1997-2006

Year	Number of catastrophic hurricanes[1]	Insured loss[2]	Year	Number of catastrophic hurricanes[1]	Insured loss[2]
1997	1	$75.4 million	2002	1	$481.9 million
1998	2	4.1 billion	2003	2	1.9 billion
1999	5	2.8 billion	2004	5	24.4 billion
2000[3]	0	NA	2005	6	60.2 billion
2001[3]	0	NA	2006[3]	0	NA

[1]Major hurricanes as defined by ISO.
[2]Adjusted to 2006 dollars.
[3]No wind event met ISO's Property Claim Services catastrophe definition of a single incident or a series of related incidents, man-made or natural disasters that causes insured property losses of at least $25 million and affects a significant number of policyholders and insurers.
NA=Not applicable.
Source: ISO's Property Claim Services unit.

The chart showing the Ten Most Costly Hurricanes in the United States on page 113 ranks historic hurricanes based on their insured losses, adjusted for inflation. The chart below uses a computer model to estimate the losses that major hurricanes of the past would produce today according to current exposures. AIR Worldwide's U.S. hurricane model simulates the specific meteorological characteristics of each storm, taking into account the current number and value of exposed properties in 2005, when the analysis was conducted.

ESTIMATED INSURED LOSSES FOR THE TOP TEN HISTORICAL HURRICANES BASED ON CURRENT EXPOSURES[1]
($ billions)

Rank	Date	Event	Insured loss (current exposures)
1	Sep. 18, 1926	Miami Hurricane	$80
2	Aug. 24, 1992	Hurricane Andrew	42
3	Aug. 29, 2005	Hurricane Katrina	41[2]
4	Sep. 21, 1938	1938 Long Island Express	35
5	Sep. 9, 1965	Hurricane Betsy	34
6	Sep. 9, 1900	Galveston Storm of 1900	33
7	Sep. 17, 1928	Great Okeechobee Hurricane	33
8	Sep. 10, 1960	Hurricane Donna	26
9	Sep. 17, 1947	1947 Fort Lauderdale Hurricane	24
10	Sep. 16, 1945	1945 Homestead Hurricane (#9)	20

[1]Modeled loss to property, contents and direct business interruption and additional living expenses for residential, mobile home, commercial, and auto exposures as of December 31, 2005.
[2]ISO estimate.

Source: AIR Worldwide Corporation.

FLOODS

TOP TEN FLOOD EVENTS, RANKED BY NATIONAL FLOOD INSURANCE PROGRAM PAYOUTS[1]

Rank	Event	Date	Number of paid losses	Amount paid	Average paid loss
1	Hurricane Katrina	Aug. 2005	164,917	$15,679,829,572	$95,077
2	Hurricane Ivan	Sep. 2004	27,304	1,515,868,005	55,518
3	Tropical Storm Allison	Jun. 2001	30,627	1,100,859,476	35,944
4	Louisiana Flood	May 1995	31,343	585,072,008	18,667
5	Hurricane Isabel	Sep. 2003	19,685	473,943,969	24,076
6	Hurricane Floyd	Sep. 1999	20,438	462,178,153	22,614
7	Hurricane Rita	Sep. 2005	9,328	442,405,134	47,428
8	Hurricane Opal	Oct. 1995	10,343	405,528,543	39,208
9	Hurricane Hugo	Sep. 1989	12,843	376,494,566	29,315
10	Hurricane Wilma	Oct. 2005	9,530	355,854,863	37,340

[1]Includes events from 1978 to February 2007. Defined by the National Flood Insurance Program as an event that produces at least 1,500 paid losses. Source: U.S. Department of Homeland Security, Federal Emergency Management Agency.

TORNADOES

A tornado is a violently rotating column of air that extends from a thunderstorm and comes into contact with the ground, according to the National Oceanic and Atmospheric Administration (NOAA). In an average year about 1,000 tornadoes are reported nationwide, according to NOAA. Tornado intensity is measured by the Fujita (F) scale. The scale rates tornadoes on a scale of 0 through 5, based on the amount and type of wind damage. The original F scale was replaced by an enhanced F scale on February 1, 2007. The new scale retains the 0 to 5 ratings, but incorporates 28 different "damage indicators" based on damage to a wide variety of structures ranging from trees to shopping malls.

THE FUJITA SCALE FOR TORNADOES

Category	Damage	Original F scale[1] Wind speed (mph)	Enhanced F scale[2] 3-second gust (mph)	Category	Damage	Original F scale[1] Wind speed (mph)	Enhanced F scale[2] 3-second gust (mph)
F-0	Light	40-72	65-85	F-3	Severe	158-207	136-165
F-1	Moderate	73-112	86-110	F-4	Devastating	208-260	166-200
F-2	Considerable	113-157	111-135	F-5	Incredible	261-318	Over 200

[1]Original scale: wind speeds represent fastest estimated speeds over ¼ mile. [2]Enhanced scale: wind speeds represent maximum 3-second gusts. Source: U.S. Department of Commerce, National Oceanic and Atmospheric Administration.

Tornadoes and related weather events caused more than $8 billion in insured losses in 2006, according to an A.M. Best study. A March 31, 1973 tornado in central and northern Georgia was the costliest tornado on record, with $5.21 billion in damage in 2007 dollars, according to the study. The next four most costly tornadoes (in 2007 dollars) occurred June 8, 1966 in Topeka, Kansas ($1.94 billion); May 11, 1970 in Lubbock, Texas ($1.43 billion); May 3, 1999 in Oklahoma City, Oklahoma ($1.30 billion) and April 3, 1974 in Xenia, Ohio ($98 million). New Jersey tops the list of states with the highest average expected losses from tornadoes, followed by Connecticut and Massachusetts, based on A.M. Best's analysis of RMS modeling data. Texas has the highest annual occurence rate, followed by Oklahoma and Kansas.

      Although tornadoes can occur at any time of the year, the weather conditions that cause tornadoes are common in the southern states in March through May. Peak months in the northern states are during the summer.

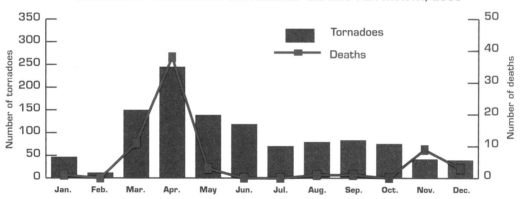

NUMBER OF TORNADOES AND RELATED DEATHS PER MONTH, 2006

Source: U.S. Department of Commerce, Storm Prediction Center, National Weather Service.

MAJOR CATASTROPHES: TORNADOES

TORNADOES AND RELATED DEATHS BY STATE, 2006[1]

State	Tornadoes	Fatalities	State	Tornadoes	Fatalities
Alabama	69	1	Nebraska	22	0
Alaska	0	0	Nevada	1	0
Arizona	6	0	New Hampshire	2	0
Arkansas	25	0	New Jersey	1	0
California	9	0	New Mexico	5	0
Colorado	20	0	New York	8	0
Connecticut	1	0	North Carolina	31	9
Delaware	0	0	North Dakota	21	0
D.C.	0	0	Ohio	36	0
Florida	42	0	Oklahoma	27	0
Georgia	21	0	Oregon	4	0
Hawaii	2	0	Pennsylvania	8	1
Idaho	9	0	Puerto Rico	1	0
Illinois	123	1	Rhode Island	0	0
Indiana	25	0	South Carolina	36	0
Iowa	38	1	South Dakota	27	0
Kansas	93	0	Tennessee	25	34
Kentucky	19	0	Texas	114	4
Louisiana	40	1	Utah	2	0
Maine	1	0	Vermont	0	0
Maryland	3	0	Virginia	16	0
Massachusetts	1	0	Washington	2	0
Michigan	10	0	West Virginia	0	0
Minnesota	25	2	Wisconsin	13	0
Mississippi	32	0	Wyoming	1	0
Missouri	103	13	**United States**	**1,121**	**67**
Montana	1	0			

[1]Includes the 15 tornadoes that tracked from a touchdown state into another state.

Source: U.S. Department of Commerce, Storm Prediction Center, National Weather Service.

TORNADOES AND RELATED DEATHS IN THE UNITED STATES, 1986-2006[1]

Year	Tornadoes	Deaths	Year	Tornadoes	Deaths	Year	Tornadoes	Deaths
1986	765	15	1993	1,173	33	2000	1,071	40
1987	656	59	1994	1,082	69	2001	1,216	40
1988	702	32	1995	1,234	30	2002	941	55
1989	856	50	1996	1,173	25	2003	1,376	54
1990	1,133	53	1997	1,148	67	2004	1,819	36
1991	1,132	39	1998	1,424	130	2005	1,264	39
1992	1,297	39	1999	1,345	94	2006	1,106	67

[1]Does not include tornadoes crossing state lines. Counts these tornadoes as one event.

Source: U.S. Department of Commerce, Storm Prediction Center, National Weather Service.

EARTHQUAKES

Since 1900, earthquakes have occurred in 39 states and have caused damage in all 50. About 5,000 quakes can be felt each year. The earthquake and fire that devastated San Francisco on April 18, 1906 was one of the worst natural disasters in the United States. It produced insured losses of $235 million at the time, equivalent to $5.1 billion in 2006 dollars. A study by AIR Worldwide estimates the loss at $108 billion, were the quake to hit under today's economic and demographic conditions.

THE TEN MOST COSTLY U.S. EARTHQUAKES
($ millions)

Rank	Year	Location	Magnitude	Estimated property damage[1] Dollars when occurred	In 2006 dollars[2]
1	1994	Northridge, CA	6.7	$13-20,000	$18-27,000
2	1989	San Francisco Bay area; Loma Prieta, CA	6.9	7,000	11,381
3	1964	Alaska and west coast of United States (tsunami damage from earthquake near Anchorage, Alaska)	9.2	500	3,252
4	1971	San Fernando, CA	6.5	553	2,753
5	2001	Washington, Oregon	6.8	2,305	2,624
6	1987	Southern California; primarily in Los Angeles–Pasadena–Whittier area	5.9	358	635
7	1933	Long Beach, CA	6.3	40	620
8	1952	Kern County, CA	7.5	60	456
9	1992	Southern California; Landers–Joshua Tree–Big Bear	7.6	92	132
10	1992	Northern California Coast; Petrolia–Eureka	7.1	66	95

[1]Includes insured and uninsured losses. [2]Adjusted to 2006 dollars by the Insurance Information Institute.

Source: U.S. Department of the Interior, U.S. Geological Survey; Munich Re; Insurance Information Institute.

The previous chart ranks historic earthquakes based on their insured losses, adjusted for inflation. The chart below uses a computer model to measure the estimated impact of historical quakes according to current exposures. The analysis, based on AIR Worldwide's U.S. earthquake model, makes use of the firm's property exposure database and takes into account the current number and value of exposed properties in 2005, when the study was conducted.

ESTIMATED INSURED LOSSES FOR THE TOP TEN HISTORICAL EARTHQUAKES BASED ON CURRENT EXPOSURES[1]
($ billions)

Rank	Date	Location	Magnitude	Insured loss (current exposures)
1	Apr. 18, 1906	San Francisco, CA	7.9	$108
2	Feb. 7, 1812	New Madrid, MO	7.7	88
3	Aug. 31, 1886	Charleston, SC	7.3	38
4	Jan. 9, 1857	Fort Tejon, CA	7.9	27
5	Oct. 21, 1868	Hayward, CA	6.8	25
6	Jan. 17, 1994	Northridge, CA	6.7	16
7	Jan. 5, 1843	Marked Tree, AR	6.5	12
8	Jun. 1, 1838	San Francisco, CA	7.2	11
9	Oct. 12, 1877	Portland, OR	6.3	11
10	Jul. 1, 1911	San Jose, CA	6.6	9

[1]Modeled loss to property, contents and direct business interruption and additional living expenses for residential, mobile home, commercial and auto exposures as of December 31, 2005. Losses include demand surge. Policy conditions and earthquake insurance take up rates are based on estimates by state insurance departments and client claims data.

Source: AIR Worldwide Corporation.

TERRORISM

A total of 2,976 people perished in the September 11, 2001 terrorist attacks in New York, Washington and Pennsylvania, excluding the 19 hijackers. Total insured losses (including liability losses) from the terrorist attacks on the World Trade Center in New York City and the Pentagon are expected to be about $36 billion (in 2006 dollars), including property, life and liability insurance claim costs (some claims are still being litigated). Loss estimates may differ from estimates calculated by other organizations. It was the worst terrorist attack on record in terms of fatalities and insured property losses, which totaled about $21 billion (in 2006 dollars).

The July 2005 bombings in the London transport system killed 56 people, injured 165 others and caused $1.72 billion in total damages, according to Swiss Re. According to Axco Information Services, the insured property damage loss was relatively minor. Losses were paid mainly by Transport for London, a captive insurer, with reinsurance coverage by Pool Re, the U.K.'s public/private mechanism for covering terrorist attacks.

WORST TERRORIST ACTS, INSURED PROPERTY LOSSES
(2006 $ millions)

Rank	Date	Country	Location	Event	Insured property loss[1]	Fatalities
1	Sep. 11, 2001	U.S.	New York City, Washington, D.C.	Hijacked airliners crash into World Trade Center and Pentagon	$21,401[2]	2,976[3]
2	Apr. 24, 1993	U.K.	London	Bomb explodes near NatWest tower in the financial district	1,005	1
3	Jun. 15, 1996	U.K.	Manchester	Irish Republican Army (IRA) car bomb explodes near shopping mall	825	0
4	Feb. 26, 1993	U.S.	New York City	Bomb explodes in garage of World Trade Center	803	6
5	Apr. 10, 1992	U.K.	London	Bomb explodes in financial district	744	3
6	Jul. 24, 2001	Sri Lanka	Colombo Intl. Airport	Rebels destroy 3 airliners, 8 military aircraft and heavily damage 3 civilian aircraft	441	20
7	Feb. 9, 1996	U.K.	London	IRA bomb explodes in South Key Docklands	287	2
8	Apr. 19, 1995	U.S.	Oklahoma City	Truck bomb crashes into government building	160	166
9	Dec. 21, 1988	Scotland	Lockerbie	PanAm Boeing 747 explodes	153	270
10	Sep. 12, 1970	Jordan	Zerqa	Hijacked Swissair DC-8, TWA Boeing 707 and BOAC VC-10 dynamited	140	0
11	Mar. 11, 2004	Spain	Madrid, Atocha	Bomb attack on trains	130	191
12	Sep. 6, 1970	Egypt	Cairo	Hijacked PanAm B-747 dynamited	123	0

[1]Includes bodily injury and aviation hull losses. Originally reported in 2001 dollars by Swiss Re. Adjusted to 2006 dollars by the Insurance Information Institute.
[2]Updated by the Insurance Information Institute to reflect latest estimate from ISO.
[3]Latest government figures.

Source: ISO's Property Claim Services unit; Swiss Re; Insurance Information Institute.

CIVIL DISORDERS

THE TEN MOST COSTLY U.S. CIVIL DISORDERS
($ millions)

Rank	Date	Location	Estimated insured loss[1]	
			Dollars when occurred	In 2006 dollars[2]
1	Apr. 29-May 4, 1992	Los Angeles, CA	$775	$1,114
2	Aug. 11-17,1965	Los Angeles, CA	44	282
3	Jul. 23, 1967	Detroit, MI	42	250
4	May 17-19, 1980	Miami, FL	65	160
5	Apr. 4-9, 1968	Washington, D.C.	24	139
6	Jul. 13-14, 1977	New York City, NY	28	93
7	Jul. 12, 1967	Newark, NJ	15	91
8	Apr. 6-9, 1968	Baltimore, MD	14	81
9	Apr. 4-11, 1968	Chicago, IL	13	75
10	Apr. 4-11, 1968	New York City, NY	4	24

[1]Includes riots and civil disorders causing insured losses to the industry of at least $1 million up to 1992, $5 million from 1992 to 1996, and $25 million thereafter.
[2]Adjusted to 2006 dollars by the Insurance Information Institute.

Source: ISO's Property Claim Services unit; Insurance Information Institute.

WILDLAND FIRES

Fire plays an important role in the life of a forest, clearing away dead wood and undergrowth to make way for younger trees. But for much of the last century, fire-suppression policies have sought to extinguish wildfires as quickly as possible to preserve timber and protect real estate. These policies have led to the accumulation of brush and other vegetation that is easily ignited and serves as fuel for wildfires. Most of the large fires with significant property damage have occurred in California, where some of the fastest developing counties are in forest areas.

2007 CALIFORNIA WILDFIRES

On October 21 wildfires broke out across Southern California, damaging thousands of homes and causing widespread evacuations. As of November 1, insured losses were expected to exceed $1.5 billion, according to early estimates by Risk Management Solutions (RMS). The fires are expected to rank among the two most damaging wildfires since 1970, in 2006 dollars. In June wildfires in the Lake Tahoe area burned 254 dwellings and other structures on the California side of Lake Tahoe. Known as the Angora Fire, the disaster caused insured losses of $100 to $150 million, as estimated by RMS. The Angora blaze did not meet ISO's catastrophe criteria in terms of the number of policyholders and insurers affected.

CATASTROPHIC WILDLAND FIRES IN THE UNITED STATES, 1970-2006[1]
($ millions)

Rank	Date	Location	Dollars when occurred	In 2006 dollars[2]
1	Oct. 20-21, 1991	Oakland, Alameda Counties, CA	$1,700.0	$2,516.3
2	Oct. 25-Nov. 4, 2003	San Diego County, CA, "Cedar"	1,060.0	1,161.4
3	Oct. 25-Nov. 3, 2003	San Bernardino County, CA, "Old"	975.0	1,068.3
4	Nov. 2-3, 1993	Los Angeles County, CA	375.0	523.2
5	Oct. 27-28, 1993	Orange County, CA	350.0	488.3
6	Jun. 27-Jul. 2, 1990	Santa Barbara County, CA	265.0	408.8
7	May 10-16, 2000	Cerro Grande, NM	140.0	163.9
8	Jun. 23-28, 2002	Rodeo-Chediski Complex, AZ	120.0	134.5
9	Sep. 22-30, 1970	Oakland-Berkeley Hills, CA	24.8	128.9
10	Nov. 24-30, 1980	Los Angeles, San Bernardino, Orange, Riverside, San Diego Counties, CA	43.0	105.2

[1]Estimated insured losses. Effective January 1, 1997, Property Claim Services (PCS) defines catastrophes as events that cause more than $25 million of insured property damage and that affect a significant number of insureds and insurers. From 1982 to 1996, PCS used a $5 million threshold in defining catastrophes. Before 1982, PCS used a $1 million threshold.
[2]Adjusted to 2006 dollars by the Insurance Information Institute.

Source: ISO's Property Claim Services unit; Insurance Information Institute.

FIRE LOSSES

Great strides have been made in constructing fire resistant buildings, reducing the incidence of fires and improving fire suppression techniques. However, in terms of property losses, these advances have been offset by increases in the number and value of buildings. According to the National Fire Protection Association, on average, a fire department responds to a fire every 19 seconds in the United States. A structure fire occurs every 60 seconds; a residential fire occurs every 76 seconds; a vehicle fire occurs every 113 seconds.

ISO estimates that fire losses associated with homeowners insurance claims (including FAIR Plans) accounted for 43 percent of total fire losses in 2006. Fire losses associated with commercial multiple peril and fire insurance claims accounted for the remainder. ISO estimates that fire losses for those lines amounted to 19 percent and 38 percent, respectively, of total fire losses in 2006.

U.S. FIRE LOSSES, 1997-2006[1]

Year	Property loss ($ millions)	Loss per capita	Year	Property loss ($ millions)	Loss per capita
1997	$12,940	$48.32	2002	$17,586	$61.07
1998	11,510	45.59	2003	21,129	72.65
1999	12,428	45.58	2004	17,344	59.06
2000	13,457	47.69	2005	20,427	68.89
2001	17,118[2]	60.04	2006	18,072	60.36

[1]Including allowances for FAIR Plan and uninsured losses. [2]Does not include insured fire losses related to terrorism.

Source: ISO; Insurance Information Institute.

STRUCTURE FIRES, 1997-2006[1]

Year	Number of fires	Year	Number of fires
1997	552,000	2002	519,000
1998	517,500	2003	519,500
1999	523,000	2004	526,000
2000	505,500	2005	511,000
2001	521,500	2006	524,000

[1]Includes public assembly, educational, institutional and residential structures, stores and offices, industry, utility, defense, storage and special structures.

Source: National Fire Protection Association.

CIVILIAN (NONFIREFIGHTER) FIRE DEATHS AND INJURIES BY PROPERTY USE, 2006

Property use	Civilian fire deaths	Percent change from 2005	Percent of all civilian fire deaths	Civilian fire injuries
Residential	2,620	-14.2%	80.7%	12,925
1- and 2-family dwellings[1]	2,155	-16.1	66.4	8,800
Apartments	425	-7.6	13.1	3,700
Other residential[2]	40	60.0	1.2	425
Nonresidential structures[3]	85	70.0	2.6	1,425
Highway vehicles	445	-11.0	13.7	1,075
Other vehicles[4]	45	125.0[5]	1.4	125
All other fires[6]	50	0.0	1.5	850
Total	**3,245**	**-11.7%**	**100.0%**	**16,400**

[1]Includes manufactured homes. [2]Includes hotels and motels, college dormitories, boarding houses, etc. [3]Includes public assembly, educational, institutional, store and office, industry, utility, storage and special structure properties. [4]Includes trains, boats, ships, farm vehicles and construction vehicles. [5]Includes an airplane crash and ensuing fire where 24 people died as a result of fire. [6]Includes outside properties with value, as well as brush, rubbish and other outside locations.

Source: National Fire Protection Association.

STRUCTURE FIRES BY TYPE OF USE, 2006[1]
($ millions)

Property use	Estimated number of fires	Percent change from 2005	Property loss[2]	Percent change from 2005
Public assembly	13,500	0.0%	$444	38.8%
Educational	6,500	8.3	105	56.7
Institutional	7,500	0.0	42	5.0
Residential	412,500	4.2	6,990	1.7
1- and 2-family dwellings[3]	304,500	6.1	5,936	2.7
Apartments	91,500	-2.7	896	-5.5
Other[4]	16,500	10.0	158	8.2
Stores and offices	20,000	-13.0	691	0.6
Industry, utility, defense[5]	11,500	0.0	573	52.4
Storage in structures	29,500	-1.7	650	10.2
Special structures	23,000	-2.1	141	-40.8
Total	**524,000**	**2.5%**	**$9,636**	**4.8%**

[1]Estimates based on data reported by fire departments responding to the 2006 National Fire Experience Survey. May not include reports from all fire departments. [2]Includes direct property loss to contents, structures, vehicles, machinery, vegetation or any other property involved in a fire. Does not include indirect losses, such as business interruption or temporary shelter costs. [3]Includes manufactured homes. [4]Includes hotels and motels, college dormitories, boarding houses, etc. [5]Does not include incidents handled only by private brigades or fixed suppression systems.

Source: National Fire Protection Association.

THE TEN MOST CATASTROPHIC MULTIPLE-DEATH FIRES OF 2006[1]

Rank	Month	State	Type of facility	Deaths
1	August	Kentucky	Aircraft crash/fire	24
2	October	Nevada	Residential hotel, 104 rooms	12
3	January	West Virginia	Sago Mine explosion, coal mine	12
4	March	Texas	Wildland fire	12
5	November	Missouri	Residential care, 19 bedrooms	11
6	March	Tennessee	Single-family house	9
7	July	Oklahoma	Single-family house	7
8	March	Indiana	Single-family house	6
9	April	Florida	Manufactured home	6
10	September	Illinois	Apartment house, 12 units	6

[1]Fires that kill five or more people in residential property, or three or more people in nonresidential or nonstructural property.

Source: National Fire Protection Association.

THE TEN MOST CATASTROPHIC MULTIPLE-DEATH FIRES IN U.S. HISTORY[1]

Rank	Date	Location/Event	Deaths
1	Sep. 11, 2001	New York, NY, World Trade Center terrorist attack	2,666[2]
2	Apr. 27, 1865	Mississippi River, SS Sultana steamship	1,547
3	Oct. 8, 1871	Peshtigo, WI, forest fire	1,152
4	Jun. 15, 1904	New York, NY, General Slocum steamship	1,030
5	Dec. 30, 1903	Chicago, IL, Iroquois Theater	602
6	Oct. 12, 1918	Cloquet, MN, forest fire	559
7	Nov. 28, 1942	Boston, MA, Cocoanut Grove night club	492
8	Apr. 16, 1947	Texas City, TX, SS Grandcamp and Monsanto Chemical Co. plant	468
9	Sep. 1, 1894	Hinckley, MN, forest fire	418
10	Dec. 6, 1907	Monongha, WV, coal mine explosion	361

[1]Fires that kill five or more people in residential property, or three or more people in nonresidential or nonstructural property.
[2]Revised to 2,976 by government officials.

Source: National Fire Protection Association.

THE TEN MOST COSTLY LARGE-LOSS FIRES OF 2006[1]

($ millions)

Rank	State	Type of facility	Estimated loss
1	Texas	Eight brush fires	$95
2	Alaska	Conflagration, started in a school	35
3	Pennsylvania	Plastics products plant	34
4	Pennsylvania	Warehouse	26
5	Virginia	Power plant	25
6	California	Passenger jet aircraft	20
7	Alabama	Food processing plant	20
8	Pennsylvania	Senior living apartment	20
9	Washington	Dormitory under construction	13
10	Arizona	Department store	13

[1]Large-loss fires of $10 million or more.

Source: National Fire Protection Association.

THE TEN MOST COSTLY LARGE-LOSS FIRES IN U.S. HISTORY
($ millions)

Rank	Date	Location/Event	Estimated loss[1] Dollars when occurred	In 2006 dollars[2]
1	Sep. 11, 2001	World Trade Center (terrorist attacks)	$33,400[3]	$38,000[3]
2	Apr. 18, 1906	San Francisco Earthquake and Fire	350	7,800
3	Oct. 8-9, 1871	Great Chicago Fire	168	2,800
4	Oct. 20, 1991	Oakland, CA, fire storm	1,500	2,200
5	Nov. 9, 1872	Great Boston Fire	75	1,300
6	Oct. 23, 1989	Pasadena, Texas, polyolefin plant	750	1,200
7	May 4, 2000	Los Alamos, NM, wildland fire	1,000	1,200
8	Oct. 25, 2003	Julian, CA, wildland fire	1,100	1,200
9	Feb. 7, 1904	Baltimore Conflagration	50	1,100
10	Oct. 25, 2003	San Bernardino, CA, Old wildland fire	975	1,100

[1]Loss estimates are from National Fire Protection Association (NFPA) records. The list is limited to fires for which some reliable dollar loss estimate exists.
[2]Adjustment to 2006 dollars made by the NFPA using the Consumer Price Index, including the U.S. Census Bureau's estimates of the index for historical times.
[3]Differs from estimates from other sources.
Source: National Fire Protection Association.

STRUCTURE FIRES IN RELIGIOUS AND FUNERAL PROPERTIES[1]
(2002-2005 annual averages)

Occupancy	Fires	Civilian deaths	Civilian injuries	Direct property damage ($ millions)
Church, mosque, temple or chapel	1,730	2	11	$91
Funeral parlor	70	0	0	5
Unclassified religious or funeral property	110	0	0	4
Total	1,910	2	11	$100

[1]Estimates of fires reported to U.S. municipal fire departments. Excludes fires reported only to federal or state agencies or industrial fire brigades. Casualty and loss projections can be heavily influenced by one unusually serious fire.
Source: National Fire Protection Association.

- Church arsons, a major problem in the 1980s, have dropped significantly. Intentional fires in religious and funeral properties fell 82 percent from 1,320 in 1980 to 240 in 2002, the last time such figures were tracked.

ARSON

Arson, the act of deliberately setting fire to a building, car or other property for fraudulent or malicious purposes, is a crime in all states.

INTENTIONALLY SET FIRES, 1997-2006
($ millions)

- The number of civilians (nonfirefighters) killed in arson fires in buildings in 2006 totaled 305, down 3.2 percent from 2005.

- Most arson fires are started by vandals. Between 20 and 25 percent are drug related. Almost half are set by children under the age of 18.

Year	Structures		Vehicles	
	Number of fires	Property loss	Number of fires	Property loss
1997	52,000	$802	NA	NA
1998	46,500	816	NA	NA
1999	43,500	828	NA	NA
2000	45,500	792	NA	NA
2001	45,500	34,453[1]	39,500	$219
2002	44,500	919	41,000	222
2003	37,500	692	30,500	132
2004	36,500	714	36,000	165
2005	31,500	664	21,000	113
2006	31,000	775	20,500	134

[1]Includes the events of September 11, 2001, which accounted for $33.44 billion in property losses. NA=Data not available.

Source: National Fire Protection Association.

PROPERTY CRIME OFFENSES

The Federal Bureau of Investigation's Uniform Crime Report defines property crime as burglary, larceny-theft and motor vehicle theft. These crimes involve the taking of money or property without the use of force or threat of force against the victims. The following chart shows the number and rate for property crimes.

PROPERTY CRIME RATES BY TYPE OF HOUSEHOLD, 2005[1]

- Rented households are burglarized at rates about 50 percent higher than owned households.

Type of household	Burglary[2]	Motor vehicle theft	Theft[3]	Total property
Renters	38.6	13.3	140.3	192.3
Owners	25.3	6.1	105.1	136.5
Percent difference (renters vs. owners)	52.6%	118.0%	33.5%	40.9%

[1]Rate per 1,000 households.
[2]Involves unlawful or forcible entry.
[3]Does not involve personal contact or forced entry.

Source: U. S. Bureau of Justice Statistics, National Crime Victimization Survey.

NUMBER AND RATE OF CRIME OFFENSES IN THE UNITED STATES, 1997-2006[1]

Year	Burglary		Larceny-theft	
	Number	Rate	Number	Rate
1997	2,460,526	918.8	7,743,760	2,891.8
1998	2,332,735	863.2	7,376,311	2,729.5
1999	2,100,739	770.4	6,955,520	2,550.7
2000	2,050,992	728.8	6,971,590	2,477.3
2001	2,116,531	741.8	7,092,267	2,485.7
2002	2,151,252	747.0	7,057,379	2,450.7
2003	2,154,834	741.0	7,026,802	2,416.5
2004	2,144,446	730.3	6,937,089	2,362.3
2005	2,155,448	726.9	6,783,447	2,287.8
2006	2,183,746	729.4	6,607,013	2,206.8

Year	Motor vehicle theft		Total property crime[2]	
	Number	Rate	Number	Rate
1997	1,354,189	505.7	11,558,475	4,316.3
1998	1,242,781	459.9	10,951,827	4,052.5
1999	1,152,075	422.5	10,208,334	3,743.6
2000	1,160,002	412.2	10,182,584	3,618.3
2001	1,228,391	430.5	10,437,189	3,658.1
2002	1,246,646	432.9	10,455,277	3,630.6
2003	1,261,226	433.7	10,442,862	3,591.2
2004	1,237,851	421.5	10,319,386	3,514.1
2005	1,235,859	416.8	10,174,754	3,431.5
2006	1,192,809	398.4	9,983,568	3,334.5

[1]Rate is per 100,000 inhabitants.
[2]Property crimes are the offenses of burglary, larceny-theft and motor vehicle theft.

Source: U.S. Department of Justice, Federal Bureau of Investigation, *Uniform Crime Reports*.

MOTOR VEHICLE CRASHES

The National Highway Traffic Safety Administration (NHTSA) reports that 42,642 people died in motor vehicle crashes in 2006, down 2.0 percent from 43,510 in 2005. However, fatalities from alcohol-related crashes rose slightly from 17,590 in 2005 to 17,602 in 2006, up 0.1 percent. Motorcycle deaths rose for the ninth consecutive year to 4,810, up 5.1 percent in 2005. NHTSA property damage figures are based on accidents reported to the police and do not include "fender bender" accidents.

MOTOR VEHICLE CRASHES, 1997-2006

Year	Fatal	Injury[1]	Property damage only[1]	Total crashes[1]
1997	37,324	2,149,000	4,438,000	6,624,324
1998	37,107	2,029,000	4,269,000	6,335,107
1999	37,140	2,054,000	4,188,000	6,279,140
2000	37,526	2,070,000	4,286,000	6,393,526
2001	37,862	2,003,000	4,282,000	6,322,862
2002	38,491	1,929,000	4,348,000	6,315,491
2003	38,477	1,925,000	4,365,000	6,328,477
2004	38,444	1,862,000	4,281,000	6,181,444
2005	39,252	1,816,000	4,304,000	6,159,252
2006	38,588	1,746,000	4,189,000	5,973,588

[1]Estimated.

Source: U.S. Department of Transportation, National Highway Traffic Safety Administration.

TRAFFIC DEATHS, 1997-2006

- The number of people injured in motor vehicle crashes fell by 4.6 percent from 2.7 million in 2005 to 2.6 million in 2006.

- The injury rates per 100 miles traveled and per 100,000 registered vehicles fell by 2.7 percent and 4.4 percent, respectively, in 2006.

Year	Fatalities	Annual percent change	Fatality rate per 100 million vehicle miles traveled	Fatality rate per 100,000 registered vehicles
1997	42,013	-0.1%	1.64	20.64
1998	41,501	-1.2	1.58	19.95
1999	41,717	0.5	1.55	19.61
2000	41,945	0.5	1.53	19.33
2001	42,196	0.6	1.51	19.07
2002	43,005	1.9	1.51	19.06
2003	42,884	-0.3	1.48	18.59
2004	42,836	-0.1	1.45	18.00
2005	43,510	1.4	1.46	17.71
2006	42,642	-2.0	1.42	16.93

Source: U.S. Department of Transportation, National Highway Traffic Safety Administration.

According to the National Highway Traffic Safety Administration, vehicle occupants accounted for 72 percent of traffic deaths in 2006. Pedestrians accounted for 11 percent of deaths. Motorcycle riders accounted for another 11 percent; pedalcyclists and other non-occupants accounted for the remainder.

MOTOR VEHICLE TRAFFIC DEATHS BY STATE, 2005-2006

State	Number of deaths 2005	Number of deaths 2006	Percent change	State	Number of deaths 2005	Number of deaths 2006	Percent change
Alabama	1,148	1,208	5.2%	Montana	251	263	4.8%
Alaska	73	74	1.4	Nebraska	276	269	-2.5
Arizona	1,179	1,288	9.2	Nevada	427	432	1.2
Arkansas	654	665	1.7	New Hampshire	166	127	-23.5
California	4,333	4,236	-2.2	New Jersey	747	772	3.3
Colorado	606	535	-11.7	New Mexico	488	484	-0.8
Connecticut	278	301	8.3	New York	1,434	1,456	1.5
Delaware	133	148	11.3	North Carolina	1,547	1,559	0.8
D.C.	48	37	-22.9	North Dakota	123	111	-9.8
Florida	3,518	3,374	-4.1	Ohio	1,321	1,238	6.3
Georgia	1,729	1,693	-2.1	Oklahoma	803	765	-4.7
Hawaii	140	161	15.0	Oregon	487	477	-2.1
Idaho	275	267	-2.9	Pennsylvania	1,616	1,525	-5.6
Illinois	1,363	1,254	-8.0	Rhode Island	87	81	-6.9
Indiana	938	899	-4.2	South Carolina	1,094	1,037	-5.2
Iowa	450	439	-2.4	South Dakota	186	191	2.7
Kansas	428	468	9.3	Tennessee	1,270	1,287	1.3
Kentucky	985	913	-7.3	Texas	3,536	3,475	-1.7
Louisiana	963	982	2.0	Utah	282	287	1.8
Maine	169	188	11.2	Vermont	73	87	19.2
Maryland	614	651	6.0	Virginia	947	963	1.7
Massachusetts	441	430	-2.5	Washington	649	630	-2.9
Michigan	1,129	1,085	-3.9	West Virginia	374	410	9.6
Minnesota	559	494	-11.6	Wisconsin	815	724	-11.2%
Mississippi	931	911	-2.1	Wyoming	170	195	14.7
Missouri	1,257	1,096	-12.8	**United States**	**43,510**	**42,642**	**-2.0%**

Source: U.S. Department of Transportation, National Highway Traffic Safety Administration.

MOTOR VEHICLES: CRASHES

VEHICLES INVOLVED IN CRASHES BY VEHICLE TYPE, 1995 AND 2005

	Fatal crashes		Injury crashes		Property damage-only crashes	
	1995	2005	1995	2005	1995	2005
Passenger cars						
Crashes	30,940	25,029	2,914,000	1,893,000	5,335,000	4,169,000
Rate per 100 million vehicle miles traveled	2.09	1.55	197	117	361	258
Rate per 100,000 registered vehicles	25.11	18.52	2,365	1,401	4,329	3,085
Light trucks[1]						
Crashes	17,587	22,838	1,024,000	1,209,000	2,149,000	2,919,000
Rate per 100 million vehicle miles traveled	2.35	2.01	137	107	287	257
Rate per 100,000 registered vehicles	28.13	24.05	1,638	1,273	3,437	3,074
Motorcycles						
Crashes	2,268	4,655	52,000	80,000	13,000	18,000
Rate per 100 million vehicle miles traveled	23.15	43.22	530	746	131	168
Rate per 100,000 registered vehicles	58.20	74.75	1,331	1,291	329	291

[1]Trucks with 10,000 pounds or less gross vehicle weight. Includes pickups, vans, truck-based station wagons and utility vehicles.

Source: U.S. Department of Transportation (USDOT), National Highway Traffic Safety Administration (NHTSA). Vehicle miles traveled–USDOT, Federal Highway Administration, revised by NHTSA; Registered passenger cars and light trucks – R.L. Polk & Co; Registered motorcycles – USDOT, Federal Highway Administration.

MOTOR VEHICLE DEATHS BY ACTIVITY OF PERSON KILLED, 2006

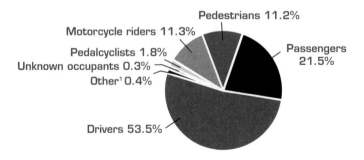

Pedestrians 11.2%
Motorcycle riders 11.3%
Pedalcyclists 1.8%
Unknown occupants 0.3%
Other[1] 0.4%
Passengers 21.5%
Drivers 53.5%

[1]Includes other nonoccupants.

Source: U.S. Department of Transportation, National Highway Traffic Safety Administration.

SEX OF DRIVERS INVOLVED IN ALL CRASHES, 1996-2005[1]

	Fatal crashes				Injury crashes			
	Male		Female		Male		Female	
Year	Number	Rate[2]	Number	Rate[2]	Number	Rate[2]	Number	Rate[2]
1996	40,899	45.19	14,723	16.54	2,378,000	2,627	1,711,000	1,922
1997	40,594	44.18	14,816	16.32	2,296,000	2,499	1,643,000	1,809
1998	40,433	43.47	14,967	16.30	2,158,000	2,319	1,576,000	1,717
1999	40,639	43.16	14,717	15.83	2,134,000	2,267	1,609,000	1,730
2000	41,443	43.27	14,682	15.48	2,192,000	2,289	1,573,000	1,659
2001	41,548	43.38	14,829	15.53	2,090,000	2,182	1,547,000	1,620
2002	41,995	43.03	14,876	15.34	2,000,000	2,049	1,481,000	1,528
2003	42,177	42.95	15,106	15.43	1,990,000	2,026	1,525,000	1,557
2004	41,876	42.06	15,272	15.38	1,912,000	1,920	1,482,000	1,493
2005	42,722	42.56	14,883	14.84	1,837,000	1,830	1,425,000	1,421

	Property damage-only crashes				Total crashes			
	Male		Female		Male		Female	
Year	Number	Rate[2]	Number	Rate[2]	Number	Rate[2]	Number	Rate[2]
1996	4,888,000	5,400	2,968,000	3,335	7,306,899	8,074	4,693,723	5,273
1997	4,808,000	5,232	2,967,000	3,268	7,144,594	7,775	4,624,816	5,094
1998	4,634,000	4,982	2,902,000	3,162	6,832,433	7,345	4,492,967	4,894
1999	4,509,000	4,789	2,800,000	3,011	6,683,639	7,099	4,423,717	4,757
2000	4,559,000	4,760	2,904,000	3,062	6,792,443	7,092	4,491,682	4,737
2001	4,518,000	4,717	2,903,000	3,041	6,649,548	6,943	4,464,829	4,677
2002	4,436,000	4,545	2,999,000	3,093	6,477,995	6,638	4,494,876	4,635
2003	4,528,000	4,610	3,020,000	3,084	6,560,177	6,680	4,560,106	4,657
2004	4,405,000	4,424	3,037,000	3,058	6,358,876	6,387	4,534,272	4,566
2005	4,357,000	4,341	3,007,000	2,999	6,236,722	6,213	4,446,883	4,435

[1]Drivers age 16 and over.
[2]Rate per 100,000 licensed drivers.

Source: U.S Department of Transportation, National Highway Safety Administration.

TEENAGE DRIVERS

Motor vehicle crashes are the leading cause of death among 15- to 20-year olds. According to the U.S. Department of Transportation, 3,467 drivers in this age group died and 281,000 were injured in motor vehicle crashes in 2005. Drivers age 15 to 20 accounted for 12.6 percent of all the drivers involved in fatal crashes and 16 percent of all the drivers involved in all police-reported crashes. Twenty-three percent of teen drivers killed were intoxicated. In 2002 the estimated economic cost of police-reported crashes involving drivers between the ages of 15 and 20 was $40.8 billion, according to the National Highway Traffic Safety Administration. Among licensed drivers, young people between the ages of 15 and 20 have the highest rate of fatal crashes relative to other age groups, including the elderly. The risk of being involved in a fatal crash for teens is three times greater than for drivers age 65 to 69.

ACCIDENTS BY AGE OF DRIVERS, 2005

Age group	Number of drivers	Percent of total	Drivers in fatal accidents	Percent of total	Drivers in all accidents	Percent of total
Under 20	9,396,000	4.7%	6,300	10.1%	2,490,000	13.5%
20–24	16,886,000	8.4	8,900	14.3	2,640,000	14.3
25–34	36,003,000	17.9	11,300	18.1	3,820,000	20.8
35–44	40,394,000	20.0	10,400	16.7	3,420,000	18.6
45–54	39,851,000	19.8	9,600	15.4	3,060,000	16.6
55–64	29,685,000	14.7	6,600	10.6	1,610,000	8.8
65–74	16,492,000	8.2	4,200	6.7	800,000	4.3
Over 74	12,793,000	6.4	5,000	8.0	560,000	3.0
Total	**201,500,000**	**100.0%**	**62,300**	**100.0%**	**18,400,000**	**100.0%**

Note: Percent of total columns may not add due to rounding; driver columns do not add because drivers under the age of 16 are not included.

Source: National Safety Council.

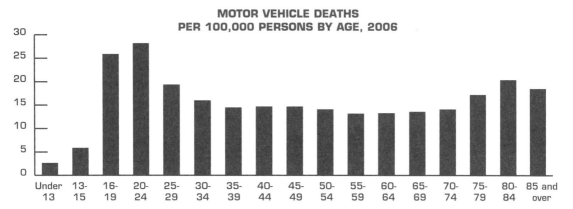

MOTOR VEHICLE DEATHS
PER 100,000 PERSONS BY AGE, 2006

Source: U.S. Department of Transportation, National Highway Traffic Safety Administration.

DRIVING BEHAVIORS REPORTED FOR DRIVERS AND MOTORCYCLE OPERATORS INVOLVED IN FATAL CRASHES, 2006[1]

Behavior	Number	Percent
Failure to keep in proper lane or running off road	16,470	28.5%
Driving too fast for conditions or in excess of posted speed limit or racing	12,262	21.3
Under the influence of alcohol, drugs, or medication	7,349	12.7
Inattentive (talking, eating, etc.)	4,560	7.9
Failure to yield right of way	4,238	7.3
Overcorrecting/oversteering	2,450	4.2
Failure to obey traffic signs, signals, or officer	2,408	4.2
Swerving or avoiding due to wind, slippery surface, other vehicle, object, nonmotorist on roadway, etc.	2,162	3.7
Operating vehicle in erratic, reckless, careless or negligent manner	2,086	3.6
Vision obscured (rain, snow, glare, lights, building, trees, etc.)	1,545	2.7
Making improper turn	1,526	2.6
Drowsy, asleep, fatigued, ill, or blacked-out	1,480	2.6
Driving wrong way on one-way traffic or wrong side of road	762	1.3
Other factors	9,426	16.3
None reported	19,990	34.6
Unknown	1,011	1.8
Total Drivers	**57,695**	**100.0**

[1]The sum of the numbers and percentages is greater than total drivers as more than one factor may be present for the same driver.

Source: U.S. Department of Transportation, National Highway Traffic Safety Administration.

PERCENT OF DRIVERS IN FATAL CRASHES WITH BACS[1]
OF 0.08 OR MORE, 1996 AND 2006

- Fatalities from alcohol-related crashes totaled 17,602 in 2006, up slightly from 17,590 in 2005.

Age	1996	2006	Point change
Under 16	9%	14%	5 pts.
16 to 20	17	19	2
21 to 24	31	33	2
25 to 34	30	29	-1
35 to 44	25	25	0
45 to 54	18	19	1
55 to 64	12	13	1
65 to 74	8	8	0
Over 74	5	5	0

[1]Blood-alcohol content. All states use 0.08 as the definition of intoxication.

Source: U.S. Department of Transportation, National Highway Traffic Safety Administration.

ALCOHOL-RELATED CRASH FATALITIES, 1997-2006[1]

Year	Number	As a percent of all crash deaths
1997	16,711	40%
1998	16,673	40
1999	15,572	40
2000	17,380	41
2001	17,400	41
2002	17,524	41
2003	17,105	40
2004	16,919	39
2005	17,590	40
2006	17,602	41

[1]Crashes are alcohol-related if either a driver or a pedestrian had a blood-alcohol content (BAC) of 0.01 or greater in a police-reported accident. All states use 0.08 as the definition of intoxication.

Source: U.S. Department of Transportation, National Highway Traffic Safety Administration.

PERSONS KILLED OR INJURED IN ALCOHOL-RELATED CRASHES BY PERSON TYPE AND INJURY SEVERITY, 2006

Person type	Persons killed[1]		Persons injured by injury severity[2]			
	Number	Percent of total	Incapacitating	Non-incapacitating	Other	Total injured
Vehicle occupants						
Driver	9,472	53.8%	26,671	61,121	94,219	182,010
Passenger	3,433	19.5	12,125	22,534	39,309	73,967
Unknown occupant	55	0.3	3	3	3	3
Total	12,960	73.6	38,796	83,654	133,527	255,977
Motorcycle riders	1,901	10.8	2,591	2,784	909	6,284
Nonmotorists						
Pedestrian	2,367	13.4	3,927	4,063	1,823	9,813
Pedalcyclist	302	1.7	724	1,738	1,259	3,721
Other/unknown	72	0.4	72	557	1,135	1,764
Total	2,741	15.6	4,723	6,358	4,216	15,298
Total	**17,602**	**100.0%**	**46,111**	**92,796**	**138,653**	**277,559**

[1]Blood-alcohol concentration (BAC) of 0.01 grams per deciliter or greater in the crash. NHTSA estimates alcohol involvement when alcohol test results are unknown.
[2]Police-reported alcohol involvement in the crash.
[3]Fewer than 500.
Source: U.S. Department of Transportation, National Highway Traffic Safety Administration.

MOTORCYCLE HELMET USE, 1994-2007[1]
(Percent)

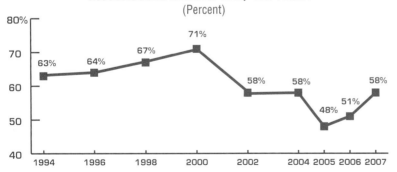

[1]Based on surveys of motorcyclists using helmets meeting Department of Transportation standards. Surveys conducted in October for 1994-2000 and in June thereafter.
Source: U.S. Department of Transportation, National Occupant Protection Use Survey, National Highway Traffic Safety Administration's National Center for Statistics and Analysis.

- The Department of Transportation estimates that motorcycle helmets are about 37 percent effective in preventing fatalities.

- In June 2007 helmet use was highest in the West, 77 percent, followed by the South and Northeast, 58 percent. Helmet use was lowest in the Midwest, 49 percent.

COLLISION LOSSES

The chart below shows the claim frequency, average loss payment per claim and average loss payment per insured vehicle year under collision coverage for recent model vehicles. The last item factors in both claim frequency and the average loss payment per claim. This combination is a measurement of both how often collision claims are filed and the magnitude of those claims.

The claim frequency is expressed as a rate per 100 insured vehicle years. A vehicle year is equal to 365 days of insurance coverage for a single vehicle.

COLLISION COVERAGE INSURANCE LOSSES IN YEARS SINCE INTRODUCTION, 2004-2006 MODEL YEAR PASSENGER VEHICLES

	2004	2005	2006	2004-2006
Claim frequency per 100 insured vehicle years				
Passenger cars and minivans	7.7	7.8	7.8	7.7
Pickups	5.5	5.6	5.7	5.6
Sport-utility vehicles	5.7	5.8	5.5	5.7
All passenger vehicles	6.7	6.9	6.9	6.8
Average loss payment per claim				
Passenger cars and minivans	$3,969	$4,029	$4,241	$4,013
Pickups	4,414	4,455	4,608	4,439
Sport-utility vehicles	4,010	3,902	3,842	3,966
All passenger vehicles	4,048	4,059	4,204	4,063
Average loss payment per insured vehicle year				
Passenger cars and minivans	$304	$315	$329	$310
Pickups	244	251	262	247
Sport-utility vehicles	228	225	213	226
All passenger vehicles	271	281	292	276

Source: Highway Loss Data Institute.

MOTOR VEHICLE THEFT

The FBI includes the theft or attempted theft of automobiles, trucks, buses, motorcycles, scooters, snowmobiles and other vehicles in its definition of motor vehicle theft.

MOTOR VEHICLE THEFT IN THE UNITED STATES, 1997-2006

Year	Vehicles stolen	Percent change
1997	1,354,189	-2.9%
1998	1,242,781	-8.2
1999	1,152,075	-7.3
2000	1,160,002	0.7
2001	1,228,391	5.9
2002	1,246,646	1.5
2003	1,261,226	1.2
2004	1,237,851	-1.9
2005	1,235,859	-0.2
2006	1,192,809	-3.5

Source: U.S. Department of Justice, Federal Bureau of Investigation, *Uniform Crime Reports.*

- A motor vehicle is stolen on average every 26 seconds in the U.S.

- The rate of motor vehicle theft was an estimated 398.4 per 100,000 people in 2006, a 4.4 percent decrease from 2005.

MOTOR VEHICLE THEFT IN CITIES

TOP TEN U.S. METROPOLITAN AREAS WITH HIGHEST MOTOR VEHICLE THEFT RATES, 2006

Rank	Metropolitan Statistical Area	Vehicles stolen	Rate[1]
1	Las Vegas/Paradise, NV	22,415	1,310.40
2	Stockton, CA	7,046	1,060.96
3	Visalia-Porterville, CA	4,238	1,031.46
4	Phoenix/Mesa/Scottsdale, AZ	39,535	1,022.88
5	Modesto, CA	5,081	1,005.13
6	Seattle/Tacoma/Bellevue, WA	31,231	974.96
7	Sacramento/Arden/Arcade/Roseville, CA	19,558	957.65
8	Fresno, CA	8,363	952.96
9	Yakima, WA	2,155	930.54
10	Tucson, AZ	8,508	920.00

[1]Ranked by the rate of vehicle thefts reported per 100,000 people based on the 2005 U.S. Census Population Estimates.

Source: National Insurance Crime Bureau.

- In 2006 all of the nation's top 10 metropolitan areas for vehicle theft were in the West, five of them in California, according to the National Insurance Crime Bureau.

TOP TEN STATES FOR VEHICLE THEFT, 2006

Rank	State	Vehicles stolen
1	California	242,693
2	Texas	95,429
3	Florida	76,437
4	Arizona	54,849
5	Michigan	50,017
6	Washington	45,899
7	Georgia	43,163
8	Illinois	37,641
9	Ohio	37,425
10	New York	32,134

Source: Natonal Insurance Crime Bureau.

TOP TEN MOST FREQUENTLY STOLEN PASSENGER VEHICLES, 2006

Rank	Model year	Make, model
1	1995	Honda Civic
2	1991	Honda Accord
3	1989	Toyota Camry
4	1997	Ford F150 Series
5	2005	Dodge Ram Pickup
6	1994	Chevrolet Full Size C/K 1500 Pickup
7	1994	Nissan Sentra
8	1994	Dodge Caravan
9	1994	Saturn SL
10	1990	Acura Integra

Source: National Insurance Crime Bureau.

RECREATIONAL BOATING

Federal law requires owners of recreational boats to register them. In 2006 there were 12.7 million registered boats, compared with 12.3 million in 1997 and 8.6 million in 1980. An accident occurring on a recreational boat must be reported to the Coast Guard if a person dies or is injured and requires medical treatment beyond first aid, if damage to the boat or other property exceeds $2,000, if the boat is lost, or if a person disappears from the boat. Out of the 4,967 accidents reported in 2006, 633 occurred in Florida, accounting for 13 percent of all incidents. Other states with high numbers of accidents were California (569), Arizona (209) and Texas (195).

Boating fatalities rose 1.9 percent from 2005 to 2006. The rate per 100,000 registered boats was 5.6, compared with 5.4 in 2005. Research has shown that alcohol, combined with typical boating conditions such as sun, wind, noise, vibration and motion, can impair a person much faster than alcohol consumption on land. Boat operators with a blood-alcohol content (BAC) above 0.10 percent are estimated to be more than 10 times as likely to be killed in a boating accident than boat operators with zero BAC.

RECREATIONAL BOATING ACCIDENTS, 2002-2006[1]

Year	Accidents		Fatalities			Property damage ($ millions)
	Total	Involving alcohol use[2]	Total	Involving alcohol use[2]	Injuries	
2002	5,705	357	750	145	4,062	$39
2003	5,438	362	703	129	3,888	40
2004	4,904	331	676	124	3,363	35
2005	4,969	402	697	157	3,451	39
2006	4,967	403	710	148	3,474	44

[1]Includes accidents involving $2,000 or more in property damage.
[2]The use of alcohol by a boat's occupants was a direct or indirect cause of the accident.
Source: U.S. Department of Transportation, U.S. Coast Guard.

- Alcohol use is the leading contributing factor in fatal boating accidents, accounting for nearly 20 percent of all reported fatalities in 2006.

- Two-thirds of all fatal boating accident victims drowned. 90 percent of the victims who drowned were not wearing life jackets.

- The most common types of boats involved in reported accidents were open motorboats (45 percent), personal watercraft (24 percent) and cabin motorboats (14 percent).

SPORTS PARTICIPATION AND INJURIES, UNITED STATES, 2006

Sport or activity	Participants	Injuries	Percent of injuries by age				
			0-4	5-14	15-24	25-64	65 and over
Archery	6,800,000[1]	3,180	0.0%	11.9%	26.6%	54.2%	7.3%
Baseball	14,600,000	163,834	2.6	49.2	27.8	19.6	0.8
Softball	12,400,000	111,094	0.3	24.5	32.6	41.8	0.8
Basketball	26,700,000	529,837	0.3	33.5	47.0	19.0	0.2
Bicycle riding[2]	35,600,000	480,299	5.7	44.0	17.4	29.5	3.3
Billiards, pool	31,800,000	4,722	9.0	22.5	17.0	48.3	2.8
Bowling	44,800,000	18,553	9.8	15.3	14.0	51.6	9.3
Boxing	NA	13,118	0.0	11.8	51.0	37.2	0.0
Cheerleading	3,800,000	25,966	0.1	45.0	52.7	2.3	0.0
Exercise	NA	197,406[3]	3.4	16.3	20.6	49.9	9.9
Fishing	40,600,000	73,206	2.8	18.5	13.3	56.5	8.9
Football	17,800,000[4,5]	460,210	0.2	47.8	41.9	10.1	0.1
Golf	24,400,000	37,891[6]	4.1	23.0	9.3	42.0	21.6
Gymnastics	NA	30,523[7]	4.1	67.6	22.0	6.2	0.0
Hockey: street, roller and field	NA	6,500[8]	0.0	28.1	62.0	9.9	0.0
Horseback riding	NA	70,915	1.4	21.7	20.5	52.2	4.2
Horseshoe pitching	NA	1,542	6.0	32.1	10.1	47.2	4.6
Ice hockey	2,600,000	21,825	0.3	37.5	48.8	13.4	0.0
Ice skating	NA	22,025[9]	0.9	48.3	21.5	28.1	1.2
Martial arts	4,700,000[4]	24,835	0.8	27.2	29.6	42.4	0.0
Mountain biking	8,500,000	10,135	0.9	8.9	25.9	63.0	1.4
Mountain climbing	NA	3,875	1.5	9.0	43.4	43.7	1.9
Racquetball, squash and paddleball	NA	6,702	0.2	4.6	18.7	69.5	6.7
Roller skating	NA	69,989[10]	0.6	59.0	13.3	26.4	0.7
Rugby	NA	10,589	0.0	4.1	77.2	18.8	0.0
Scuba diving	NA	1,963	0.0	4.1	6.9	89.0	0.0
Skateboarding	9,700,000	125,713	1.2	50.6	38.8	9.0	0.3

SPORTS PARTICIPATION AND INJURIES, UNITED STATES, 2006 (Cont'd)

Sport or activity	Participants	Injuries	Percent of injuries by age				
			0-4	5-14	15-24	25-64	65 and over
Snowboarding	5,200,000	50,660	0.0%	28.2%	54.6%	17.0%	0.1%
Snowmobiling	NA	7,293	0.0	8.7	38.2	49.2	3.9
Soccer	14,000,000	186,544	0.6	43.5	37.3	18.4	0.2
Swimming	56,500,000	178,412[11]	10.3	41.3	18.3	27.3	2.8
Tennis	10,400,000	22,425	0.6	15.4	22.1	48.1	13.8
Track and field	NA	20,459	0.3	44.7	50.5	4.2	0.3
Volleyball	11,100,000	57,387	0.1	28.0	41.9	28.9	1.0
Water skiing	6,300,000	9,928	0.1	8.4	39.2	52.3	0.0
Weight lifting	32,900,000	73,425	3.1	9.0	39.1	46.8	1.9
Wrestling	NA	36,943	0.0	35.2	59.6	5.0	0.2

[1]Data for 2005. [2]Excludes mountain biking. [3]Includes exercise equipment (407,708 injuries) and exercise activity (149,698 injuries). [4]Data for 2004. [5]Includes 9,600,000 in touch football and 8,200,000 in tackle football. [6]Excludes golf carts (13,411 injuries). [7]Excludes trampolines (109,522 injuries). [8]Includes field hockey (5,238 injuries) and roller hockey (1,262 injuries). Excludes 29,597 injuries in hockey, unspecified. [9]Excludes 11,394 injuries in skating, unspecified. [10]Includes roller skating (42,305 injuries) and in-line skating (27,684 injuries). [11]Includes injuries associated with swimming, swimming pools, pool slides, diving or diving boards and swimming pool equipment. NA=Data not available.

Source: National Safety Council.

ATV ACCIDENTS

An increasing number of children are being injured in accidents involving all-terrain vehicles (ATVs), open air vehicles with three, four or six wheels designed for off road use. Many states require ATV insurance for vehicles operated on state-owned land.

ATV-RELATED EMERGENCY ROOM-TREATED INJURIES, 2001-2005[1]

Year	Estimated number of injuries		Percent of total
	All ages	Younger than 16 years	Younger than 16 years
2001	110,100	34,300	31%
2002	113,900	37,100	33
2003	125,500	38,600	31
2004	136,100	44,700	33
2005	136,700	40,400	30

[1]ATVs with 3, 4 or unknown number of wheels.

Source: United States Consumer Product Safety Commission.

AVIATION LOSSES

UNITED STATES

- There were 1,603 civil aviation accidents in 2006, down from 1,779 in 2005. Total fatalities rose from 600 to 766.

- There were 50 fatalities on large scheduled commercial airlines in 2006, compared with 22 in 2005.

- There were no fatalities on large nonscheduled airlines (charter airlines) from 2004 to 2006.

- Small commuter airlines had three accidents in 2006, compared with six in 2005.

- Small on-demand airlines such as air taxis had 54 accidents in 2006, down from 66 in 2005. 16 people died in these accidents, compared with 18 in 2005.

- There were 1,515 general aviation accidents in 2006, the lowest number in 40 years. However, these accidents resulted in 698 deaths, compared with 562 deaths in 2005.

The National Transportation Safety Board compiles data on aviation flight hours, accidents and fatalities for commercial and general aviation.

Since 1997, commercial airlines have been divided into two categories according to the type of aircraft used: aircraft with 10 or more seats and aircraft with fewer than 10 seats. The nonscheduled commercial aircraft with more than 10 seats are also called charter airlines. Commercial airlines flying aircraft with fewer than 10 seats include commuter (scheduled) airlines, and on-demand air taxis. General aviation includes all U.S. noncommercial or privately owned aircraft.

In 2006, 744 million people flew on commercial airlines in the United States, compared with 739 million in 2005 and 665 million in 2000. The Federal Aviation Administration projected that 769 million people would fly on commercial airlines in the United States in 2007 and 1 billion would fly annually by 2015.

AIRCRAFT ACCIDENTS IN THE UNITED STATES, 2006[1]

	Flight hours (000)	Total accidents	Fatal accidents	Total fatalities[2]	Total accidents per 100,000 flight hours
Commercial airlines					
10 or more seats					
Scheduled	18,900	25	2	50	0.132
Nonscheduled	660	6	0	0	0.909
Less than 10 seats					
Commuter	280	3	1	2	1.071
On-demand	3,600	54	10	16	1.50
General aviation	22,800	1,515	303	698	6.64
Total civil aviation	**NA**	**1,603**	**316**	**766**	**NA**

[1]Preliminary data. Totals do not add because of collisions involving aircraft in different categories.
[2]Includes nonpassenger deaths.
NA=Data not available.

Source: National Transportation Safety Board.

U.S. LARGE AIRLINE ACCIDENTS, 1997-2006[1]

Year	Flight hours	Total accidents	Fatal accidents	Total fatalities[2]	Total accidents per 100,000 flight hours
1997	15,838,109	49	4	8	0.309
1998	16,816,555	50	1	1	0.297
1999	17,555,208	51	2	12	0.291
2000	18,299,257	56	3	92	0.306
2001	17,814,191	46[3]	6	531	0.236
2002	17,290,198	41	0	0	0.237
2003	17,476,700	54	2	22	0.309
2004	18,882,503	30	2	14	0.159
2005	19,390,029	40	3	22	0.206
2006[4]	19,560,000	31	2	50	0.158

[1]Scheduled and unscheduled planes with more than 10 seats.
[2]Includes nonpassenger deaths.
[3]Illegal acts, such as terrorism or sabotage, were responsible for accidents in this year. Accidents caused by such acts are not included in total accidents per 100,000 flight hours.
[4]Preliminary.

Source: National Transportation Safety Board.

WORLD AVIATION LOSSES

Worldwide passenger deaths in scheduled air services are compiled by the International Civil Aviation Organization, a United Nations agency with 185 member states.

WORLDWIDE SCHEDULED AIR SERVICE FATAL ACCIDENTS, 1997-2006

Year	Fatal aircraft accidents[1]	Passenger fatalities	Passenger fatalities per 100 million passenger kilometers	Year	Fatal aircraft accidents[1]	Passenger fatalities	Passenger fatalities per 100 million passenger kilometers
1997	25	921	0.04	2002	14	791	0.03
1998	20	904	0.03	2003	7	466	0.02
1999	21	499	0.02	2004	9	203	0.01
2000	18	757	0.03	2005	17	712	0.02
2001	13	577	0.02	2006	13	755	0.02

[1]Involving a passenger fatality only.

Source: International Civil Aviation Organization.

WORKPLACE LOSSES

According to the National Safety Council (NSC), the total cost of unintentional workplace deaths and injuries in 2005 was an estimated $160.4 billion. This figure includes wage and productivity losses of injured workers of $80.0 billion, medical costs of $31.3 billion and administrative expenses of $34.4 billion. Other employers' costs include the value of time lost by workers dealing with injured employees and the time required to investigate injuries and write up injury reports. These add another $10.7 billion. Also included are fire losses of $2.3 billion and $1.7 billion in motor vehicle damage. In general, economic losses from work injuries are not comparable from year to year; as additional or more precise data become available to the NSC, they are used from that year forward. Previously estimated figures are not revised.

WORKPLACE LOSSES AND DEATHS, 1998-2005

| Year | Workers[3] | Economic loss[1] ($ millions) | | Loss per worker (In 2005 dollars)[4] | Fatalities[2] | |
		Dollars when occurred	In 2005 dollars[4]		Number	Per 100,000 workers
1998	132,772	$125,100	$149,890	$1,129	5,117	3.9
1999	134,688	122,600	143,720	1,067	5,184	3.8
2000	136,402	131,200	148,800	1,091	5,022	3.7
2001	136,246	132,100	145,675	1,069	5,042	3.7
2002	137,731	146,600	159,149	1,156	4,726	3.4
2003	138,988	156,200	165,793	1,193	4,725	3.4
2004	140,504	142,200	142,018	1,046	4,999	3.6
2005	142,946	160,400	160,400	1,122	4,961	3.5

[1]Economic loss from unintentional injuries. These estimates are not comparable from year to year.
[2]From unintentional injuries.
[3]Age 16 and over, gainfully employed, including owners, managers and other paid employees, the self-employed, unpaid family workers and active duty resident military personnel.
[4]Adjusted to 2005 dollars by the Insurance Information Institute.

Source: National Safety Council; U.S. Department of Labor, Bureau of Labor Statistics, Census of Fatal Occupational Injuries; Insurance Information Institute.

OCCUPATIONAL DISEASE

According to the U.S. Department of Labor's Bureau of Labor Statistics, an occupational disease is any new abnormal condition or disorder, other than one resulting from an occupational injury, caused by exposure to factors associated with employment. Included are acute and chronic diseases which may be caused by inhalation, absorption, ingestion or direct contact in the workplace.

The overwhelming majority of reported new illnesses are those that directly relate to workplace activity (e.g., contact dermatitis or carpal tunnel syndrome) and are easy to identify. However, some conditions, such as long-term latent illnesses caused by exposure to carcinogens, often are difficult to relate to the workplace and may be understated.

ASBESTOS-RELATED ILLNESS

Exposure to asbestos can cause lung cancer and other respiratory diseases. The first asbestos-related lawsuit was filed in 1966. A large number of workers who may have physical signs of exposure but not a debilitating disease are filing claims now out of concern that if they later develop an illness, the company responsible may be bankrupt, due to other asbestos claims. It can take as long as 40 years after exposure for someone to be diagnosed with an asbestos-related illness.

ESTIMATED ASBESTOS LOSSES, 2000-2006
($ billions)

Year	Beginning reserve	Losses Incurred[1]	Paid	Ending reserve[2]
2000	$10.7	$1.5	$1.4	$10.8
2001	10.8	3.8	1.6	13.0
2002	12.6	7.6	2.0	18.2
2003	18.1	6.5	2.2	22.4
2004	22.4	4.3	3.3	23.4
2005	23.4	3.6	2.3	24.7
2006	24.7	1.6	2.6	23.7

- Incurred asbestos losses dropped to $1.6 billion in 2006, the lowest level since 2000 when they totaled $1.5 billion.

[1]Incurred losses are losses related to events that have occurred, regardless of whether or not the claims have been paid.
[2]Because of changes in the population of insurers reporting data each year, the beginning reserve may not equal the ending reserve of the prior year.

Source: ISO.

TOP TEN OCCUPATIONS WITH THE LARGEST NUMBER OF INJURIES AND ILLNESSES, 2005[1]
(000)

Occupation	Number	Percent of total
Laborers (nonconstruction)	92.2	7.5%
Truckdrivers, heavy	65.9	5.3
Nursing aides, orderlies	52.2	4.2
Construction laborers	39.3	3.2
Truckdrivers, light	32.7	2.6
Retail salespersons	32.3	2.6
Janitors and cleaners	31.4	2.5
Carpenters	31.3	2.5
Maintenance and repair workers (general)	23.2	1.9
Stock clerks and order fillers	23.1	1.9
Total, 10 occupations	423.6	34.3
All occupations	**1,234.7**	**100.0%**

[1]Nonfatal injuries and illnesses involving days off from work for private industries; excludes farms with less than 11 employees.
Source: U.S. Department of Labor, Bureau of Labor Statistics.

CAUSES OF WORKPLACE DEATHS

According to the U.S. Department of Labor, the most dangerous occupations in 2006 were fishing workers, with 141.7 deaths per 100,000 employees, followed by aircraft pilots and flight engineers, logging workers, iron and steel workers and waste collectors. The all-industry average was 3.9 deaths per 100,000 workers.

WORKPLACE DEATHS BY CAUSE, 2001-2006[1]

Cause	2001-2005 average	2005	2006 Number	2006 Percent of total
All transportation (includes vehicle crashes)	2,451	2,493	2,413	42%
Vehicle crashes	1,394	1,437	1,329	23
Contact with objects and equipment	952	1,005	983	17
Assaults and violence (includes homicides)	850	792	754	13
Homicides	602	567	516	9
Falls	763	770	809	14
Exposure to harmful substances or environments	498	501	525	9
Fires and explosions	174	159	201	4
Total workplace fatalities	**5,704**	**5,734**	**5,703**	**100%**

[1]From intentional and unintentional sources.
Source: U.S. Department of Labor, Bureau of Labor Statistics, Census of Fatal Occupational Injuries.

DEATH RATES

U.S. DEATH RATES FROM MAJOR CAUSES, 2004

Cause of death	Number of deaths	Percent of deaths	Age-adjusted rate[1] per 100,000 population
Heart disease	652,486	27.2%	217.0
Cancers	553,888	23.1	185.8
Strokes	150,074	6.3	50.0
Respiratory disease	121,987	5.1	41.1
Accidents	112,012	4.7	37.7
Diabetes	73,138	3.1	24.5
Alzheimer's disease	65,965	2.8	21.8
Influenza/pneumonia	59,664	2.5	19.8
Kidney disease	42,480	1.8	14.2
Septicemia	33,373	1.4	11.2
Suicide	32,439	1.4	10.9
Chronic liver disease	27,013	1.1	9.0
Hypertension[2]	23,076	1.0	7.7
Parkinson's disease	17,989	0.8	6.1
Homicide	17,357	0.7	5.9
All other causes	414,674	17.3	NA
All deaths	**2,397,615**	**100.0%**	**800.8**

[1] Factors out differences based on age.
[2] Essential (primary) hypertension and hypertensive renal disease.
NA=Not applicable.

Source: National Center for Health Statistics.

ODDS OF DYING, BY SPECIFIC TYPES OF ACCIDENTS

The chart below shows the likelihood, or odds, of dying as a result of a specific type of accident. The odds of dying over a one-year period are based on the U.S. population as a whole, not on participants in any particular activity or on how dangerous that activity may be. For example, more people are killed in auto accidents than in motorcycle accidents or airplane crashes, not because riding a motorcycle or traveling in an airplane is more or less dangerous, but because far more people travel by car. To arrive at lifetime odds, one-year odds were factored in with the average life expectancy of 77.9 years for a person born in the United States in 2004.

- The odds of dying from an injury in 2004 were 1 in 1,756 according to the latest data available.

- The lifetime odds of dying from an injury for a person born in 2004 were 1 in 23.

ODDS OF DEATH IN THE UNITED STATES BY CAUSE OF INJURY, 2004[1]

Cause of death	Deaths	One-year odds	Lifetime odds
Motor vehicle accidents	44,933	6,535	84
Assault by firearm	11,624	25,263	324
Motorcycle riding	4,018	73,085	938
Exposure to smoke, fire and flames	3,229	90,944	1,167
Fall on and from stairs and steps	1,638	179,278	2,301
Air and space transport accidents	679	432,484	5,552
Firearms discharge	649	452,476	5,808
Drowning and submersion while in or falling into swimming pool	625	469,851	6,031
Fall on and from ladder or scaffolding	392	749,125	9,616
Cataclysmic storm[2]	63	4,661,220	59,836
Lightning	46	6,383,844	81,949
Earthquake and other earth movements	30	9,788,561	125,655
Bitten or struck by dog	27	10,876,179	139,617
Flood	22	13,348,038	171,348

[1]Ranked by deaths in 2004.

[2]Includes hurricanes, tornadoes, blizzards, dust storms and other cataclysmic storms.

Source: National Center for Health Statistics; National Safety Council.

The Bureau of Labor Statistics' Consumer Expenditures Survey describes the buying habits of American consumers using household expenditure records and surveys. Expenditures include goods and services purchased, whether or not payment was made at the time of purchase, and all sales and excise taxes.

Income, age of family members, geographic location, taste and personal preference influence expenditures. Location often affects the cost of auto and homeowners insurance. Rural households spend less than urban households on auto insurance; regional variations in residential building costs affect spending on homeowners insurance. In addition to the number and type of cars, where they are driven and by whom, auto insurance prices are influenced by such factors as how rates are set (by the state or in a competitive market) and how claimants are compensated (through the no-fault or traditional tort systems).

INSURANCE AND OTHER CONSUMER EXPENDITURES AS A PERCENT OF TOTAL HOUSEHOLD SPENDING, 1990-2006[1]

	1990	1995	2000	2002	2004	2005	2006
Housing	30.0%	31.7%	31.7%	31.9%	31.3%	31.9%	33.1%
Transportation	15.9	16.4	17.5	16.9	15.8	16.0	15.7
Food	15.0	14.0	13.6	13.2	13.3	12.8	12.6
Other	10.6	10.2	10.5	10.3	10.3	10.4	10.6
Retirement[2]	8.8	8.0	7.8	8.6	10.2	10.4	10.2
Total insurance	5.8	6.8	6.3	6.8	6.9	6.5	6.3
Health	2.0	2.7	2.6	2.9	3.1	2.9	3.0
Vehicle	2.0	2.2	2.0	2.2	2.2	2.0	1.8
Life	1.2	1.1	1.0	1.0	0.9	0.8	0.7
Homeowners	0.5	0.7	0.7	0.7	0.8	0.7	0.8
Other	0.1	0.1	0.1	[3]	[3]	0.1	[3]
Entertainment	5.0	5.0	4.9	5.1	5.1	5.1	4.9
Clothing	5.7	5.3	4.9	4.3	4.2	4.1	3.9
Health care	3.1	2.7	2.8	2.9	2.9	2.8	2.7

[1]Ranked by 2006 data.
[2]Mostly payroll deductions for retirement purposes such as Social Security (77%) and private pension plans (14%) and nonpayroll deposits such as IRAs (9%) in 2006.
[3]Less than 0.1 percent.
Note: Percentages may not add due to rounding.

Source: U.S. Department of Labor, Bureau of Labor Statistics.

- Insurance accounted for 6.3 percent of household spending in 2006, down 0.2 percentage points from 2005. Retirement expenditures fell from 10.4 percent of household spending to 10.2 percent during the same period.

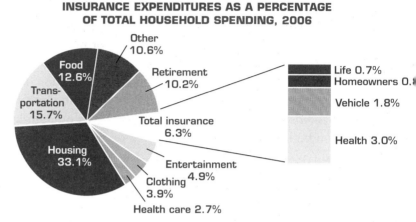

INSURANCE EXPENDITURES AS A PERCENTAGE OF TOTAL HOUSEHOLD SPENDING, 2006

Other 10.6%
Food 12.6%
Retirement 10.2%
Transportation 15.7%
Total insurance 6.3%
Housing 33.1%
Entertainment 4.9%
Clothing 3.9%
Health care 2.7%

Life 0.7%
Homeowners 0.8
Vehicle 1.8%
Health 3.0%

Source: U.S. Department of Labor, Bureau of Labor Statistics.

CONSUMER PRICES

The Bureau of Labor Statistics collects the prices of a fixed "basket" of consumer goods and services every month to compile the consumer price index. The price of all types of insurance is heavily influenced by the cost of goods and services paid by insurers to meet claims.

CONSUMER PRICE INDICES FOR INSURANCE AND RELATED ITEMS AND ANNUAL RATES OF CHANGE, 1997-2006
(Base: 1982-84=100)

Year	Cost of living (all items) Index	Percent change	Motor vehicle insurance Index	Percent change	Medical care items Index	Percent change	Physicians' services Index	Percent change	Hospital services[1] Index	Percent change
1997	160.5	2.3%	251.6	3.2%	234.6	2.8%	222.9	3.0%	101.7	NA
1998	163.0	1.6	254.3	1.1	242.1	3.2	229.5	3.0	105.0	3.2%
1999	166.6	2.2	253.8	-0.2	250.6	3.5	236.0	2.8	109.3	4.1
2000	172.2	3.4	256.7	1.1	260.8	4.1	244.7	3.7	115.9	6.0
2001	177.1	2.8	268.1	4.4	272.8	4.6	253.6	3.6	123.6	6.6
2002	179.9	1.6	291.6	8.8	285.6	4.7	260.6	2.8	134.7	9.0
2003	184.0	2.3	314.4	7.8	297.1	4.0	267.7	2.7	144.7	7.4
2004	188.9	2.7	323.2	2.8	310.1	4.4	278.3	4.0	153.4	6.0
2005	195.3	3.4	329.9	2.1	323.2	4.2	287.5	3.3	161.6	5.3
2006	201.6	3.2	331.8	0.6	336.2	4.0	291.9	1.5	172.1	6.5
Percent change 1997-2006		**25.6**		**31.9**		**43.3**		**31.0**		**69.2**

CONSUMER PRICE INDICES FOR INSURANCE AND
RELATED ITEMS AND ANNUAL RATES OF CHANGE, 1997-2006 (Cont'd)
(Base: 1982-84=100)

Year	Motor vehicle body work Index	Percent change	New vehicles Index	Percent change	New cars Index	Percent change	New trucks[2] Index	Percent change	Used cars and trucks Index	Percent change
1997	172.9	4.2%	144.3	0.4%	141.7	0.2%	151.4	1.3%	151.1	-3.8%
1998	179.5	3.8	143.4	-0.6	140.7	-0.7	151.1	-0.2	150.6	-0.3
1999	182.2	1.5	142.9	-0.3	139.6	-0.8	152.0	0.6	152.0	0.9
2000	187.8	3.1	142.8	-0.1	139.6	0.0	151.7	-0.2	155.8	2.5
2001	194.9	3.8	142.1	-0.5	138.9	-0.5	150.7	-0.7	158.7	1.9
2002	199.6	2.4	140.0	-1.5	137.3	-1.2	147.8	-1.9	152.0	-4.2
2003	202.9	1.7	137.9	-1.5	134.7	-1.9	146.1	-1.2	142.9	-6.0
2004	208.2	2.6	137.1	-0.6	133.9	-0.6	145.0	-0.8	133.3	-6.7
2005	215.0	3.3	137.9	0.6	135.2	1.0	145.3	0.2	139.4	4.6
2006	224.8	4.6	137.6	-0.2	136.4	0.9	142.9	-1.7	140.0	0.4
Percent change 1997-2006		**30.0**		**-4.6**		**-3.7**		**-5.6**		**-7.3**

Year	Tenants and household insurance[3] Index	Percent change	Repair of household items[3] Index	Percent change	Legal services Index	Percent change	Existing single-family homes Median price	Percent change
1997	NA	NA	NA	NA	163.8	4.3%	$126,000	5.1%
1998	99.8	NA	101.8	NA	171.7	4.8	132,800	5.4
1999	101.3	1.5%	107.2	5.3%	180.0	4.8	138,000	3.9
2000	103.7	2.4	111.6	4.1	189.3	5.2	143,600	4.1
2001	106.2	2.4	119.4	7.0	199.5	5.4	153,100	6.6
2002	108.7	2.4	125.1	4.8	211.1	5.8	165,000	7.8
2003	114.8	5.6	131.0	4.7	221.7	5.0	178,800	8.4
2004	116.2	1.2	139.4	6.4	232.3	4.8	195,400	9.3
2005	117.6	1.2	147.4	5.7	241.8	4.1	219,600	12.4
2006	116.5	-0.9	154.7	5.0	250.0	3.4	221,900	1.0
Percent change 1997-2006		**16.7[4]**		**52.0[4]**		**52.6**		**76.1**

[1]December 1996=100. [2]December 1983=100. [3]December 1997=100. [4]1998-2006
NA=Data not available.

Source: U.S. Department of Labor, Bureau of Labor Statistics; National Association of Realtors.

FRAUD

- The Insurance Information Institute estimates that fraud accounts for 10 percent of the property/casualty insurance industry's incurred losses and loss adjustment expenses, or about $30 billion a year.

Insurance fraud is a deliberate deception perpetrated against or by an insurance company or agent for the purpose of financial gain. Fraud may be committed at different points in the insurance transaction by applicants for insurance, policyholders, third-party claimants or professionals who provide services to claimants. Insurance agents and company employees may also commit insurance fraud. Common frauds include "padding," or inflating actual claims, misrepresenting facts on an insurance application, submitting claims for injuries or damage that never occurred, and "staging" accidents.

Insurance fraud may be classified as "hard" or "soft." Hard fraud is a deliberate attempt either to stage or invent an accident, injury, theft, arson or other type of loss that would be covered under an insurance policy.

Soft fraud, which is sometimes called opportunity fraud, occurs when a policyholder or claimant exaggerates a legitimate claim. A car owner involved in a "fender bender" who pads the claim to cover the policy deductible is committing soft fraud. Another example is exaggerating the number and value of items stolen from a home or business. Soft fraud may also occur when people purposely provide false information to influence the underwriting process in their favor when applying for insurance. To lower insurance premiums or increase the likelihood that the application for insurance will be accepted, people may underreport the number of miles driven, misrepresent where a car is garaged, fail to provide an accurate medical history when applying for health insurance, or falsify the number of employees and the nature of their work for workers compensation coverage.

About 40 states have set up fraud bureaus. Some bureaus have limited powers, and some states have more than one bureau to address fraud in different lines of insurance.

KEY STATE LAWS AGAINST INSURANCE FRAUD

State	Insurance fraud classified as a crime	Immunity statutes	Fraud bureau	Mandatory insurer fraud plan	Mandatory auto photo inspection
Alabama	X[1]	X[2]			
Alaska	X	X	X		
Arizona	X	X	X		
Arkansas	X	X	X	X	
California	X	X	X	X	
Colorado	X	X	X	X	
Connecticut	X	X	X[1,3]		
Delaware	X	X	X		
D.C.	X	X	X	X	
Florida	X	X	X	X	X
Georgia	X	X	X		
Hawaii	X[4]	X[5]	X[5]		
Idaho	X	X	X		
Illinois	X	X			
Indiana	X	X			
Iowa	X	X	X		
Kansas	X	X	X	X	
Kentucky	X	X	X	X	
Louisiana	X	X	X		
Maine	X	X		X	
Maryland	X	X	X	X	
Massachusetts	X	X	X		X
Michigan	X	X			
Minnesota	X	X	X	X	
Mississippi	X	X[2]	X[3]		
Missouri	X	X	X		
Montana	X	X	X[1,3]		
Nebraska	X	X	X		
Nevada	X	X	X[3]		
New Hampshire	X	X	X	X	
New Jersey	X	X	X	X	X

- Immunity statutes protect the person or insurance company that reports insurance fraud from criminal and civil prosecution.

- Fraud bureaus are state law enforcement agencies, mostly set up in the department of insurance, where investigators review fraud reports and begin the prosecution process.

(table continues)

KEY STATE LAWS AGAINST INSURANCE FRAUD (Cont'd)

- Mandatory insurer fraud plans require companies to formulate a program for fighting fraud and sometimes to establish special investigation units to identify fraud patterns.

State	Insurance fraud classified as a crime	Immunity statutes	Fraud bureau	Mandatory insurer fraud plan	Mandatory auto photo inspection
New Mexico	X	X	X	X	
New York	X	X	X	X	X
North Carolina	X	X	X		
North Dakota	X	X	X		
Ohio	X	X	X	X	
Oklahoma	X	X	X		
Oregon		X			
Pennsylvania	X	X	X	X	
Rhode Island	X	X[1]	X[1,6]		X
South Carolina	X	X	X[3]		
South Dakota	X	X	X		
Tennessee	X	X	X	X	
Texas	X	X	X	X	
Utah	X	X	X		
Vermont	X[1]	X			
Virginia		X	X[7]		
Washington	X	X	X[1,6]	X	
West Virginia	X	X	X		
Wisconsin	X	X			
Wyoming	X	X[2]			

[1]Workers compensation insurance only. [2]Arson only. [3]Fraud bureau set up in the state Attorney General's office. [4]Auto insurance and workers compensation fraud only. [5]Auto insurance only. [6]Fraud bureau set up in the state Department of Labor. [7]Fraud bureau set up in the state police office.

Source: Coalition Against Insurance Fraud, Property Casualty Insurers Association of America.

LITIGIOUSNESS

INSURERS' LEGAL DEFENSE COSTS

Lawsuits against businesses affect the cost of insurance and the products and services of the industries sued. According to Tillinghast, an actuarial consulting firm, the American civil liability (tort) system cost $260.8 billion in 2005, up slightly from $259.7 billion the previous year. Most lawsuits are settled out of court. Of those that are tried and proceed to verdict, Jury Verdict Research data show that in 2005 the median, or midpoint, plaintiff award in personal injury cases was $45,000, about the same as the previous year but considerably higher than the $32,000 level in 2002.

Insurers are required to defend their policyholders against lawsuits. The costs of settling a claim are reported on insurers' financial statements as "defense and cost containment expenses incurred." These expenses includes defense, litigation and medical cost containment. Expenditures for surveillance, litigation management and fees for appraisers, private investigators, hearing representatives and fraud investigators are included. In addition, attorney legal fees may be incurred owing to a duty to defend, even when coverage does not exist, because attorneys must be hired to issue opinions about coverage. Insurers' defense costs as a percentage of incurred losses are going up significantly in some lines, such as products liability. There are many possible reasons for this: cases are becoming more complex; insurers are spending more money to defend individual cases; and the cost of defending certain types of lawsuits, such as asbestos cases, may be increasing.

DEFENSE COSTS AND COST CONTAINMENT EXPENSES AS A PERCENT OF INCURRED LOSSES, 2004-2006[1]
($000)

	2004		2005		2006	
	Amount	As a percent of incurred losses	Amount	As a percent of incurred losses	Amount	As a percent of incurred losses
Products liability	$1,347,178	53.8%	$1,427,045	70.0%	$ 876,030	134.5%
Medical malpractice	2,214,495	40.5	2,427,241	48.0	2,438,039	56.6
Commercial multiple peril[2]	2,232,547	39.7	2,198,205	42.2	2,322,743	36.7
General liability[3]	5,891,398	22.6	6,970,797	28.3	5,727,225	27.1
Workers compensation	2,459,706	10.0	2,735,166	11.1	2,734,225	11.0
Commercial auto liability	1,220,868	11.3	1,039,773	10.0	1,062,935	10.1
Private passenger auto liability	4,263,149	7.6	3,775,160	6.6	3,716,987	6.6
All liability lines	$19,629,341	14.9%	$20,573,387	15.9%	$18,878,184	15.3%

[1]Net of reinsurance, excluding state funds.
[2]Liability portion only.
[3]Excludes products liability.

Source: National Association of Insurance Commissioners (NAIC) Annual Statement Database, via Highline Data, LLC. Copyrighted information. No portion of this work may be copied or redistributed without the express written permission of Highline Data, LLC.

COST OF U.S. TORT SYSTEM, 1990-2005
($ billions)

Source: Tillinghast-Towers Perrin.

- U.S. tort costs grew by 0.5 percent in 2005, the smallest increase in tort costs since 1997.

- Tort costs amounted to $880 per person in 2005. This compares with $12 per person in 1950.

- Over the 10-year period, 1996-2005, tort costs grew 68.8 percent.

- Tort costs accounted for 2.09 percent of gross domestic product (GDP) in 2005.

GROWTH OF TORT COSTS, 1951-2005
(Percent)

Years	Average annual increase in tort system costs
1951-1960	11.6%
1961-1970	9.8
1971-1980	11.9
1981-1990	11.8
1991-2000	3.2
2001	14.7
2002	13.4
2003	5.5
2004	5.7
2005	0.5
55 years (1950-2005)	9.5%

Source: Tillinghast-Towers Perrin.

COST OF CLAIMS AND LIABILITY LIMITS

Litigiousness is not only pushing up the cost of insurance but also the amount of insurance that businesses must buy to protect themselves against lawsuits, potentially driving up the price of goods and services for all consumers.

Each year the broker Marsh reviews the excess liability insurance buying decisions of more than 7,000 organizations worldwide, including some 2,900 U.S. companies. Excess liability insurance, also known as excess-casualty insurance, increases the liability protection provided by a company's liability insurance. It is designed to provide protection from infrequent catastrophic accidents or occurrences. The following chart indicates the percentage of U.S. firms experiencing a loss of $5 million or more. Those that experienced such a loss tended to purchase much higher limits of liability coverage.

U.S. FIRMS EXPERIENCING A LOSS OF $5 MILLION OR MORE, 2002-2006[1]

(Percent)

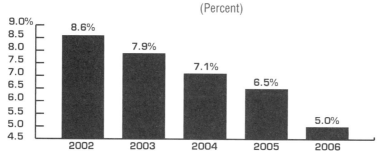

[1]Loss experience in the past 5 years.

Source: 2006 Limits of Liability Report, © Marsh Inc. 2006.

U.S. AVERAGE EXCESS LIABILITY LIMITS RELATIVE TO LOSS EXPERIENCE, 2002-2006

(Average limits purchased, $ millions)

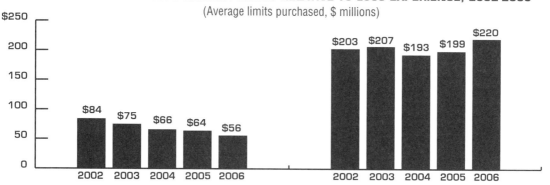

Firms *not* experiencing $5 million+ loss[1]   Firms experiencing $5 million+ loss[1]

[1]Loss experience in the past 5 years.

Source: 2006 Limits of Liability Report, © Marsh Inc. 2006.

- Policyholders reduced their cost of casualty risk by 3 percent in 2005, according to a Marsh survey of over 1,600 businesses.

CASUALTY COST OF RISK PER $1,000 OF REVENUE, 2004-2005

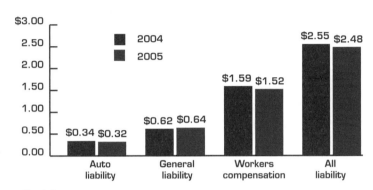

Source: Marsh Inc.

MEDIAN[1] AND AVERAGE PERSONAL INJURY JURY AWARDS, 1999 AND 2005
($000)

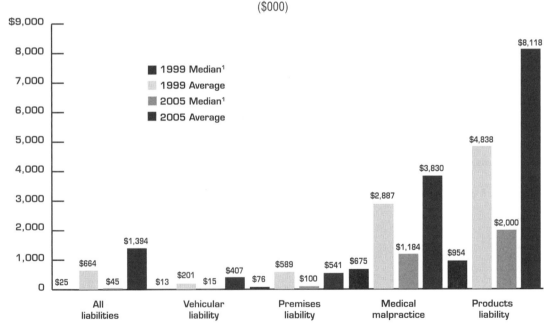

[1]Represents the midpoint jury award. Half of awards are above the median and half are below.

Source: Reprinted with permission from *Current Award Trends in Personal Injury*. Copyright 2007 by LRP Publications, 747 Dresher Road, P.O. Box 980, Horsham, PA 19044-0980. All rights reserved.

DIRECTORS AND OFFICERS LIABILITY INSURANCE

Directors and officers liability insurance (D&O) covers directors and officers of a company for negligent acts or omissions and for misleading statements that result in suits against the company. There are various forms of D&O coverage. Corporate reimbursement coverage indemnifies directors and officers of the organization. Side-A coverage provides D&O coverage for personal liability when directors and officers are not indemnified by the firm. Entity coverage for claims made specifically against the company is also available. D&O policies may be broadened to include coverage for employment practices liability (EPL). EPL coverage may also be purchased as a stand-alone policy.

A survey of 2,875 U.S. corporations by the Tillinghast unit of Towers Perrin shows that the D&O premium index, a measure of insurance costs, dropped 18 percent in 2006, after dropping 9 percent in 2005 and 10 percent in 2004. Claims susceptibility, the percentage of participants who reported one or more claims in a ten-year period, was 14 percent in 2006, a 2 percent drop from the previous year. Public companies showed significantly higher claim susceptibility, with 31 percent reporting at least one claim, compared with private companies (9 percent) and nonprofit organizations (4 percent). The average closed claim fell from $4.8 million in 2005 to $4.3 million in 2006.

DIRECTORS AND OFFICERS LIABILITY CLAIMS BY TYPE OF CLAIMANT IN THE UNITED STATES, 1996-2006

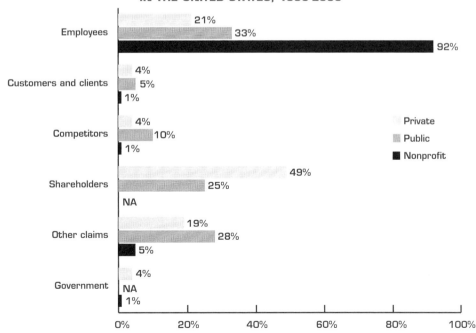

NA=Not applicable.
Source: 2006 Directors and Officers Liability Survey, Tillinghast-Towers Perrin.

- The overall average policy limit for U.S. participants in the 2006 Tillinghast D&O survey ranged from $34 million for public companies to $3 million for nonprofits. The average was $11.55 million.

- AIG was the leading D&O insurer in premium volume in the 2006 survey, with a 37 percent market share, followed by Chubb and XL with 22 percent and 6.6 percent shares, respectively. Chubb led in policy count, with 22 percent of the market. ACE was second with a 16.6 percent share followed by AIG with 16.3 percent.

DIRECTORS AND OFFICERS LIABILITY CLAIM INCIDENCE BY BUSINESS CLASS, 1996-2006

Business class	Susceptibility[1]	Frequency[2]
Banking	26%	0.74
Biotechnology and pharmaceuticals	11	0.15
Durable goods	22	0.33
Education	25	0.46
Governmental and other nonprofit	2	0.03
Health services	30	14.66
Merchandising	21	0.39
Nonbanking financial services	17	0.42
Nondurable goods	15	0.25
Personal and business services	18	0.32
Petroleum, mining, agriculture	15	0.30
Real estate, construction	10	0.19
Technology	16	0.24
Transportation and communications	22	0.33
Utilities	35	0.71
Other	0	0.00
All business classes	**14%**	**0.45**

[1]Percentage of participants that reported one or more claims over the 10-year experience period, 1996-2006.

[2]Average number of claims per participant over the 10-year experience period. A claim frequency of 0.25 indicates that 100 entities reported a total of 25 claims over the 10-year period.

Source: 2006 Directors and Officers Liability Survey, Tillinghast-Towers Perrin.

DIRECTORS AND OFFICERS LIABILITY CLAIM TRENDS BY OWNERSHIP, 2004-2006

	Susceptibility[1]			Frequency[2]		
	2004	2005	2006	2004	2005	2006
Public	27%	35%	31%	0.559	0.618	0.569
Private	8	10	9	0.124	0.178	0.141
Nonprofit	5	6	4	1.342	1.532	1.160

[1]Percentage of participants that reported one or more claims over the 10-year experience period, 1996-2006.

[2]Average number of claims per participant over the 10-year experience period. A claim frequency of 0.25 indicates that 100 entities reported a total of 25 claims over the 10-year period.

Source: 2006 Directors and Officers Liability Survey, Tillinghast-Towers Perrin.

DIRECTORS AND OFFICERS CLAIMANT DISTRIBUTION, 1996-2006[1]

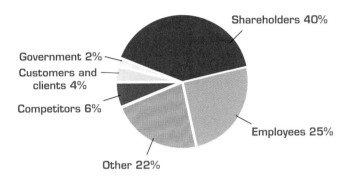

Shareholders 40%

Government 2%

Customers and clients 4%

Competitors 6%

Employees 25%

Other 22%

[1]Claims against for-profit companies.
Source: 2006 Directors and Officers Liability Survey, Tillinghast-Towers Perrin.

EMPLOYMENT PRACTICES LIABILITY

Employment practices are a frequent source of claims against directors, officers and their organizations. Organizations that purchase insurance for employment practices liability (EPL) claims typically either buy a stand-alone EPL insurance policy or endorse their D&O policy to cover employment practices liability.

In the 2006 Tillinghast D&O survey, 91 percent of participants purchased EPL coverage, up from 79 percent in 2005. Thirty-six percent of participants purchased stand-alone EPL coverage, up from 14 percent in 2005. Fifty-five percent purchased EPL insurance with their D&O policy, down from 65 percent in 2005.

TRENDS IN EMPLOYMENT PRACTICES LIABILITY, 1996-2005

Year	Median (midpoint) award	Probability range[1]
1996	$128,000	$40,350–400,000
1997	133,691	45,412–376,046
1998	164,200	43,125–400,000
1999	150,000	50,000–463,919
2000	169,813	50,000–500,000
2001	145,777	43,387-450,125
2002	200,000	56,884-500,000
2003	161,000	49,649-514,130
2004	199,000	57,000-505,224
2005	276,711	90,532-658,000

[1]The middle 50 percent of all awards arranged in ascending order in a sampling, 25 percent above and below the median award.

Source: Reprinted with permission from *Employment Practice Liability*. Copyright 2006 by LRP Publications, 747 Dresher Road, P.O. Box 980, Horsham, PA 19044-0980. All rights reserved.

SHAREHOLDER LAWSUITS

Cornerstone Research has conducted annual studies of securities litigation each year since the passage of the 1995 Private Securities Litigation Reform Act, enacted to curb frivolous shareholder lawsuits. In 2006 the total value of cases settled in securities class-action settlements soared to $17.2 billion, nearly double the previous record of $9.4 billion set in 2005. The increase was largely due to five settlements in excess of $1 billion, including a $6.6 billion partial settlement in the Enron Corporation case that bought the total Enron settlement to $7.1 billion. The average settlement increased almost five-fold in 2006, reflecting an increase in the average settlement size, rather than an increase in the number of cases settled. (The number of cases actually fell from 723 in 2005 to 93 in 2006.) Even without the 5 megasettlements, the average settlement in 2006 was $45 million, an all-time high and more than twice the average for all post-Reform Act settlements through 2005. By contrast, the median, or midpoint, settlement was $7.0 million in 2006, on par with the $6.7 million median for all post-Reform Act settlements through 2005.

POST-REFORM ACT SETTLEMENTS OF SECURITIES LAWSUITS, 1996-2006[1]

	1996-2005	2006
Minimum	$0.1 million	$0.3 million
Median	6.7 million	7.0 million
Average	22.6 million	106.6 million
Maximum	0.6 billion	2.7 billion
Total amount	**16.5 billion**	**10.0 billion**

[1]Private Securities Litigation Reform Act of 1995; adjusted for inflation.
Note: Statistics for settlements exclude the Enron Corporation settlement totaling $7.1 billion as of year-end 2006, the WorldCom, Inc. settlement totaling $6.2 billion as of year-end 2005 and the Cendant Corporation settlement of $3.1 billion in 2000. Including these cases, the average and total values are $180.6 million and $17.2 billion, respectively, for 2006 and $36.2 million and $26.5 billion, respectively, for all post-Reform Act cases through 2005.

Source: Cornerstone Research.

Capital
Shareholder's equity (for publicly traded insurance companies) and retained earnings (for mutual insurance companies). There is no general measure of capital adequacy for property/casualty insurers. Capital adequacy is linked to the riskiness of an insurer's business. A company underwriting medical device manufacturers needs a larger cushion of capital than a company writing Main Street business, for example.

Combined ratio
Percentage of each premium dollar a property/casualty insurer spends on claims and expenses. A decrease in the combined ratio means financial results are improving; an increase means they are deteriorating.

Direct premiums
Property/casualty premiums collected by the insurer from policyholders, before reinsurance premiums are deducted. Insurers share some direct premiums and the risk involved with their reinsurers.

Dividend
Money returned to policyholders from an insurance company's earnings. Considered a partial premium refund rather than a taxable distribution, reflecting the difference between the premium charged and actual losses. Many life insurance policies and some property/casualty policies pay dividends to their owners. Life insurance policies that pay dividends are called participating policies.

Earned premium
The portion of premium that applies to the expired part of the policy period. Insurance premiums are payable in advance but the insurance company does not fully earn them until the policy period expires.

Expense ratio
Percentage of each premium dollar that goes to insurers' expenses including overhead, marketing and commissions.

Generally accepted accounting principles/GAAP
Generally accepted accounting principles (GAAP) accounting is used in financial statements that publicly held companies prepare for the Securities and Exchange Commission.

Incurred losses
Losses occurring within a fixed period, whether or not adjusted or paid during the same period.

Lloyds
Corporation formed to market services of a group of underwriters. Does not issue insurance policies or provide insurance protection. Insurance is written by individual underwriters, with each assuming a part of every risk. Has no connection to Lloyd's of London, and is found primarily in Texas.

Loss adjustment expenses
The sum insurers pay for investigating and settling insurance claims, including the cost of defending a lawsuit in court.

Loss ratio
Percentage of each premium dollar an insurer spends on claims.

Mutual insurance company
A company owned by its policyholders that returns part of its profits to the policyholders as dividends. The insurer uses the rest as a surplus cushion in case of large and unexpected losses.

Net premiums written
Premiums written after reinsurance transactions.

Policyholders' surplus
The amount of money remaining after an insurer's liabilities are subtracted from its assets. It acts as a financial cushion above and beyond reserves, protecting policyholders against an unexpected or catastrophic situation.

Reciprocal exchange

Unincorporated association organized to write insurance for its members, each of whom assumes a share of the risks covered.

Statutory accounting principles/SAP

More conservative standards than under GAAP accounting rules, they are imposed by state laws that emphasize the present solvency of insurance companies. SAP helps ensure that the company will have sufficient funds readily available to meet all anticipated insurance obligations by recognizing liabilities earlier or at a higher value than GAAP and assets later or at a lower value. For example, SAP requires that selling expenses be recorded immediately rather than amortized over the life of the policy.

Stock insurance company

An insurance company owned by its stockholders who share in profits through earnings distributions and increases in stock value.

Underwriting income

The insurer's profit on the insurance sale after all expenses and losses have been paid. When premiums aren't sufficient to cover claims and expenses, the result is an underwriting loss. Underwriting losses are typically offset by investment income.

Note: An expanded glossary is available on the I.I.I. Web site at www.iii.org/media/glossary/

PUBLICATIONS

In addition to the Insurance Fact Book, the Insurance Information Institute produces a number of online and print publications. To order, call 212-346-5500, email publications@iii.org or order online at www.iii.org

Insurance Handbook For Reporters

A journalist's guide to the insurance industry, providing concise explanations of auto, home, life, disability and business insurance. Features include a comprehensive glossary, listings of hundreds of insurance organizations and a guide to insurance industry resources.

Online version available at www.iii.org/media/research/insurancehandbook

The Financial Services Fact Book

Unique and comprehensive guide with more than 350 graphs and charts on insurance, banking, securities and on financial services as a whole. Published jointly with The Financial Services Roundtable.

Online version available at www.financialservicesfacts.org

A Firm Foundation: How Insurance Supports The Economy

Shows the myriad ways in which insurance provides economic support—from offering employment and fueling the capital markets, to providing financial security and income to individuals and local businesses through the payment of claims. The resource includes a wide array of charts and tables. The online version has a special tool that generates state specific compilations.

Online version available at www.economicinsurancefacts.org

International Insurance Fact Book

Facts and statistics on the property/casualty and life insurance industries of dozens of countries. No print edition. Available in CD ROM format.

Online version available at www.internationalinsurance.org

Insuring Your Business

A comprehensive insurance guide for small business owners.

Online at www.iii.org/smallbusiness

Commercial Insurance

A comprehensive guide to the business of commercial insurance—its 20-plus major coverages and dozens of specialty products. The resource provides clear, concise explanations of all aspects of the sector, including distribution, surplus lines and reserving. No print edition.

Online version available at www.commercialinsurancefacts.org

I.I.I. Insurance Daily

Keeps thousands of readers up-to-date on important events, issues and trends in the insurance industry each business morning. This unique electronic newsletter contains abstracts of insurance-related articles from newspapers and magazines from across the U.S. and abroad.

Transmitted early each business day via email.

I.I.I. Insurance Issues Updates

Frequently updated background papers on key insurance issues.

Online at www.iii.org/media

WEB CONTENT

Thousands of Web sites presently use I.I.I. content on their pages or link to I.I.I. Web sites. Some of the following content is available as automated content feeds and links. Please send requests to andreab@iii.org.

I.I.I. Wire
Up-to-the minute insurance-related news
www.iii.org

Hot Topics
The latest studies and issues papers
www.iii.org

Facts & Statistics
The latest insurance industry facts and statistics.
www.iii.org/media/facts

Latest Studies
The latest insurance industry reports and studies.
www.iii.org/media/lateststud

Know Your Stuff
An easy-to-use free home inventory program that can be downloaded by consumers.
www.knowyourstuff.org

My Financial House
An easy-to-use free financial inventory program that can be downloaded by consumers.
www.myfinancialhouse.org

Disaster Insurance Information
Web site posting information on major disasters within the United States.
www.disasterinformation.org

Terms and Conditions Blog
Topical discussions of insurance issues.
www.iii.org/insuranceindustryblog

YEAR	EVENT
1601	First insurance legislation in the United Kingdom was enacted. Modern insurance has its roots in this law which concerned coverage for merchandise and ships.
1666	Great Fire of London demonstrated destructive power of fire in an urban environment, leading entrepreneur Nicholas Barbon to form a business to repair houses damaged by fire.
1684	Participants in the Friendly Society in England formed a mutual insurance company to cover fire losses.
1688	Edward Lloyd's coffee house, the precursor of Lloyd's of London, became the central meeting place for ship owners seeking insurance for a voyage.
1696	Hand in Hand mutual fire company was formed. Aviva, the world's oldest continuously operating insurance company, traces its origins to this company.
1710	Charles Povey formed the Sun, the oldest insurance company in existence which still conducts business in its own name. It is the forerunner of the Royal & Sun Alliance Group.
1735	The Friendly Society, the first insurance company in the United States, was established in Charleston, South Carolina. This mutual insurance company went out of business in 1740.
1752	The Philadelphia Contributionship for the Insurance of Houses from Loss by Fire, the oldest insurance carrier in continuous operation in the United States, was established.
1759	Presbyterian Ministers Fund, the first life insurance company in the United States, was founded.
1762	Equitable Life Assurance Society, the world's oldest mutual life insurer, was formed in England.
1776	Charleston Insurance Company and the South Carolina Insurance Company, the first two United States marine insurance companies, were formed in South Carolina.
1779	Lloyd's of London introduced the first uniform ocean marine policy.
1792	Insurance Company of North America, the first stock insurance company in the United States, was established.
1813	Eagle Fire Insurance Company of New York assumed all outstanding risks of the Union Insurance Company, in the first recorded fire reinsurance agreement in the United States.
1849	New York passed the first general insurance law in the United States.
1850	Franklin Health Assurance Company of Massachusetts offered the first accident and health insurance.
1851	New Hampshire created the first formal agency to regulate insurance in the United States.
1861	First war-risk insurance policies were issued, written by life insurance companies during the Civil War.
1866	National Board of Fire Underwriters was formed in New York City, marking the beginning of insurance rate standardization.
	Hartford Steam Boiler Inspection and Insurance Company, the first boiler insurance company, was established in Hartford, Connecticut.
1873	The Massachusetts Legislature adopted the first standard fire insurance policy.
1878	Fidelity and Casualty Company of New York began providing fidelity and surety bonds.
1885	Liability protection was first offered with the introduction of employers liability policies.

BRIEF HISTORY

YEAR	EVENT
1890	First policies providing benefits for disabilities from specific diseases were offered.
1894	National Board of Fire Underwriters established Underwriters' Laboratories to investigate and test electrical materials to ensure they meet fire safety standards.
1898	Travelers Insurance Company issued the first automobile insurance policy in the United States.
1899	First pedestrian killed by an automobile, in New York City.
1910	New York passed the first United States workers compensation law. It was later found to be unconstitutional.
1911	Wisconsin enacted the first permanent workers compensation law in the United States.
1912	Lloyd's of London introduced aviation insurance coverage.
1925	Massachusetts passed the first compulsory automobile insurance legislation.
	Connecticut passed the first financial responsibility law for motorists.
1938	Federal Crop Insurance Act created the first federal crop insurance program.
1945	McCarran-Ferguson Act (Public Law 15) was enacted. It provided the insurance industry with a limited exemption to federal antitrust law, assuring the pre-eminence of state regulation of the industry.
1947	New York established the Motor Vehicle Liability Security Fund to cover auto insurance company insolvencies. This organization was a precursor of the state guaranty funds established by insurers in all states to absorb the claims of insolvent insurers.
1950	First package insurance policies for homeowners coverage were introduced.
1960	Boston Plan was established to address insurance availability problems in urban areas in Boston.
1968	First state-run Fair Access to Insurance Requirements (FAIR) Plans were set up to ensure property insurance availability in high-risk areas.
	The federal flood insurance program was established with the passage of the National Flood Insurance Act. It enabled property owners in communities that participate in flood reduction programs to purchase insurance against flood losses.
1971	Massachusetts became the first state to establish a true no-fault automobile insurance plan.
1981	Federal Risk Retention Act of 1981 was enacted. The law fostered the growth of risk retention groups and other nontraditional insurance mechanisms.
	The Illinois Legislature created the Illinois Insurance Exchange, a cooperative effort of individual brokers and risk bearers operating as a single market, similar to Lloyd's of London.
1985	Mission Insurance Group failed. The insolvency incurred the largest payout by state guaranty funds for a single property/casualty insurance company failure at that time. This and other insolvencies in the 1980s led to stricter state regulation of insurer solvency.
	Montana became the first state to forbid discrimination by sex in the setting of insurance rates.
1992	European Union's Third Nonlife Insurance Directive became effective, establishing a single European market for insurance.

YEAR	EVENT
1996	Florida enacted rules requiring insurers to offer separate deductibles for hurricane losses, marking a shift to hurricane deductibles based on a percentage of loss rather than a set dollar figure.
	Catastrophe bonds, vehicles for covering disaster risk in the capital markets, were introduced.
1997	World Trade Organization agreement to dismantle barriers to trade in financial services, including insurance, banking and securities, was signed by the United States and some 100 other countries.
1998	Travelers became first insurer to sell auto insurance on the Internet.
1999	Financial Services Modernization Act (Gramm-Leach-Bliley) enacted, allowing insurers, banks and securities firms to affiliate under a financial holding company structure.
2001	Terrorist attacks upon the World Trade Center in New York City and the Pentagon in Washington, D.C. caused about $40 billion in insured losses.
	New York became the first state to ban the use of hand-held cell phones while driving.
2002	Terrorism Risk Insurance Act enacted to provide a federal backstop for terrorism insurance losses.
2003	In a landmark ruling, upheld in 2004, the U.S. Supreme Court placed limits on punitive damages, holding in State Farm v. Campbell that punitive damages awards should generally not exceed nine times compensatory awards.
2004	New York Attorney General Eliot Spitzer and a number of state regulators launched investigations into insurance industry sales and accounting practices.
2005	Citigroup sold off its Travelers life insurance unit, following the spin-off of its property/casualty business in 2002. This dissolved the arrangement that led to the passage of Gramm-Leach-Bliley in 1999.
	The federal Class Action Fairness Act moved most class-action lawsuits to federal courts, offering the prospect of lower defense costs and fewer and less costly verdicts.
	A string of hurricanes, including Hurricane Katrina, hit the Gulf Coast, making 2005 the most active hurricane season on record.
2006	Massachusetts became the first state to pass a universal health insurance law.
	Congress passed legislation extending the Terrorism Risk Insurance Act to December 2007. The act, originally passed in 2002 to provide a federal backstop for terrorism insurance losses, had been set to expire at the end of 2005.
2007	Florida passed legislation shifting more of the cost of paying for hurricane damage from private insurers to the state.
	Washington became the first state to ban the practice of texting with a cell phone while driving.

The majority of state commissioners are appointed by state governors and serve at their pleasure. The states designated with an asterisk (*) presently elect insurance commissioners to four-year terms.

Alabama • Walter A. Bell, Commissioner of Insurance, 201 Monroe St., Suite 1700, Montgomery, AL 36104. Tel. 334-269-3550. Fax. 334-241-4192. www.aldoi.org

Alaska • Linda S. Hall, Director of Insurance, 550 W. 7th Ave., Suite 1560, Anchorage, AK 99501-3567. Tel. 907-269-7900. Fax. 907-269-7910. www.dced.state.ak.us/insurance

American Samoa • Elisara Togiai, Insurance Commissioner, Pago Pago, AS 96799. Tel. 011-684-633-4116 Ext. 55. Fax. 011-684-633-2269. www.americansamoa.gov

Arizona • Christina Urias, Director of Insurance, 2910 North 44th St., Suite 210, Phoenix, AZ 85018-7269. Tel. 602-364-3100. Fax. 602-364-2505. www.id.state.az.us

Arkansas • Julie Benafield Bowman, Insurance Commissioner, 1200 W. 3rd St., Little Rock, AR 72201-1904. Tel. 501-371-2600. Fax. 501-371-2618. www.arkansas.gov/insurance

*California • Steve Poizner, Commissioner of Insurance, 300 South Spring Street, South Tower, Los Angeles, CA 90013. Tel. 213-897-8921. www.insurance.ca.gov

Colorado • David F. Rivera, Commissioner of Insurance, 1560 Broadway, Suite 850, Denver, CO 80202. Tel. 303-894-7499. Fax. 303-894-7455. www.dora.state.co.us/insurance

Connecticut • Thomas R. Sullivan, Commissioner of Insurance, PO Box 816, Hartford, CT 06142-0816. Tel. 860-297-3900. Fax. 860-566-7410. www.ct.gov/cid

*Delaware • Matthew Denn, Insurance Commissioner, The Rodney Bldg., 841 Silver Lake Blvd., Dover, DE 19904. Tel. 302-674-7300. Fax. 302-739-5280. www.delawareinsurance.gov

District of Columbia • Thomas E. Hampton, Commissioner of Insurance, 810 First St., NE, Suite 701, Washington, DC 20002. Tel. 202-727-8000. Fax. 202-535-1196. www.disb.dc.gov

Florida • Kevin McCarty, Director of the Office of Insurance Regulation, 200 E. Gaines St., Tallahassee, FL 32399-0300. Tel. 850-413-3132. Fax. 850-488-2349. www.floir.com

*Georgia • John W. Oxendine, Insurance Commissioner, 2 Martin L. King, Jr. Dr., West Tower, Suite 704, Atlanta, GA 30334. Tel. 404-656-2070. Fax. 404-657-8542. www.gainsurance.org

Guam • Theresa C. Santos, Director of the Department of Insurance, Securities & Banking, Mariner Ave., 1240 Route 16, Barrigada, GU 96913. Tel. 671-635-1843. Fax. 671-633-2643. www.admin.gov.gu/admin.html

Hawaii • J.P. Schmidt, Insurance Commissioner, PO Box 3614, Honolulu, HI 96811. Tel. 808-586-2790. Fax. 808-568-2806. www.state.hi.us/dcca/ins

Idaho • William Deal, Director of the Department of Insurance, 700 West State St., PO Box 83720, Boise, ID 83720-0043. Tel. 208-334-4250. Fax. 208-334-4398. www.doi.state.id.us

Illinois • Michael T. McRaith, Director of Insurance, 320 W. Washington St., Springfield, IL 62767-0001. Tel. 217-782-4515. Fax. 217-782-5020. www.state.il.us/ins

Indiana • Jim Atterholt, Commissioner of Insurance, 311 West Washington St., Suite 300, Indianapolis, IN 46204-2787. Tel. 317-232-2385. Fax. 317-232-5251. www.in.gov/idoi

Iowa • Susan E. Voss, Commissioner of Insurance, 330 Maple St., Des Moines, IA 50319-0065. Tel. 515-281-6348. Fax. 515-281-3059. www.iid.state.ia.us

*Kansas • Sandy Praeger, Commissioner of Insurance, 420 South West Ninth St., Topeka, KS 66612-1678. Tel. 785-296-3071. Fax. 785-296-2283. www.ksinsurance.org

Kentucky • Julie M. McPeak, Insurance Commissioner, PO Box 517, Frankfort, KY 40602. Tel. 502-564-6027. Fax. 502-564-1650. http://doi.ppr.ky.gov

*Louisiana • James J. Donelon, Commissioner of Insurance, 1702 North Third Street, Baton Rouge, LA 70802. Tel. 225-342-5423. Fax. 225-342-8622. www.ldi.la.gov

Maine • Eric A. Cioppa, Acting Superintendent of the Bureau of Insurance, 34 State House Station, Augusta, ME 04333-0034. Tel. 207-624-8475. Fax. 207-624-8599. http://www.maineinsurancereg.org

Maryland • Ralph S. Tyler, Insurance Commissioner, 525 St. Paul Pl., Baltimore, MD 21202. Tel. 410-468-2090. Fax. 410-468-2020. http://www.mdinsurance.state.md.us

Massachusetts • Nonie Burnes, Commissioner of Insurance, 1 South Station, Boston, MA 02110. Tel. 617-521-7301. Fax. 617-521-7575. www.state.ma.us/doi

Michigan • Linda A. Watters, Commissioner of Insurance, PO Box 30220, Lansing, MI 48909-7220. Tel. 517-335-3167. Fax. 517-335-4978. www.michigan.gov/ofis

Minnesota • Glenn Wilson, Commissioner of Commerce, 85 7th Place East, Suite 500, St. Paul, MN 55101. Tel. 651-296-4026. Fax. 651-297-1959. www.commerce.state.mn.us

*Mississippi • Mike Chaney, Commissioner of Insurance, 1001 Woolfolk State Office Building, 501 N. West St., Jackson, MS 39201. Tel. 601-359-3569. Fax. 601-359-2474. www.doi.state.ms.us

Missouri • Douglas M. Ommen, Director of Insurance, 301 W. High St., PO Box 690, Jefferson City, MO 65102-0690. Tel. 573-751-4126. Fax. 573-751-1165. www.insurance.state.mo.us

*Montana • John Morrison, Commissioner of Insurance, 840 Helena Ave., Room 270, Helena, MT 59601. Tel. 406-444-2040. Fax. 406-444-3497. http://sao.mt.gov/insurance/index.asp

Nebraska • Ann Frohman, Acting Director of Insurance, Terminal Bldg., 941 O St., Suite 400, Lincoln, NE 68508-3639. Tel. 402-471-2201. Fax. 402-471-2990. www.nol.org/home/NDOI

Nevada • Alice A. Molasky-Arman, Commissioner of Insurance, 788 Fairview Dr., Suite 300, Carson City, NV 89701. Tel. 775-687-4270. Fax. 775-687-3937. http://doi.state.nv.us

New Hampshire • Roger Sevigny, Insurance Commissioner, 21 South Fruit St., Suite 14, Concord, NH 03301-7317. Tel. 603-271-2261. Fax. 603-271-1406. www.state.nh.us/insurance

New Jersey • Steven M. Goldman, Commissioner of Banking & Insurance, PO Box 325, Trenton, NJ 08625. Tel. 609-292-5360. Fax. 609-292-5865. www.njdobi.org

New Mexico • Morris J. Chavez, Superintendent of Insurance, PO Box 1269, Santa Fe, NM 87504-1269. Tel. 505-827-4601. Fax. 505-827-4734. www.nmprc.state.nm.us/insurance/inshm.htm

New York • Eric R. Dinallo, Superintendent of Insurance, 25 Beaver Street, New York, NY 10004. Tel. 212-480-6400. Fax. 212-480-2310. www.ins.state.ny.us

*North Carolina • James E. Long, Commissioner of Insurance, 1201 Mail Service Center, Raleigh, NC 27699-1201. Tel. 919-733-3058. Fax. 919-733-6495. www.ncdoi.com

*North Dakota • Adam Hamm, Commissioner of Insurance, State Capitol, Fifth Fl., 600 East Boulevard Ave., Dept. 401, Bismarck, ND 58505-0320. Tel. 701-328-2440. Fax. 701-328-4880. www.state.nd.us/ndins

Ohio • Mary Jo Hudson, Director of Insurance, 2100 Stella Court, Columbus, OH 43215-1067. Tel. 614-644-2658. Fax. 614-644-3743. www.ohioinsurance.gov

*Oklahoma • Kim Holland, Commissioner of Insurance, 2401 NW 23rd Street, Oklahoma City, OK 73107. Tel. 405-521-2828. Fax. 405-521-6635. www.oid.state.ok.us

Oregon • Carl Lundberg, Acting Insurance Administrator, PO Box 14480, Salem, OR 97309-0405. Tel. 503-947-7980. Fax. 503-378-4351. www.cbs.state.or.us/external/ins

Pennsylvania • Joel Scott Ario, Insurance Commissioner, 1326 Strawberry Square, Harrisburg, PA 17120. Tel. 717-787-2317. Fax. 717-787-8585. www.ins.state.pa.us/ins/site/default.asp

Puerto Rico • Dorelisse Juarbe Jimenez, Commissioner of Insurance, PO Box 8330, San Juan, PR 00910-8330. Tel. 787-722-8686. Fax. 787-722-4400. www.ocs.gobierno.pr

Rhode Island • A. Michael Marques, Director, 233 Richmond St., Suite 233, Providence, RI 02903-4233. Tel. 401-222-2223. Fax. 401-222-5475. www.dbr.state.ri.us

South Carolina • Scott Richardson, Director of Insurance, PO Box 100105, Columbia, SC 29202-3105. Tel. 803-737-6160. Fax. 803-737-6229. www.doi.state.sc.us

South Dakota • Merle D. Scheiber, Director of Insurance, 445 E. Capitol Ave., Pierre, SD 57501-3185. Tel. 605-773-4104. Fax. 605-773-5369. www.state.sd.us/dcr/insurance

Tennessee • Leslie A. Newman, Commissioner of Commerce & Insurance, 500 James Robertson Pkwy., Suite 660, Nashville, TN 37243-0565. Tel. 615-741-2241. Fax. 615-532-6934. www.state.tn.us/commerce

Texas • Mike Geeslin, Commissioner of Insurance, 333 Guadalupe St., Austin, TX 78701. Tel. 512-463-6464. Fax. 512-475-2005. www.tdi.state.tx.us

Utah • D. Kent Michie, Commissioner of Insurance, 3110 State Office Building, Salt Lake City, UT 84114-6901. Tel. 801-538-3800. Fax. 801-538-3829. www.insurance.utah.gov

Vermont • Paulette J. Thabault, Commissioner of Banking, Insurance, Securities and Health Care Administration, 89 Main St., Drawer 20, Montpelier, VT 05620-3101. Tel. 802-828-3301. Fax. 802-828-3306. www.bishca.state.vt.us

Virgin Islands • John McDonald, Director of Division of Banking & Insurance, 18 Kongens Gade, St. Thomas, VI 00801. Tel. 340-773-6459. Fax. 340-774-9458. www.itg.gov.vi

Virginia • Alfred W. Gross, Commissioner of Insurance, PO Box 1157, Richmond, VA 23218. Tel. 804-371-9694. Fax. 804-371-9349. www.scc.virginia.gov/division/boi

*Washington • Mike Kreidler, Insurance Commissioner, PO Box 40255, Olympia, WA 98504-0255. Tel. 360-725-7100. Fax. 360-586-2018. www.insurance.wa.gov

West Virginia • Jane L. Cline, Insurance Commissioner, 1124 Smith St., Charleston, WV 25301. Tel. 304-558-3354. Fax. 304-558-4965. www.wvinsurance.gov

Wisconsin • Sean Dilweg, Commissioner of Insurance, PO Box 7873, Madison, WI 53707. Tel. 608-267-1233. Fax. 608-266-9935. www.oci.wi.gov

Wyoming • Kenneth G. Vines, Insurance Commissioner, Herschler Bldg., 106 East 6th Ave., Cheyenne, WY 82002. Tel. 307-777-7401. Fax. 307-777-2446. http://insurance.state.wy.us

The following organizations are supported by insurance companies or have activities closely related to insurance. National and state organizations which subscribe to the services of the Insurance Information Institute are identified by an asterisk (*).

ACORD • Two Blue Hill Plaza, 3rd Fl., PO Box 1529, Pearl River, NY 10965-8529. Tel. 845-620-1700. Fax. 845-620-3600. www.acord.com — An industry-sponsored institute serving as the focal point for improving the computer processing of insurance transactions through the insurance agency system.

The Actuarial Foundation • 475 N. Martingale Rd., Suite 600, Schaumburg, IL 60173-2226. Tel. 847-706-3535. Fax. 847-706-3599. www.actuarialfoundation.org — Develops, funds and executes education and research programs that serve the public by harnessing the talents of actuaries.

Advocates for Highway and Auto Safety • 750 First St., NE, Suite 901, Washington, DC 20002. Tel. 202-408-1711. Fax. 202-408-1699. www.saferoads.org — An alliance of consumer, safety and insurance organizations dedicated to highway and auto safety.

AIR Worldwide Corporation • 131 Dartmouth St., Boston, MA 02116. Tel. 617-267-6645. Fax. 617-267-8284. www.air-worldwide.com — Risk modeling and technology firm that develops models of global natural hazards, enabling companies to identify, quantify and plan for the financial consequences of catastrophic events.

A.M. Best Company, Inc. • Ambest Rd., Oldwick, NJ 08858. Tel. 908-439-2200. www.ambest.com — Rating organization and publisher of reference books and periodicals relating to the insurance industry.

America's Health Insurance Plans • 601 Pennsylvania Ave., NW, South Building, Suite 500, Washington, DC 20004. Tel. 202-778-3200. Fax. 202-331-7487. www.ahip.org — National trade association representing health insurance plans providing medical, long-term care, disability income, dental supplemental, stop-gap and reinsurance coverage.

American Academy of Actuaries • 1100 17th St., NW, 7th Fl., Washington, DC 20036. Tel. 202-223-8196. Fax. 202-872-1948. www.actuary.org — Professional association for actuaries. Issues standards of conduct and provides government liaison and advisory opinions.

American Association of Crop Insurers • 1 Massachusetts Ave., NW, Suite 800, Washington, DC 20001-1401. Tel. 202-789-4100. Fax. 202-408-7763. www.cropinsurers.com — Trade association of insurance companies to promote crop insurance.

American Association of Insurance Services • 1745 S. Naperville Rd., Wheaton, IL 60187-8132. Tel. 630-681-8347. Fax. 630-681-8356. www.aaisonline.com — Rating, statistical and advisory organization, made up principally of small and medium-sized property/casualty companies.

American Association of Managing General Agents • 150 South Warner Rd., Suite 156, King of Prussia, PA 19406. Tel. 610-225-1999. Fax. 610-225-1996. www.aamga.org — Membership association of managing general agents of insurers.

American Bankers Insurance Association • 1120 Connecticut Ave., NW, Washington, DC 20036. Tel. 202-663-5163. Fax. 202-828-4546. www.theabia.com — A separately chartered affiliate of the American Bankers Association. A full service association for bank insurance interests dedicated to furthering the policy and business objectives of banks in insurance.

The American College • 270 S. Bryn Mawr Ave., Bryn Mawr, PA 19010. Tel. 888-263-7265. Fax. 610-526-1465. www.theamericancollege.edu — An independent, accredited nonprofit institution, originally The American College of Life Underwriters. Provides graduate and professional education in insurance and other financial services.

American Council of Life Insurers • 101 Constitution Ave., NW, Suite 700, Washington, DC 20001-2133. Tel. 202-624-2000. www.acli.com — Trade association responsible for the public affairs, government, legislative and research aspects of the life insurance business.

American Institute for Chartered Property Casualty Underwriters • 720 Providence Rd., PO Box 3016, Malvern, PA 19355-0716. Tel. 800-644-2101. Fax. 610-640-9576. www.aicpcu.org — An independent, nonprofit educational organization that confers the Chartered Property Casualty Underwriter (CPCU) professional designation on those individuals who meet its education, experience and ethics requirements.

*American Institute of Marine Underwriters • 14 Wall St., New York, NY 10005. Tel. 212-233-0550. Fax. 212-227-5102. www.aimu.org — Provides information of concern to marine underwriters and promotes their interests.

American Insurance Association • 1130 Connecticut Ave., NW, Suite 1000, Washington, DC 20036. Tel. 202-828-7100. Fax. 202-293-1219. www.aiadc.org — Trade and service organization for property/casualty insurance companies. Provides a forum for the discussion of problems as well as safety, promotional and legislative services.

American Land Title Association • 1828 L St., NW, Suite 705, Washington, DC 20036. Tel. 800-787-ALTA. Fax. 888-787-ALTA. www.alta.org — Trade organization for title insurers, abstractors and agents. Performs statistical research and lobbying services.

American Nuclear Insurers • 95 Glastonbury Blvd., Glastonbury, CT 06033. Tel. 860-682-1301. Fax. 860-659-0002. www.amnucins.com — A nonprofit unincorporated association through which liability insurance protection is provided against hazards arising out of nuclear reactor installations and their operations.

American Prepaid Legal Services Institute • 321 N. Clark St., Chicago, IL 60610. Tel. 312-988-5751. Fax. 312-988-5710. www.aplsi.org — National membership organization providing information and technical assistance to lawyers, insurance companies, administrators, marketers and consumers regarding group and prepaid legal service plans.

American Tort Reform Association • 1101 Connecticut Ave., NW, Suite 400 Washington, DC 20036. Tel. 202-682-1163. Fax. 202-682-1022. www.atra.org — A broad based, bipartisan coalition of more than 300 businesses, corporations, municipalities, associations, and professional firms that support civil justice reform.

APIW. • 555 Fifth Ave., 8th Fl., New York, NY 10017. Tel. 212-867-0228. Fax. 212-867-2544. www.apiw.org — A professional association of women in the insurance and reinsurance industries and related fields. Provides professional education, networking and support services to encourage the development of professional leadership among its members.

*Arbitration Forums, Inc. • 3350 Buschwood Park Dr., Bldg. 3, Suite 295, Tampa, FL 33618-1500. Tel. 888-272-3453. Fax. 813-931-4618. www.arbfile.org — Nonprofit provider of interinsurance dispute resolution services for self-insureds, insurers and claim service organizations.

Association of Financial Guaranty Insurers • c/o TowersGroup, 15 West 39th St., 14th Fl., New York, NY 10018. Tel. 212-354-5020. Fax. 212-391-6920. www.afgi.org — Trade association of the insurers and reinsurers of municipal bonds and asset-backed securities.

Automobile Insurance Plans Service Office • 302 Central Ave., Johnston, RI 02919. Tel. 401-946-2310. Fax. 401-528-1350. www.aipso.com — Develops and files rates and provides other services for state-mandated automobile insurance plans.

Bank Insurance & Securities Association • 303 West Lancaster Ave., Suite 2D, Wayne, PA 19087. Tel. 610-989-9047. Fax. 610-989-9102. www.bisanet.org — Fosters the full integration of securities and insurance businesses with depository institutions' traditional banking businesses. Participants include executives from the securities, insurance, investment advisory, trust, private banking, retail, capital markets and commercial divisions of depository institutions.

Captive Insurance Companies Association • 4248 Park Glen Rd., Minneapolis, MN 55416. Tel. 952-928-4655. Fax. 952-929-1318. www.cicaworld.com — Organization that disseminates information useful to firms that utilize the captive insurance company concept to solve corporate insurance problems.

*Casualty Actuarial Society • 4350 N. Fairfax Dr., Suite 250, Arlington, VA 22203. Tel. 703-276-3100. Fax. 703-276-3108. www.casact.org — Promotes actuarial and statistical science in property/casualty insurance fields.

Certified Automotive Parts Association • 1518 K St., NW, Suite 306, Washington, DC 20005. Tel. 202-737-2212. Fax. 202-737-2214. www.capacertified.org — Nonprofit organization formed to develop and oversee a test program guaranteeing the suitability and quality of automotive parts.

Coalition Against Insurance Fraud • 1012 14th St., NW, Suite 200, Washington, DC 20005. Tel. 202-393-7330. Fax. 202-393-7329. www.insurancefraud.org — An alliance of consumer, law enforcement and insurance industry groups dedicated to reducing all forms of insurance fraud through public advocacy and education.

The Committee of Annuity Insurers • c/o Davis & Harman LLP, 1455 Pennsylvania Ave., NW, Suite 1200, Washington, DC 20004. Tel. 202-347-2230. Fax. 202-393-3310. www.annuity-insurers.org — Group whose goal is to address federal legislative and regulatory issues relevant to the annuity industry and to participate in the development of federal tax and securities policies regarding annuities.

Conning Research and Consulting Inc. • One Financial Plaza, Hartford, CT 06103-2627. Tel. 888-266-6464. www.conningresearch.com — Research and consulting firm that offers a growing array of specialty information products, insights and analyses of key issues confronting the insurance industry.

Council of Insurance Agents and Brokers • 701 Pennsylvania Ave., NW, Suite 750, Washington, DC 20004-2608. Tel. 202-783-4400. Fax. 202-783-4410. www.ciab.com — A trade organization representing leading commercial insurance agencies and brokerage firms.

CPCU (Chartered Property Casualty Underwriters) Society • 720 Providence Rd., PO Box 3009, Malvern, PA 19355-0709. Tel. 800-932-2728. Fax. 610-251-2780. www.cpcusociety.org — Professional society established to foster the higher education of those engaged in insurance and risk management; encourages and conducts research.

Crop Insurance Research Bureau • 10800 Farley, Suite 330, Overland Park, KS 66210. Tel. 913-338-0470. Fax. 913-339-9336. www.cropinsurance.org — Crop insurance trade organization.

Defense Research Institute • 150 North Michigan Ave., Suite 300, Chicago, IL 60601. Tel. 312-795-1101. Fax. 312-795-0747. www.dri.org — A national and international membership association of lawyers and others concerned with the defense of civil actions.

Employee Benefit Research Institute • 2121 K St., NW, Suite 600, Washington, DC 20037-1896. Tel. 202-659-0670. Fax. 202-775-6312. www.ebri.org — The Institute's mission is to advance the public's, the media's and policymakers' knowledge and understanding of employee benefits and their importance to the U.S. economy.

Eqecat • 475 14th St., Suite 550, Oakland, CA 94612-1900. Tel. 510-817-3100. www.eqecat.com — Provider of products and services for managing natural and man-made risks. Provides innovative catastrophe management solutions for property and casualty insurance underwriting, accumulation management and transfer of natural hazard and terrorism risk.

Federal Insurance Administration • 500 C St., SW, Washington, DC 20472. Tel. 800-621-3362. Fax. 800-827-8112. www.fema.gov — Administers the federal flood insurance program.

Fitch Credit Rating Company • One State Street Plaza, New York, NY 10004. Tel. 212-908-0500. www.fitchratings.com — Assigns claims-paying ability ratings to insurance companies.

Global Aerospace, Inc. • 51 John F. Kennedy Pkwy., Short Hills, NJ 07078. Tel. 973-379-0800. Fax. 973-379-0900. www.aau.com — A pool of property/casualty companies engaged in writing all classes of aviation insurance.

Global Association of Risk Professionals • 100 Pavonia Ave., Suite 405, Jersey City, NJ 07310. Tel. 201-222-0054. Fax. 201-222-5022. www.garp.com/index.asp — International group whose aim is to encourage and enhance communications between risk professionals, practitioners and regulators worldwide.

Group of North American Insurance Enterprises • 40 Exchange Place, Suite 1707, New York, NY 10005. Tel. 212-480-0808. Fax. 212-480-9090. www.gnaie.net — Group focusing on financial reporting, accounting and solvency issues.

Highline Data LLC • One Alewife Center, Suite 460, Cambridge, MA 02140. Tel. 877-299-9424. www.highlinedata.com — An information and data services company comprised of two principal product lines: National Underwriter Insurance Data Services and Highline Banking Data Services.

Highway Loss Data Institute • 1005 North Glebe Rd., Suite 800, Arlington, VA 22201. Tel. 703-247-1600. Fax. 703-247-1588. www.hwysafety.org — Nonprofit organization to gather, process and provide the public with insurance data concerned with human and economic losses resulting from highway accidents.

Independent Insurance Agents & Brokers of America, Inc. • 127 S. Peyton St., Alexandria, VA 22314. Tel. 800-221-7917. Fax. 703-683-7556. www.iiaba.org — Trade association of independent insurance agents and brokers.

Inland Marine Underwriters Association • 14 Wall St., 8th Fl., New York, NY 10005. Tel. 212-233-0550. Fax. 212-227-5102. www.imua.org — Forum for discussion of problems of common concern to inland marine insurers.

*Institute for Business & Home Safety • 4775 E. Fowler Ave., Tampa, FL 33617. Tel. 813-286-3400. Fax. 813-286-9960. www.ibhs.org — An insurance industry-sponsored nonprofit organization dedicated to reducing losses, deaths, injuries and property damage resulting from natural hazards.

Insurance Accounting and Systems Association, Inc. • 3511 Shannon Rd., Suite 160, PO Box 51340, Durham, NC 27707. Tel. 919-489-0991. Fax. 919-489-1994. www.iasa.org — An international organization to promote the study, research and development of modern techniques in insurance accounting and systems.

Insurance Industry Charitable Foundation • 990 N. California Blvd., Suite 230, Walnut Creek, CA 94596. Tel. 925-280-8009. Fax: 925-280-8059. www.iicf.org — This group seeks to help communities and enrich lives by combining the collective strengths of the insurance industry to provide grants, volunteer service and leadership.

Insurance Committee for Arson Control • 3601 Vincennes Rd., Indianapolis, IN 46268. Tel. 317-876-6226. Fax. 317-879-8408. www.arsoncontrol.org — All-industry coalition that serves as a catalyst for insurers' anti-arson efforts and a liaison with government agencies and other groups devoted to arson control.

Insurance Data Management Association, Inc. (IDMA) • 545 Washington Blvd., 22-16, Jersey City, NJ 07310-1686. Tel. 201-469-3069. Fax. 201-748-1690. www.idma.org — An independent, nonprofit, professional, learned association dedicated to increasing the level of professionalism, knowledge and visibility of insurance data management.

Insurance Education Institute • 3601 Vincennes Rd., Indianapolis, IN 46268-0700. Tel. 800-433-8408. Fax. 317-879-8408. www.theief.org — Organization dedicated to educating Main Street America about how insurance works.

Insurance Information Institute • 110 William St., New York, NY 10038. Tel. 212-346-5500. Fax. 212-732-1916. www.iii.org — A primary source for information, analysis and referral on insurance subjects.

Insurance Institute for Highway Safety • 1005 North Glebe Rd., Suite 800, Arlington, VA 22201. Tel. 703-247-1500. Fax. 703-247-1588. www.highwaysafety.org — Research and education organization dedicated to reducing loss, death, injury and property damage on the highways. Fully funded by property/casualty insurers.

Insurance Institute of America, Inc. • 720 Providence Rd., PO Box 3016, Malvern, PA 19355-0716. Tel. 800-644-2101. Fax. 610-640-9576. www.aicpcu.org — Provides educational programs and professional certification to people in property and liability insurance. Offerings range from entry-level to advanced, specialized programs. Certification is determined through the administration of national exams.

Insurance Library Association of Boston • 156 State St., Boston, MA 02109. Tel. 617-227-2087. Fax. 617-723-8524. www.insurancelibrary.org — A nonprofit, independent membership library serving the research and education interests of all branches of the insurance industry.

Insurance Marketplace Standards Association • 4550 Montgomery Ave., Suite 700N, Bethesda, MD 20814. Tel. 240-744-3030. Fax. 240-744-3031. www.imsaethics.org — A nonprofit, independent organization created to strengthen consumer trust and confidence in the marketplace for individually sold life insurance, long-term care insurance and annuities.

Insurance Regulatory Examiners Society • 12710 S. Pflumm Rd., Suite 200, Olathe, KS 66062. Tel. 913-768-4700. Fax. 913-768-4900. www.go-ires.org — Nonprofit professional and educational association for examiners and other professionals working in the insurance industry.

Insurance Research Council • 718 Providence Rd., PO Box 3025, Malvern, PA 19355-0725. Tel. 610-644-2212. Fax. 610-640-5388. www.ircweb.org — A division of the American Institute for CPCU. Provides research relevant to public policy issues affecting risk and insurance.

Integrated Benefits Institute • 595 Market St., Suite 810, San Francisco, CA 94105. Tel. 415-222-7280. Fax. 415-222-7281. www.ibiweb.org — A private, nonprofit organization that provides research, discussion and analysis, data services and legislative review to measure and improve integrated benefits programs, enhance efficiency in delivery of all employee-based benefits and promote effective return-to-work.

Intermediaries and Reinsurance Underwriters Association, Inc. • 971 Route 202 North, Branchburg, NJ 08876. Tel. 908-203-0211. Fax. 908-203-0213. www.irua.com — Educational association to encourage the exchange of ideas among reinsurers worldwide writing principally treaty reinsurance.

International Association of Insurance Fraud Agencies, Inc. • PO Box 10018, Kansas City, MO 64171. Tel. 816-756-5285. Fax. 816-756-5287. www.iaifa.org — An international association opening the doors of communication, cooperation and exchange of information in the fight against sophisticated global insurance and related financial insurance fraud.

International Association of Special Investigation Units • 8015 Corporate Dr., Suite A, Baltimore, MD 21236. Tel. 410-931-3332. Fax. 410-931-2060. www.iasiu.com — Group whose goals are to promote a coordinated effort within the industry to combat insurance fraud and to provide education and training for insurance investigators.

*International Insurance Society, Inc. • 101 Murray St., New York, NY 10007. Tel. 212-815-9291. Fax. 212-815-9297. www.IIsonline.org — A nonprofit membership organization whose mission is to facilitate international understanding, the transfer of ideas and innovations, and the development of personal networks across insurance markets through a joint effort of leading executives and academics throughout the world.

*ISO • 545 Washington Blvd., Jersey City, NJ 07310-1686. Tel. 800-888-4476. Fax. 201-748-1472. www.iso.com — Provider of products and services that help measure, manage and reduce risk. Provides data, analytics and decision-support solutions to professionals in many fields, including insurance, finance, real estate, health services, government and human resources.

IVANS • 100 First Stamford Place, Stamford, CT 06902. Tel. 800-288-4826. Fax. 203-698-7299. www.IVANS.com — An industry-sponsored organization offering a data communications network linking agencies, companies and providers of data to the insurance industry.

Kehrer-LIMRA • 300 Day Hill Rd, Windsor, CT 06095-4761. Tel. 860-298-3910. Fax. 860-298-9555. www.kehrerlimra.com/ — Consultant focusing on the financial services marketplace. Conducts studies of sales penetration, profitability, compensation and compliance.

Latin American Agents Association • PO Box 5890, El Monte, CA 91734. Tel. 626-444-0999. Fax. 626-444-2999. www.latinagents.com — An independent group of Hispanic agents and brokers, whose goal is to educate, influence and inform the insurance community about the specific needs of the Latino community in the United States.

Latin American Association of Insurance Agencies • 2550 NW 72nd Ave., Suite 318, Miami, FL 33122. Tel. 305-477-1442. Fax. 305-477-5298. www.laaia.com — An association of insurance professionals whose purpose is to protect the rights of its members, benefit the consumer through education, provide information and networking services, and promote active participation in the political environment and community service.

The Life and Health Insurance Foundation for Education • 2175 K St. NW, Suite 250, Washington, DC, 20037-1809. Tel. 202-464-5000. www.life-line.org — Nonprofit organization dedicated to addressing the public's growing need for information and education about life, health, disability and long-term care insurance.

LIMRA International • 300 Day Hill Rd., Windsor, CT 06095. Tel. 860-285-7787. Fax. 860-298-9555. www.limra.com — Worldwide association providing research, consulting and other services to insurance and financial services companies in more than 60 countries. LIMRA helps its member companies maximize their marketing effectiveness.

LOMA • 2300 Windy Ridge Pkwy., Suite 600, Atlanta, GA 30339-8443. Tel. 770-951-1770. Fax. 770-984-0441. www.loma.org — Worldwide association of insurance companies specializing in research and education, with a primary focus on home office management.

Loss Executives Association • PO Box 37, Tenafly, NJ 07670. Tel. 732-388-5700. Fax. 732-388-0171. www.lossexecutivesassoc.org — A professional association of property loss executives providing education to the industry.

Marshall & Swift/Boeckh • 2885 S. Calhoun Rd., New Berlin, WI 53151. Tel. 262-780-2800. Fax. 262-780-0306. www.msbinfo.com — Building cost research company providing data and estimating technologies to the property insurance industry.

MIB, Inc. • PO Box 105, Essex Station, Boston, MA 02112. Tel. 866-692-6901. www.mib.com/html/lost-life-insurance.html — Database of individual life insurance applications processed since 1995.

Moody's Investors Service • 99 Church St., New York, NY 10007. Tel. 212-553-1658. www.moodys.com — Global credit analysis and financial information firm.

Mortgage Insurance Companies of America (MICA) • 727 15th St., NW, 12th Fl., Washington, DC 20005. Tel. 202-682-2683. Fax. 202-393-5557. www.micanews.com — Represents the private mortgage insurance industry. MICA provides information on related legislative and regulatory issues, and strives to enhance understanding of the role private mortgage insurance plays in housing Americans.

National African-American Insurance Association (NAAIA) • 1718 M St., NW, PO Box 1110, Washington, DC 20036. Tel. 866-56-NAAIA. www.naaia.org — NAAIA fosters the nationwide presence, participation and long-term financial success of African-American insurance professionals within the greater insurance community and provides its members and the insurance industry a forum for sharing information and ideas that enhance business and professional development.

National Arbitration Forum • PO Box 50191, Minneapolis, MN 55405-0191. Tel. 800-474-2371. Fax. 952-345-1160. www.arbitration-forum.com — A leading neutral administrator of arbitration, mediation and other forms of alternative dispute resolution worldwide.

National Association for Fixed Annuities • 2300 E. Kensington Blvd., Milwaukee, WI 53211. Tel. 414-332-9306. Fax. 415-946-3532. www.nafa.us/ — Promotes the growth, acceptance and understanding of annuity and life products; provides educational and informational resources.

National Association for Variable Annuities • 11710 Plaza America Dr., Suite 100, Reston, VA 20190. Tel. 703-707-8830. Fax. 703-707-8831. www.navanet.org — Promotes the growth, acceptance and understanding of annuity and variable life products to retirement-focused Americans; provides educational and informational resources.

National Association of Health Underwriters • 2000 N. 14th St., Suite 450, Arlington, VA 22201. Tel. 703-276-0220. Fax. 703-841-7797. www.nahu.org — Professional association of people who sell and service disability income, and hospitalization and major medical health insurance.

National Association of Independent Insurance Adjusters • 825 West State St., Suite 117-C&B, Geneva, IL 60134. Tel. 630-397-5012. Fax. 630-397-5013. www.naiia.com — Association of claims adjusters and firms operating independently on a fee basis for all insurance companies.

National Association of Insurance and Financial Advisors • 2901 Telestar Ct., PO Box 12012, Falls Church, VA 22042-1205. Tel. 703-770-8100. Fax. 703-770-8224. www.naifa.org — Professional association representing health and life insurance agents.

National Association of Insurance Commissioners • 2301 McGee St., Suite 800, Kansas City, MO 64108-2662. Tel. 816-842-3600. Fax. 816-783-8175. www.naic.org — Organization of state insurance commissioners that promotes uniformity in state supervision of insurance matters and recommends legislation in state legislatures.

National Association of Insurance Women • 6528 E. 101st St. PMB #750, Tulsa, OK 74133. Tel. 800-766-6249. Fax. 918-743-1968. www.naiw.org — Fosters educational programs for members. Promotes public safety and service programs.

National Association of Mutual Insurance Companies • 3601 Vincennes Rd., PO Box 68700, Indianapolis, IN 46268. Tel. 317-875-5250. Fax. 317-879-8408. www.namic.org — Trade association of property/casualty mutual insurance companies.

National Association of Professional Insurance Agents • 400 N. Washington St., Alexandria, VA 22314. Tel. 703-836-9340. Fax. 703-836-1279. www.pianet.com — Trade association of independent insurance agents.

National Association of Professional Surplus Lines Offices, Ltd. • 200 NE 54th St., Kansas City, MO 64118. Tel. 816-741-3910. Fax. 816-741-5409. www.napslo.org — Professional association of wholesale brokers, excess and surplus lines companies, affiliates and supporting members.

National Association of Surety Bond Producers • 1828 L St., NW, Suite 720, Washington, DC 20036-5104. Tel. 202-686-3700. Fax. 202-686-3656. www.nasbp.org — Trade association of surety bond producers.

*National Conference of Insurance Guaranty Funds • 300 North Meridian St., Suite 1020, Indianapolis, IN 46204. Tel. 317-464-8199. Fax. 317-464-8180. www.ncigf.org — Advisory organization to the state guaranty fund boards; gathers and disseminates information regarding insurer insolvencies.

National Conference of Insurance Legislators • 385 Jordan Rd., Troy, NY 12180. Tel. 518-687-0178. Fax. 518-687-0401. www.ncoil.org — Organization of state legislators whose main area of public policy concern is insurance and insurance regulation.

National Crop Insurance Services, Inc. • 8900 Indian Creek Parkway, Suite 600, Overland Park, KS 66210-1567. Tel. 913-685-2767. Fax. 913-685-3080. www.ag-risk.org — National trade association of insurance companies writing hail insurance, fire insurance and insurance against other weather perils to growing crops, with rating and research services for crop-hail and rain insurers.

National Fire Protection Association • One Batterymarch Park, Quincy, MA 02169-7471. Tel. 617-770-3000. Fax. 617-770-0700. www.nfpa.org — Independent, nonprofit source of information on fire protection, prevention and suppression.

National Highway Traffic Safety Administration • 400 Seventh St., SW, Washington, DC 20590. Tel. 888-327-4236. Fax. 202-366-2106. www.nhtsa.dot.gov — Carries out programs and studies aimed at reducing economic losses in motor vehicle crashes and repairs.

National Independent Statistical Service • PO Box 68950, 3601 Vincennes Rd., Indianapolis, IN 46268. Tel. 317-876-6200. Fax. 317-876-6210. www.niss-stat.org — National statistical agent and advisory organization for all lines of insurance, except workers compensation.

National Insurance Association • 411 Chapel Hill Dr., Suite 633, Durham, NC 27701. Tel. 919-683-5328. — Association of minority-owned life insurance companies.

*National Insurance Crime Bureau • 1111 East Touhy Ave., Suite 400, Des Plaines, IL 60018. Tel. 800-447-6282. Fax. 847-544-7101. www.nicb.org — Not-for-profit organization dedicated to combating insurance fraud and vehicle theft.

National Organization of Life and Health Insurance Guaranty Associations (NOLHGA) • 13873 Park Center Rd., Suite 329, Herndon, VA 20171. Tel. 703-481-5206. Fax. 703-481-5209. www.nolhga.com — A voluntary association composed of the life and health insurance guaranty associations of all 50 states, the District of Columbia, and Puerto Rico. When insolvency involves multiple states, NOLHGA assists its members in fulfilling their statutory obligations to policyholders.

National Risk Retention Association • 4248 Park Glen Rd., Minneapolis, MN 55416. Tel. 952-928-4656. Fax. 952-929-1318. www.nrra-usa.org — The voice of risk retention group and purchasing group liability insurance programs, organized pursuant to the Federal Liability Risk Retention Act.

National Safety Council • 1121 Spring Lake Dr., Itasca, IL 60143-3201. Tel. 630-285-1121. Fax. 630-285-1315. www.nsc.org — Provides national support and leadership in the field of safety, publishes safety material and conducts public information and publicity programs.

*NCCI Holdings, Inc. • 901 Peninsula Corporate Circle, Boca Raton, FL 33487. Tel. 561-893-1000. Fax. 561-893-1191. www.ncci.com — Develops and administers rating plans and systems for workers compensation insurance.

National Structured Settlements Trade Association • 1800 K St., NW, Suite 718, Washington, DC 20006. Tel. 202-466-2714. Fax. 202-466-7414. www.nssta.com — Trade association representing consultants, insurers and others who are interested in the resolution and financing of tort claims through periodic payments.

NeighborWorks Insurance Alliance • 1325 G St., NW, Suite 800, Washington, DC 20005-3100. Tel. 202-220-2300. Fax. 202-376-2600. www.nw.org/network/neighborworksprogs/insurance/default.asp — The goal of this group is to develop partnerships between the insurance industry and NeighborWorks organizations to better market the products and services of both, for the benefit of the customers and communities they serve.

*The New York Alliance Against Insurance Fraud • c/o New York Insurance Association, Inc., 130 Washington Ave., Albany, NY 12210. Tel. 518-432-3576. Fax. 518-432-4220. www.fraudny.com — A cooperative effort of insurance companies in New York State to educate the industry about the costs of insurance fraud, the many forms it can take and what can be done to fight it.

INSURANCE AND RELATED SERVICE ORGANIZATIONS

New York Board of Fire Underwriters • 40 Fulton St., New York, NY 10038. Tel. 212-227-3700. Fax. 212-385-3700. www.nybfu.org — Conducts fire safety and electrical inspections, helps develop fire safety standards and assists in the adjustment of fire insurance claims.

*New York Insurance Association, Inc. • 130 Washington Ave., Albany, NY 12210. Tel. 518-432-4227. Fax. 518-432-4220. www.nyia.org — A trade association of property/casualty insurance companies that provide insurance coverage for autos, homes and businesses throughout New York State.

*New York Property Insurance Underwriting Association • 100 William St., 4th Fl., New York, NY 10038. Tel. 212-208-9700. Fax. 212-344-9879. www.nypiua.com — Provides basic property insurance for New York State residents not able to obtain the coverage through the voluntary market. Administers the C-MAP and FAIR Plan.

Nonprofit Risk Management Center • 1130 Seventeenth St., NW, Suite 210, Washington, DC 20036. Tel. 202-785-3891. Fax. 202-296-0349. www.nonprofitrisk.org — Conducts research and education on risk management and insurance issues of special concern to nonprofit organizations.

Organisation for Economic Co-operation and Development • 2001 L St., NW Suite 650, Washington, DC 20036-4922. Tel. 202-785-6323. Fax. 202-785-0350. www.oecdwash.org — Markets the publications of the OECD in the United States and serves as an information center for the U.S. market. The Center is engaged in public outreach activities and acts as a liaison office to the U.S. legislative and executive branches.

Overseas Private Investment Corporation • 1100 New York Ave., NW, Washington, DC 20527. Tel. 202-336-8400. Fax. 202-336-7949. www.opic.gov — Self-sustaining U.S. government agency providing political risk insurance and finance services for U.S. investment in developing countries.

Physician Insurers Association of America • 2275 Research Blvd., Suite 250, Rockville, MD 20850. Tel. 301-947-9000. Fax. 301-947-9090. www.thepiaa.org — Trade association representing physician-owned mutual insurance companies that provide medical malpractice insurance.

*Professional Liability Underwriting Society • 5353 Wayzata Blvd., Suite 600, Minneapolis, MN 55416. Tel. 952-746-2580. Fax. 952-746-2599. www.plusweb.org — An international, nonprofit association that provides educational opportunities and programs to enhance the professionalism of its members.

Property Casualty Insurers Association of America • 2600 South River Rd., Des Plaines, IL 60018-3286. Tel. 847-297-7800. Fax. 847-297-5064. www.pciaa.net — Serves as a voice on public policy issues and advocates positions that foster a competitive market place for property/casualty insurers and insurance consumers.

Property Insurance Plans Service Office • 27 School St., Suite 302, Boston, MA 02108. Tel. 617-371-4175. Fax. 617-371-4177. www.pipso.com — Provides technical and administrative services to state property insurance plans.

Property Loss Research Bureau • 3025 Highland Parkway, Suite 800, Downers Grover, IL 60515. Tel. 630-724-2200. Fax. 630-724-2260. www.plrb.org — Trade organization that promotes productivity and efficiency in the property and liability loss and claim adjustment processes, disseminates information on property and liability issues and fosters education and new and beneficial developments within the industry.

Public Risk Management Association • 500 Montgomery St., Suite 750, Alexandria, VA 22314. Tel. 703-528-7701. Fax. 703-739-0200. www.primacentral.org — Membership organization representing risk managers in state and local public entities.

RAND Institute for Civil Justice • 1776 Main St., PO Box 2138, Santa Monica, CA 90407-2138. Tel. 310-451-6979. www.rand.org/centers/icj — Organization formed within the RAND Corporation to perform independent, objective research and analysis concerning the civil justice system.

Reinsurance Association of America • 1301 Pennsylvania Ave., NW, Suite 900, Washington, DC 20004. Tel. 202-638-3690. Fax. 202-638-0936. www.reinsurance.org — Trade association of property/casualty reinsurers; provides legislative services for members.

Risk and Insurance Management Society, Inc. • 1065 Avenue of the Americas, 13th Fl., New York, NY 10018. Tel. 212-286-9292. www.rims.org — Organization of corporate buyers of insurance that makes known to insurers the insurance needs of business and industry, supports loss prevention, and provides a forum for the discussion of common objectives and problems.

Risk Management Solutions, Inc. • 7015 Gateway Blvd., Newark, CA 94560. Tel. 510-505-2500. Fax. 510-505-2501. www.rms.com — Provides products and services for the quantification and management of catastrophe risk associated with natural perils as well as products for weather derivatives and enterprise risk management for the property/casualty insurance industry.

School of Risk Management, Insurance and Actuarial Science of the Tobin College of Business at St. John's University • 101 Murray St., New York, NY 10007. Tel. 212-277-5193. Fax. 212-277-5189. www.stjohns.edu/academics/graduate/tobin/srm — Insurance industry-supported college providing a curriculum leading to bachelor's and master's degrees in business administration, financial management of risk, insurance finance and actuarial science. The Kathryn and Shelby Cullom Davis Library (212-217-5135) provides services, products and resources to its members.

Self-Insurance Institute of America • PO Box 1237, Simpsonville, SC 29681. Tel. 800-851-7789. Fax. 864-962-2483. www.siia.org — Organization that fosters and promotes alternative methods of risk protection.

SNL Financial LC • One SNL Plaza, PO Box 2124, Charlottesville, VA 22902. Tel. 434-977-1600. Fax. 434-977-4466. www.snl.com — Research firm that collects, standardizes and disseminates all relevant corporate, financial, market and M&A data as well as news and analytics for the industries it covers: banking, specialized financial services, insurance, real estate and energy.

Society of Actuaries • 475 North Martingale, #600, Schaumburg, IL 60173. Tel. 847-706-3500. Fax. 847-706-3599. www.soa.org — An educational, research and professional organization dedicated to serving the public and its members. The Society's vision is for actuaries to be recognized as the leading professionals in the modeling and management of financial risk and contingent events.

Society of Certified Insurance Counselors • The National Alliance for Insurance Education & Research, 3630 North Hills Dr., PO Box 27027, Austin, TX 78755-2027. Tel. 800-633-2165. Fax. 512-349-6194. www.scic.com — National education program in property, liability and life insurance, with a continuing education requirement upon designation.

Society of Financial Examiners • 174 Grace Blvd. Altamonte Springs, FL 32714. Tel. 800-787-7633. Fax. 407-682-3175. www.sofe.org — Professional society for examiners of insurance companies, banks, savings and loans, and credit unions.

Society of Insurance Research • 631 Eastpointe Dr., Shelbyville, IN 46176. Tel. 317-398-3684, Fax. 317-642-0535. www.sirnet.org — Stimulates insurance research and fosters exchanges among society members on research methodology.

Society of Insurance Trainers and Educators • 2120 Market St., Suite 108, San Francisco, CA 94114. Tel. 415-621-2830. Fax. 415-621-0889. www.insurancetrainers.org — Professional organization of trainers and educators in insurance.

Standard & Poor's Rating Group • 55 Water St., New York, NY 10041. Tel. 212-438-1000. www.standardandpoors.com — Monitors the credit quality of bonds and other financial instruments of corporations, governments and supranational entities.

Surety Association of America • 1101 Connecticut Ave., NW, Suite 800, Washington, DC 20036. Tel. 202-463-0600. Fax. 202-463-0606. www.surety.org — Statistical, rating, development and advisory organization for surety companies.

Surety Information Office • 1828 L St. NW, Suite 720, Washington, DC 20036-5104. Tel. 202-686-7463. Fax. 202-686-3656. www.sio.org — Statistical, rating, development and advisory organization for surety companies. Membership includes insurance companies licensed to write fidelity or surety insurance in one or more states and foreign affiliates.

Underwriters' Laboratories, Inc. • 333 Pfingsten Rd., Northbrook, IL 60062-2096. Tel. 847-272-8800. Fax. 847-272-8129. www.ul.com — Investigates and tests electrical materials and other products to determine whether fire prevention and protection standards are being met.

Viatical and Life Settlement Association of America • 1504 E. Concord St., Orlando, FL 32803. Tel. 407-894-3797. Fax. 407-897-1325. www.viatical.org — Nonprofit trade association for members of the viatical and life settlement industry, associated businesses and consumers; a leader in promoting responsible legislation and regulation of the industry.

Weather Risk Management Association (WRMA) • 1156 15th St., NW, Suite 900, Washington, DC 20005. Tel. 202-289-3800. Fax. 202-223-9741. wrma.org — The goal of the WRMA is to serve the weather risk management industry by providing forums for discussion and interaction with others associated with financial weather products.

*Wisconsin Insurance Alliance • 44 E. Mifflin St., Suite 201, Madison, WI 53703-2895. Tel. 608-255-1749. Fax. 608-255-2178. www.wisinsal.org — A state trade association of property/casualty insurance companies conducting legislative affairs and public relations on behalf of the industry.

*Workers Compensation Research Institute • 955 Massachusetts Ave., Cambridge, MA 02139. Tel. 617-661-9274. www.wcrinet.org — A nonpartisan, not-for-profit membership organization conducting public policy research on workers compensation, health care and disability issues. Members include employers, insurers, insurance regulators and state regulatory agencies, as well as several state labor organizations.

ACE USA

Acuity

Aegis Insurance Services Inc.

Allianz of America, Inc.

Allstate Insurance Group

American Agricultural Insurance Company

American International Group, Inc.

Atlantic Mutual Companies

Auto Club South Insurance Company

Beazley Group plc

Bituminous Insurance Companies

Chubb Group of Insurance Companies

Church Mutual Insurance Company

CNA

CUMIS Insurance Society, Inc.

De Smet Farm Mutual Insurance Company of South Dakota

Dryden Mutual Insurance Company

Erie Insurance Group

Farmers Group, Inc.

GEICO

Gen Re

Germania Insurance

Glencoe U.S. Holding Group

Grange Insurance Companies

GuideOne Insurance

The Hanover Insurance Group Inc.

The Harford Mutual Insurance Companies

Harleysville Insurance

The Hartford Financial Services Group

Holyoke Mutual Insurance Company

James River Group, Inc.

Liberty Mutual Group

Lloyd's

Lockton Companies

Marsh Inc.

MetLife Auto & Home

Millville Mutual Insurance Company

Missouri Employers Mutual Insurance

Munich Reinsurance America, Inc.

Nationwide

New York Life Insurance Company

The Norfolk & Dedham Group

North Pointe Insurance Group

Ohio Mutual Insurance Group

OneBeacon Insurance Group

Palisades Safety and Insurance Association

Pennsylvania Lumbermens Mutual Insurance Company

Plymouth Rock Assurance Corporation

Safeco Insurance Companies

Scor U.S. Corporation

SECURA Insurance Companies

Selective Insurance Group

State Farm Mutual Automobile Insurance Company

The Sullivan Group

Swiss Reinsurance America Corporation

TIAA-CREF

The Tokio Marine and Fire Insurance Co., Ltd.

Travelers

Unitrin Property and Casualty Insurance Group

USAA

Utica National Insurance Group

West Bend Mutual Insurance Company

Westfield Group

W. R. Berkley Corporation

XL Global Services

XL Insurance Company, Ltd.

Zurich North America

Associate Members

Allegany Co-op Insurance Company

Deloitte

Farmers Mutual Fire Insurance of Tennessee

Livingston Mutual Insurance Company

Mutual Assurance Society of Virginia

Randolph Mutual Insurance Company

Sompo Japan Research Institute, Inc.

Insurance Information Institute
110 William Street
New York, NY 10038

Tel. 212-346-5500. Fax. 212-732-1916. http://www.iii.org

President – Robert P. Hartwig, Ph.D., CPCU
Executive Vice President – Cary Schneider
Senior Vice President – Public Affairs – Jeanne Salvatore

Research
Vice President and Chief Economist – Steven N. Weisbart, Ph.D, CLU
Vice President – Global Issues – Claire Wilkinson

Fact Book
Vice President – Publications and Information Services – Madine Singer
Managing Editor – Neil Liebman
Research and Production – Mary-Anne Firneno
Director – Technology and Web Production – Shorna Lewis
Production Assistant – Charlene Lewis
Editorial Advisor – Andréa C. Basora
Special Consultant – Ruth Gastel, CPCU

Media
    New York:
        Vice President – Media Relations – Michael Barry
        Vice President – Web and Editorial Services – Andréa C. Basora
        Vice President – Communications – Loretta Worters

    Washington, DC:
        Vice President – Carolyn Gorman
        Tel. 202-833-1580. Fax. 202-785-4676.

    West Coast:
    Insurance Information Network of California:
    Executive Director – Candysse Miller
    Tel. 213-624-4462. Fax. 213-624-4432.
        Northern California:
        Communications Specialist – Tully Lehman
        Tel. 925-969-2223. Fax. 925-969-2188.

Representatives
    Special Counsel – William E. Bailey, Ph.D., CPCU
        Tel. 617-884-2461. Fax. 617-884-2593.
    Davis Communications – William J. Davis, Atlanta
        Tel. 770-321-5150. Fax. 770-321-5150.

C

capacity, 34
capital, 34
capital gains, 29
captive domiciles, top twenty, 8
car insurance. *See* automobile insurance
casualty, cost of risk, 160
catastrophes
    costliest, worldwide, 105,106
    deadliest, worldwide, 107
    global, 105-107
    historical, 112, 113, 115, 119, 120, 126, 127
    insured losses, *v*, 29, 109-111
    U.S., 109-123
    See also civil disorders, earthquakes; fires; floods;
        hurricanes; terrorism; tornadoes
cell phone/driver distraction laws, 75
charitable causes, insurance industry contribution, 12
choice no-fault automobile insurance, 66-67
civil disorders, 122
claim costs, litigation, 156-157, 159
claims
    as percentage of premium dollar, 30
    automobile insurance, 59
    collision, 138
    homeowners insurance, 85
class-action lawsuits, shareholder, 164
coastal properties, value of insured, 80
coastal states, population growth, 79
combined ratio, 30, 35
    automobile insurance, 52, 54
    homeowners multiple peril, 78
    See also individual lines
commercial insurance, 45-49, 92
commercial multiple peril insurance, 96-97
companies. *See* insurance companies
compulsory automobile insurance, 63-65
consumer expenditures, 151, 152
consumer price indices, 152-153
costs. *See* expenditures
crime, 128-129, 139-140
credit insurance, 45, 47, 51
credit life insurance, 19
crop insurance, 51
    multiple peril insurance 104
    See also farmowners insurance
cross-border sales, 7

D

death rates, by cause, 149
deaths. *See* fatalities
defense and cost containment expenses, 156-157
direct writers, 15

direct written premiums, 10
    by line, 45
        by line and by state, 48-51
    by state, 41
    health insurance, 21
    leading countries, 1
    leading writers, 10, 11, 53, 54, 79, 92
    worldwide, 2
directors and officers liability insurance, 161-163
disability insurance, 22
    leading companies, 28
    premiums, 28
disasters. *See* catastrophes
distribution channels, 15
    annuities, 21
dividends, policyholder, 29
    policyholder, 33
drunk driving, 70-71, 72, 136, 137
    laws, 70-71

E

earned premiums, 29
earthquake insurance, 45, 47, 51, 91
earthquakes, 119-120
    most costly, 119
earthquakes, top ten, historical, 120
employment, 12, 13
employment practices liability, trends, 163
endowment insurance, 26
expenditures
    by household, 151, 152
    by state
        automobile insurance, 55-57
        renters and homeowners insurance, 84
    health insurance, 11
        premium dollar, 59, 85
        underwriting dollar, 30
expense ratio, 35

F

FAIR plans, 81-82
farmowners insurance, 45, 47, 48, 97
fatalities
    aircraft, 144, 145
    alcohol-related, 136, 137
    automobile/motor vehicles, 130-132, 134-137
    avian flu, 108, 149
    aviation, 144, 145
    fire, 124-126
    hurricanes, 112
    tornadoes, 117, 119
    workplace, 146, 148

federal flood insurance, 45, 47, 51, 87-90

fidelity bonds, 45, 47, 50, 101

financial guaranty insurance, 45, 47, 50

financial responsibility laws, automobile insurance, 63-65

financial results, overview, 29

fire claims, 85

fire insurance, 45, 46, 49, 50, 99

fires
    arson, 127-128
    by property use, 125
    deaths and injuries, 124, 125-126
    intentionally set, 128
    largest loss, 126, 127
    structure, 124
        religious and funeral properties, 127
    top ten, historical, 126, 127

first-party and liability insurance, 66, 67

flood insurance
    federal, 45, 47, 51, 87-90
    losses, 88

floods, losses, top ten events, 116

foreign reinsurers, 3

foreign sales by U.S. companies, 7

foreign-owned companies, sales in U.S., 7

forest fires. *See* wildland fires

fraud, insurance, 154
    laws, 155-156

freezing losses, 86, 87

Fujita Scale for tornado classification, 116

G

general (other) liability insurance, 95
    See also product liability insurance

glossary, 165-166

graduated drivers licenses, 75, 76-77

gross domestic product, insurance industry
    contribution, 12, 13

group annuities, 19
    leading writers, 27

guaranty funds, 43
    net assessments
        by state, 44
        by year, 43

H

health care dollar, 11

health care insurance, 11, 21
    See also accident and health insurance

health expenditures, 12

health insurance, direct written premiums, 21
    premiums, 21

Herfindahl scale, 39

high risk markets, by state, 79
    by state, 83

highway safety laws. *See* laws affecting motorists

highway safety. *See* automobile/motor vehicle categories

history of insurance, 169-171

homeowners insurance
    causes of losses, 86
    combined ratio, 78
    expenditures, by household, 151, 153
    mold, 86
    ownership, 83
    premium dollar distribution, 85
    premiums, 45, 47, 48, 50
        average premiums, by state, 84
        direct written, by state, 48
        net written, by year, 78

homeowners losses, 86

household expenditures, 151, 152

Hurricane Andrew, 106, 110, 113

Hurricane Katrina, 105, 106, 110, 112, 113, 115
    flood losses, 116

hurricanes, 110-115
    by year, 112
    by year, 114
    claims, by year, 114
    deadliest, 112
    historical, 112, 113, 115
    most costly, 113, 115
    named storms, 2007, 113
    top ten, historical, 115
    value of vulnerable properties, 80

I

income, net, *v*, 29, 33

incurred losses, 29

individual term life, leading writers, 26

individual whole life insurance, 26

industrial life insurance, 19

injuries, odds of death, 150

injuries. *See also* accidents; automobile/motor vehicle
    crashes; fires

inland marine insurance, 45, 47, 49, 100

insolvency funds. *See* guaranty funds

insurance and service organizations, 175-186

insurance companies
    by state, 16
    leading writers, 10, 11, 53, 54, 92
    number of, domestic property/casualty, *v*
    top ten, global, 4

insurance departments, 172-174

insurance industry cycle, 32

Insurance Information Institute, staff, 188
    member companies, 187

insurance ownership, 83

intentionally set fires, 128
investment income, 29, 33
investments, by type, 36, 37
    life/health insurers, 18
        bond portfolio, 18

J

jury awards, 160

L

larceny-theft, 129
laws
    affecting motorists
        alcohol server liability, 72
        cell phone/driver distraction, 75
        compulsory automobile insurance, 63
        drunk driving, 70-71
        financial responsibility/compulsory, 63, 64-65
        license renewal, 73-74
        no-fault insurance, 66, 67
        seat-belts, 68-69
        young driver laws, 75, 76-77
    insurance fraud, 155-156
    See also state-by-state tables
leading companies, 10, 53, 54, 92
    by direct premiums written, 11
    disability, premiums, 28
    global, 4-6
    group annuities, net written, by year, 27
    individual annuities, net written, 27
    individual term life insurance, 26
    life insurance, 26
    long-term care insurance, 23
legal defense costs, 156-157
legislation, by state, 64-65, 67, 68-69, 70-71, 72, 73-74, 76-77
liability, homeowners insurance, 86
liability insurance. *See* specific lines of insurance, example, general liability
liability limits, 159
life insurance, global, 1, 2
life insurance, market share, 15
life/health insurance, companies, number of, 16
    employment, 13
    investments, 18
    leading writers, 11
    operating data, 17
    premiums, 9
        by state, 24-25
    top ten companies, global, 5
lightning insurance claims, 87
liquor liability laws, 72
    See also drunk driving laws

litigation, costs, 156-157, 158,
long-term care (LTC) insurance, 23
loss ratio, 35
losses
    asbestos, 147
    automobile liability, by year, 60
    by U.S. firms, 159
    by year, catastrophes, U.S., 110
    catastrophes, *v*, 105-111
        worldwide, 106
    fire, 123-127
    floods, 88
    homeowners, causes of, 86
    hurricanes, 114-115
    incurred, property casualty insurance, 29
    inflation adjusted catastrophe losses, by cause of loss, 111
    liability by U.S. firms, 159, 121
    most costly catastrophes
        U.S., 110
        worldwide, 105, 106
    underwriting, 29, 33
    workplace, 146-148
    World Trade Center, 106

M

mandatory automobile insurance. *See* compulsory automobile insurance
marine insurance
    inland marine insurance, 45, 47, 49, 100
    ocean marine insurance, 45, 47, 50, 100
market share trends, insurer size, 39
medical care costs. *See* health expenditures
medical malpractice insurance, 45, 47, 49, 98
mergers and acquisitions, *v*, 14
mold, 86
monetary thresholds, 66, 67
mortgage guaranty insurance, 45, 47, 51, 102
mortgage loans, 36
motor vehicles. *See* automobile/motor vehicle categories
motorcycle, crashes, 132
    deaths, 132, 137
motorcycles, helmet use, 137
multiple peril insurance
    commercial, 45, 47, 49, 96-97
    crop, 104
    farmowners, 45, 47, 48, 97
    homeowners, 45, 47, 48, 78

N

National Flood Insurance Program, 87-90, 116
net income, *v*, 29, 33
net premiums written, 9, 30, 32, 34, 46-47
    by line, 45, 46-47
    by year, 53, 54
    growth in, 32
    See also individual lines
no-fault automobile insurance, 66, 67
nonlife premiums, 1, 2
Northridge earthquake, 106, 110, 119

O

occupational disease, 147, 148
ocean marine insurance, 45, 47, 50, 100
odds of dying, by cause, 150
older drivers
    automobile/motor vehicle crashes, 134, 135
    license renewal laws, 73-74
operating results, 29, 33
    life/health insurance, 17
other liability. *See* general liability insurance
overseas sales of property/casualty insurance. *See* foreign sales

P

personal injury protection (PIP), 66, 67
personal insurance, 46-47, 48
policyholder dividends, 29, 33
policyholders' surplus, 29, 34
premium dollar distribution, 30, 59, 85
premium taxes, 42
premiums, *v*, 9-10
    average renters and homeowners, by state, 84
    by line, life/health, 19
    by type of insurer, 9
    direct written
        by line, by state, 48-51
        by state, 41
        leading countries, 1
        leading writers, 10, 53, 54
        worldwide, 2
    growth in, 10
        by line, 45, 46-47
        by year, 30, 34
        net written, 9, 34
    life/health insurance, by state, 24-25
    See also individual lines; direct premiums written;
      net premiums written
private mortgage insurance. *See* mortgage guaranty
  insurance
private passenger cars, accidents
    bodily injury, 60

property damage, 60
Private Securities Reform Act, 164
product liability insurance, 45, 47, 49, 95
profitability, 31
property crime offenses, 128, 129

R

rate of return, *v*, 31
real estate investments, 36
reinsurance, 3, 40, 45, 47
    domicile of alien reinsurers, 3
    top ten brokers, global, 6
    top ten companies, global, 5
reinsurance companies, top ten, U.S., 40
renters insurance, 83, 84
repair costs, automobile, 138
residual market. *See* shared automobile market
riots. *See* civil disorders

S

Saffir/Simpson classification system for hurricanes, 111
sales expenses, 30
seat-belt laws, 68-69
securities lawsuits, 164
September 11, 2001, 106, 120, 121, 126, 127
    See also terrorist attacks; World Trade Center
shared automobile market, 62-63
shareholder class-action lawsuits, 164
special flood hazard areas, 88
special revenue bonds, 37
sports injuries, by sport, 142-143
Stamping Offices, 38
State-by-state tables
    alcohol server liability laws, 72
    automobile financial responsibility laws, 64-65
    automobile first-party and liability insurance laws,
      67
    automobile insurance expenditures, 56-57
    automobile shared market, 62-63
    automobile theft, 140
    automobile/motor vehicle deaths, 131
    beach and windstorm plans, 83
    coastal population growth, 79
    coastal properties, 80
    companies, number of, 16
    direct premiums, 41
      by line, 48-51
    drunk driving laws, 70-71
    FAIR plans, 82
    flood insurance, 89-90
    fraud laws, 155-156
    guaranty fund assessments, 44
    homeowners insurance premiums, 84

legislation, 64-65, 67, 68-69, 70-71, 72, 73-74, 76-77

license renewal laws, 73-74

life/health insurance, premiums, 24-25

liquor liability laws, 72

older driver laws, 73-74

premiums, by state, 48-51
    direct written, by state, 41

private passenger cars insured, 62-63

renters insurance premiums, 84

residual market, 61, 62-63

seat-belt laws, 68-69

taxes, premium, 42

tornadoes and tornado deaths, 118

vehicles insured, 62-63

young driver laws, 76-77

state shared market, vehicles insured, 61, 62-63

stocks, 18, 36, 37

storms, losses. See catastrophes; hurricanes; tornadoes

surety, 45, 47, 50, 101

surplus, policyholders', 29, 34

surplus lines, 38
    top ten companies, 39

T

taxes, 17, 29, 30, 59, 85
    premiums written, by state, 42

teenage drivers. See young drivers

terrorism. See terrorist attacks

terrorist attacks, 106, 110, 120, 121

theft, automobiles, 59, 128, 129, 139
    top ten states, 140

tornadoes, 116-119

tort costs, 158

tort liability, automobile insurance, 66, 67

U

underwriting results, 29, 30, 33

uninsured motorists, 61

unintentional injuries. See accidents; automobile/ motor vehicle crashes; workplace losses

V

vehicles insured, by state, shared market, 62-63

verbal thresholds, automobile insurance, 67

voluntary automobile market, 61, 62-63

W

water damage, claims, 85, 86, 87

wildland fires, 122-123

wind and hail coverage, 83

windstorm plans. See beach and windstorm plans

workers compensation benefits, coverage and costs, 94

workers compensation insurance, 45, 47, 49, 93-94
    medical costs, 94

workplace
    deaths, 148
        by cause, 148
    disease, 147, 148
    losses, 146

work-related illnesses, 148

world insurance market, 1-2
    by year, 2
    leading countries, 1
    premiums, v
    top ten companies, world, 4, 5

World Trade Center, 106, 110

Write-Your-Own Flood Insurance Program, 87, 89-90

Y

young drivers
    automobile/motor vehicle crashes, 134, 135
    laws, 75, 76-77